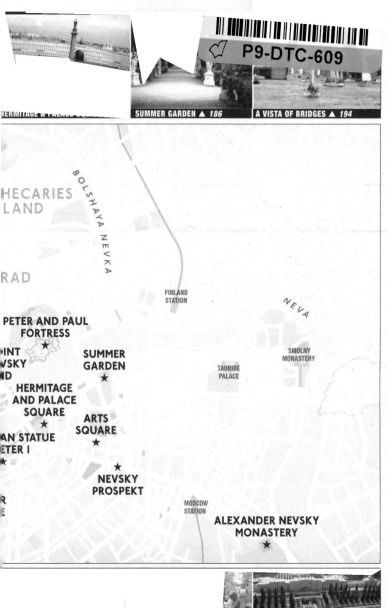

SUMMER GARDEN ▲ 186

A VISTA OF BRIDGES ▲ 194

HERMITAGE & PALACE

APOTHECARIES
ISLAND

BOLSHAYA NEVKA

GRAD

FINLAND
STATION

NEVA

PETER AND PAUL
FORTRESS

POINT
NEVSKY
ISLAND

SUMMER
GARDEN

SMOLNY
MONASTERY

TAURIDE
PALACE

HERMITAGE
AND PALACE
SQUARE

ARTS
SQUARE

MAN STATUE
PETER I

NEVSKY
PROSPEKT

MOSCOW
STATION

ALEXANDER NEVSKY
MONASTERY

A. NEVSKY MONASTERY ▲ 253

PETERHOF ▲ 256

show that attracts many devotees.

THEATER SQUARE
The Mariinsky Theater has made this square the city's artistic hub.

KOLOMNA DISTRICT
The four islands, nine embankments and twenty bridges of this 19th-century district can be explored by boat.

NEVSKY PROSPEKT
The city's main thoroughfare is lined with shops, churches and various palaces. Malaya Sadovaya Street is especially worth a visit.

ARTS SQUARE
Three museums, two theaters, the Philharmonia, and the crafts market nearby make up this historic area.

NEVSKY MONASTERY
It contains the Artists' Necropolis, where great Russian artists are buried.

PETERHOF
This great Baroque palace and its parks are the venue for popular festivities.

ST PETERSBURG

KNOPF GUIDES

● Encyclopedia section

■ **NATURE** The natural heritage: species and habitats characteristic to the area covered by the guide, annotated and illustrated by naturalist authors and artists.

HISTORY The impact of international historical events on local history, from the arrival of the first inhabitants to the present day, with key dates appearing in a timeline above the text.

ARTS AND TRADITIONS The region's local customs and traditions and their continuing role in contemporary life.

ARCHITECTURE The architectural heritage, focusing on style and topology, a look at rural and urban buildings, major civil, religious and military monuments.

AS SEEN BY PAINTERS A selection of paintings of the city or country by different artists and schools, arranged chronologically or thematically.

AS SEEN BY WRITERS An anthology of texts focusing on the city or country, taken from works of all periods and countries, arranged thematically.

▲ Itineraries

Each itinerary begins with a map of the area to be explored.

✪ **SPECIAL INTEREST** These sites are not to be missed. They are highlighted in gray boxes in the margins.

★ **EDITOR'S CHOICE** Sites singled out by the editor for special attention.

INSETS On richly illustrated double pages, these insets turn the spotlight on subjects deserving more in-depth treatment.

◆ Practical information

All the travel information you will need before you go and when you get there.

USEFUL ADDRESSES A selection of the best hotels and restaurants compiled by an expert.

PLACES TO VISIT A handy table of addresses and opening hours.

APPENDICES Bibliography, list of illustrations and general index.

MAP SECTION Maps of all the areas covered by the guide, preceded by a street index; these maps are marked out with letters and figures making it easy for the reader to pinpoint a town, region or site.

Each map in the map section is designated by a letter. In the practical information, each place can be pinpointed on the map (for example: ◆ **A** B1).

The itinerary map shows the main sites of interest.

■ ● ▲ ◆
The above symbols within the text provide cross-references to a place or a theme discussed elsewhere in the guide.

★ The star symbol signifies sites singled out by the editor for special attention.

FROM THE HERMITAGE TO THE SUMMER PALACE

1. THE HERMITAGE
2. PALACE SQUARE
3. ALEXANDER COLUMN
4. ARCH OF THE GENERAL STAFF
5. MOIKA EMBANKMENT
6. PUSHKIN MUSEUM
7. IMPERIAL STABLES
8. PALACE EMBANKMENT
9. WINTER CANAL BRIDGE
10. MARBLE PALACE
11. MENSHIKOV PIER (FIELD OF MARS)
12. PAVLOVSKY REGIMENTAL BARRACKS
13. SUMMER GARDEN
14. SUMMER PALACE
15. FONTANKA EMBANKMENT
16. LAW SCHOOL
17. CHURCH OF ST PANTELEIMON
18. DECORATIVE ARTS

THE HERMITAGE AND PALACE SQUARE ✪
The Hermitage, symbol of St Petersburg, is one of the largest museums in the world, with collections comprising about three million items. Now extending to the former General Staff Headquarters on Palace Square ▲ 180, the museum constitutes a major cultural center. "Under the Aegis of the Eagle", one of the displays there, is an exhibition of Empire artifacts.

THE HERMITAGE

THE FIRST WINTER PALACES. The Winter Palace, now known as the Hermitage Museum, is the fourth building to have been constructed on this site. After the first "small Dutch-style house" built by Peter I it was probably the Italian architect Domenico Trezzini who built the first Winter Palace (1711–12). This building was destroyed in 1726. Meantime, the architect Mattarnovy had built a "winter house" next door (1716–19) for Peter I. In 1732 the Empress Anna Ivanovna from the Rastrelli another palace. It was razed in 1754 to make way for the current palace, built for Elizabeth Petrovna.
PALACE OF ELIZABETH. Built from 1754 to 1762 by Bartolomeo Rastrelli; this palace is renowned for its profusion of Baroque decoration: two stories of columns cover the facades.

☐ One day
◆ E

CATHERINE II'S WINTER PALACE. The interiors were still uncompleted when Rastrelli was dismissed by Catherine in August 1762. The director of the Buildings Chancellery, I. Betsky, called in several foreign architects to replace him: Jean-Baptiste Vallin de la Mothe, Antonio Rinaldi and the German Yury Velten. De la Mothe decorated Catherine II's private apartments (later destroyed in the 1837 fire), the Throne Room, the church, the apartments of the ladies of honor on the third floor, and the apartments of Count Grigory Orlov on the mezzanine floor. Felten reorganized the Portrait and the Mirror galleries, and Rinaldi changed the Throne Room into an oval salon. Catherine II had ten grandchildren, and the imperial apartments (including the theater) were altered to meet their needs by Giacomo Quarenghi and Ivan Starov. But the really major changes were to come with new construction work.

166

167

At the beginning of each itinerary, the time it will take to cover the area is indicated beneath the mini-map, as are the grid references to the map section

The mini-map pinpoints the itinerary within the wider area covered by the guide.

✪ This symbol indicates places of special interest.

● **Encyclopedia section**

▲ Itineraries in St Petersburg

◆ Practical information

FROM THE FORTRESS TO THE ISLANDS OF THE DELTA ▲ 143
A historic place from which to explore the city, the Fortress contains the Peter and Paul Cathedral, the History Museum and the Old Arsenal. The Petrograd Side, a district on the right bank of the Neva, has buildings in the Art Nouveau style. To the west lie the islands of the delta, which, with their parks and gardens, are a favorite place of relaxation for St Petersburgers.

VASILYEVSKY ISLAND ▲ 155
The part of the island known as the Point (Strelka) has a large population of students and academics, and many monuments, museums, colleges and research institutes connected to the university or the Russian Navy. Menshikov Palace, with splendid apartments, and the Kunstkammer, Peter the Great's gallery of curiosities, both on University Embankment, are open to visitors.

FROM THE HERMITAGE TO THE SUMMER PALACE ▲ 165
Oppposite the Fortress, on the left bank of the Neva, stand palaces, gardens and major monuments, all of them examples of the Peter-the-Great style. They include the Hermitage, one of the largest museums in the world, Palace Square and, between the Marble Palace and the Summer Palace, the huge Field of Mars. Fine 18th-century statues grace the Summer Garden.

FROM THE ADMIRALTY TO THE HAYMARKET ▲ 189
Highlights include the Admiralty and New Holland districts, built on the site of former shipyards; the beautiful St Isaac's Cathedral, the largest church in St Petersburg; Theater Square, hub of the city's artistic life and home of the acclaimed Mariinsky Theater; St Nicholas' Cathedral, a fine example of Baroque elegance in blue, white and gold; and the 19th-century Dostoevsky District.

AROUND NEVSKY PROSPEKT ▲ 211
Nevsky Prospekt is the city's main thoroughfare and its finest commercial street. On Arts Square and Ostrovsky Square stand major artistic institutions: among them are the Russian Museum in Mikhail Palace, Engineers' Castle, the Shostakovich Philarmonia and the Alexandrinsky Theater. The Church of the Resurrection, with its famous twisted onion domes, is also not to be missed.

FROM THE FONTANKA TO INSURRECTION SQUARE ▲ 235
Running from Fountains House to the Rimsky-Korsakov Museum and Dostoevsky Museum, and taking in the Samoilov Museum and Pushkin Street, this literary and musical itinerary follows in the footsteps of great Russian writers and composers. An additional highlight is Beloselsky-Belozersky Palace, now used as a cultural center that also features a waxworks museum.

FROM SMOLNY TO ALEXANDER NEVSKY MONASTERY ▲ 245
Smolny Monastery and Cathedral, masterpieces of Russian Baroque architecture, contrast with the restrained style of the Smolny Institute , which played a prominent role in the 1917 Revolution. This historical itinerary takes in Kikin Palace, Tauride Palace and the Alexander Nevsky Monastery, where major figures in Russian intellectual life are buried.

PALACES ON THE OUTSKIRTS OF ST PETERSBURG ▲ 255
Major festivities takes place at Peterhof, a palace set in grounds with elaborate fountains. Oranienbaum, which has been open to visitors for several years now, contains some remarkable examples of marquetry. Also open to the public are Tsarskoe Selo, whose well-known façade is 985 feet wide, and Pavlovsk, by far the most sophisticated of all Russian summer palaces.

Numerous specialists and academics have contributed to this guide.
All the information that it contains has been approved by them.

• Encyclopedia section

NATURE
Vladimir Leftchenko,
Alexey Nekrassov, Jean-Pierre Verdet,
Philippe Dubois
LANGUAGE
Annette Lefebvre
HISTORY
Tamara Kondratieva
ARTS AND TRADITIONS
Antoine Nivière, Alexandra Schouwaloff,
Emmanuel Ducamp, Béatrice Picon-Vallin,
Natalia Metelitsa, Igor Dimitriev,
Prascovie de Saint-Hippolyte
ARCHITECTURE
Brigitte de Montclos, Ewa Bérard,
Andrey Punin, Vladimir Rivline
ST PETERSBURG AS SEEN BY PAINTERS
Alexandra Schouwaloff
THE RUSSIAN AVANT-GARDE
Andrey Nakov
ST PETERSBURG AS SEEN BY WRITERS
Lucinda Gane
ALEXANDER PUSHKIN
Anne Klimoff

▲ Itineraries in St Petersburg

Anne Nercessian, Alexander Noskov,
Brigitte de Montclos, Natalya Brodskaya,
Vera Biron, Vitaly Sychev, Natalya Metelitsa,
Vladimir Leon, Alexandra Schouwaloff,
Tamara Kondratieva, Emmanuel Ducamp

◆ Practical information

Olga Yartseva
Hotels and restaurants: Olga Yartseva,
Robert Cottrell of the *Financial Times*
and Catherine Sharpe

This is a Borzoi Book
published by Alfred A. Knopf

Completely revised and
updated in 2007

www.aaknopf.com

ISBN 10: 0-375-71104-X
ISBN 13: 978-0-375-71104-6

Originally published in France by
Nouveaux-Loisirs, a subsidiary of Editions
Gallimard, Paris, 1993. Copyright © 1993
by Editions Nouveaux-Loisirs

Series editors
Shelley Wanger and Clémence Jacquinet

Translated by
Anthony Roberts and Yvonne Worth

Edited and typeset by
Book Creation Services, London

Printed and bound in Italy by
Zanardi Group

ST PETERSBURG
Original French-language edition

Editors
Sophie Mastelinck and Agnès Baubault,
with Odile Simon (Nature)
Layout
Yann Le Duc assisted by Annie Civard
and Carole Gaborit
Picture research
Catherine Boncenne
Updating
Olga Yartseva and Sophie Besançon
(editing)

ILLUSTRATIONS
Nature: Jean Chevallier, François
Desbordes, Claire Felloni,
Catherine Lachaux, Dominique Mansion,
Pascale Robin, John Wilkinson
Architecture: Michel Aubois, Jean-
François Binet, Vincent Brunot, François
Desbordes, Jean-Marie Guillou, Jean-
Michel Kacedan, Maurice Pommier,
Sylvain Roueri, Amato Soro, Catherine
Totems
Itineraries: Jean-Michel Kacedan,
Maurice Pommier, Laure Massin
(coloring), Jean-Philippe Chabot,
Frédéric Bony
Maps: Vincent Brunot, Éric Gillion,
Marc Lagarde (coloring)
Computer graphics: Édigraphie, Paul
Coulbois, Xavier Garnerin (Latitude),
Patrick Merienne

PHOTOGRAPHY
V. Baranovsky, V. Buss, Roger Gain,
Koncharov, V. Savik, V. Terebenin

SPECIAL THANKS TO
Anne Nercessian, Vera Biron
(Dostoevsky Museum, St Petersburg),
Véronique Schiltz, Galina Vassiliev
(Historic Archives of St Petersburg),
Georges Willembachov (Hermitage
Museum), Martine Kahane (Opéra
Garnier-Bastille), Alexandre Illinsky,
Vladimir Terebebin, Helena Asséeva,
Isabelle Haas and Stéphanie François

Encyclopedia section

"The quays of St Petersburg are among the loveliest things in Europe: why? Because they embody both luxury and solidity."
Astolphe de Custine

Photograph: bicentary celebrations of the founding of St Petersburg, May 1900

"The aspect of St Petersburg is more conducive of astonishment than admiration . . . if it is not quite perfectly beautiful, it is none the less completely strange."

Olympe Audovard

Photograph: The Fontanka from Anichkov Bridge, 1900

"On the left was a little
black canal, which lay
against the colossus of the
Admiralty . . . gilded at
every edge, and adorned
by a glinting statue of
Fame, all in gold . . ."

Louis-Ferdinand Céline

*Photograph: entrance to
the Admiralty, c. 1900*

"There is nothing finer than Nevsky Prospekt,
not in St Petersburg at any rate; for in
St Petersburg it is everything. And, indeed,
is there anything more gay, more brilliant,
more resplendent than this beautiful
street of our capital?"

Nikolai Gogol

Photograph: Nevsky Prospekt, 1906

Nature

The St Petersburg region extends 280 miles west to east and between 65 and 200 miles north to south. Its southeast extremity is washed by the waters of the Gulf of Finland; and to the north of it is Lake Ladoga. The region lies to the northwest of the Russian plateau, the substratum of which is crystalline rock. The various ice ages produced morainic elevations and lakes, which in general give the land its undulating aspect. The climate is one of strong contrasts, being conditioned on the one hand by the movement of air masses off the Atlantic and on the other by polar continental air, which is dry and very cold in winter. St Petersburg itself is situated more or less where the northern and temperate climatic regions meet.

0   3 miles

Kotlin Island

Bay of Neva

Isthmus of Carelia

Neva

- Sandy banks along the seaboard
- Argillaceous plains, with forests and marshes in sandy soil areas
- Plains and plateaux with glacial moraines (mixed and coniferous forests)
- Marshes and peat-bogs
- Arable land and conifer forests (foothills)
- Calcareous plateau with deciduous or coniferous forests and grassland
- Prone to flooding

Autumn weather is characterized by frequent depressions, with strong winds causing occasional floods.

In December Atlantic depressions bring rain and snow; in January and February the arrival of dry air from the Arctic makes for cloudless skies.

The black tern lives in noisy colonies among the marshes skirting the Bay of the Neva.

On the island of Kotlin the construction of a dyke was begun in the 1980's as a measure to protect the city from flooding. The dyke is still unfinished, because it has been shown to disturb the Neva estuary's ecosystem.

The marshy, island-strewn delta in which Peter the Great chose to build his capital ● 78 benefits from Atlantic weather, without which the region would probably be icebound for much of the year.

| Marsh |

AVERAGE TEMPERATURES AT GROUND LEVEL (°C)

—16— July isotherm (61°F)

— -8 — January isotherm (18°F)

33 Maximum temperatures (91°F)

-40 Minimum temperatures (-40°F)

AVERAGE PRECIPITATION (mm)

less   more

 Isohyet

PREVAILING WINDS

→ July

→ January

In the spring the weather changes frequently on account of the continual confrontation of air masses.

In July the average temperature is 67°F. July is also a season of thunderstorms; cloudbursts can be very violent.

■ THE NEVA

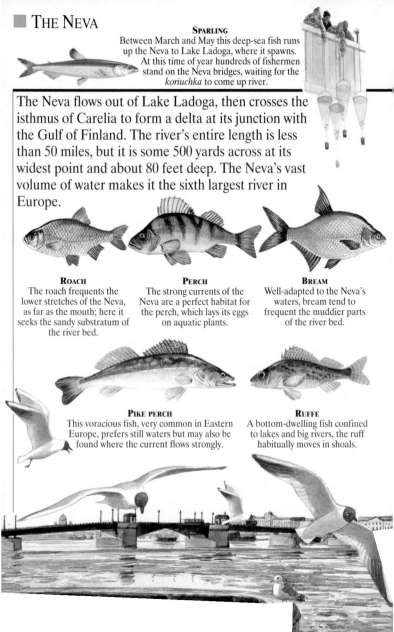

SPARLING
Between March and May this deep-sea fish runs
up the Neva to Lake Ladoga, where it spawns.
At this time of year hundreds of fishermen
stand on the Neva bridges, waiting for the
koriuchka to come up river.

The Neva flows out of Lake Ladoga, then crosses the
isthmus of Carelia to form a delta at its junction with
the Gulf of Finland. The river's entire length is less
than 50 miles, but it is some 500 yards across at its
widest point and about 80 feet deep. The Neva's vast
volume of water makes it the sixth largest river in
Europe.

ROACH
The roach frequents the
lower stretches of the Neva,
as far as the mouth; here it
seeks the sandy substratum of
the river bed.

PERCH
The strong currents of the
Neva are a perfect habitat for
the perch, which lays its eggs
on aquatic plants.

BREAM
Well-adapted to the Neva's
waters, bream tend to
frequent the muddier parts
of the river bed.

PIKE PERCH
This voracious fish, very common in Eastern
Europe, prefers still waters but may also be
found where the current flows strongly.

RUFFE
A bottom-dwelling fish confined
to lakes and big rivers, the ruff
habitually moves in shoals.

House martin

Swift

These birds nest on the great riverfront
buildings of St Petersburg, notably the
Hermitage ▲ 168. They feed on insects,
skimming close to the water's surface.

During the winter
the Neva may be
impassable for a
period varying
between two and five
months. In the winter
of 1941–2 ● 50 the
Neva was covered by
ice over 3 feet thick.
The river's powerful
current sometimes
brings very high water.

The worst flooding on record took place in
1824 ● 35. Dykes have been constructed in
the bay of the Neva to protect the city.

Following the thaw the Neva may still
remain impassable to ships for over a month.
Every spring great blocks of ice sweep down
the river from Lake Ladoga to the open sea.

BLACK-HEADED GULL
Present on the river all year round, this
half-tame gull will often eat from the
hand during the winter.

The Summer Garden ▲ *186* is a combination of rigorous landscaping and exuberant animal life.

The building of the city of St Petersburg led inevitably to a significant change in the vegetation of the surrounding region. The new artificial plantations brought with them a number of foreign exotic plant species to live alongside the indigenous varieties. Nowadays St Petersburg still remains a "green city", with historic spaces – such as the Summer Garden and the enormous parks of Krestovsky and Elagin islands – which serve as urban reminders of the great forests that lie further afield.

RED SQUIRREL
The shy, agile rodent is widespread throughout the parks and cemeteries of St Petersburg.

PINE MARTEN
A carnivorous member of the weasel family, which habitually feeds on birds as well as small mammals, beetles and carrion.

HOODED CROW
Omnipresent in the city, this crow is especially numerous in the smaller parks and around the Alexander Nevsky Monastery ▲ 253.

SISKIN
The siskin is common in the mountain and forest regions of Europe – and in the parks of St Petersburg.

SCARLET ROSEFINCH
This oriental species is currently expanding its range deep into Western Europe.

Male

Female

FIELDFARE
The fieldfare nests in noisy colonies, especially in the Summer Garden.

THRUSH NIGHTINGALE
A legendary songbird, the eastern European version of our common nightingale.

Tourists may be surprised by the sight of men scything the grass by hand in Elagin Park ▲ 154.

ALDER
The berries of this small tree, which favors cool, humid soils, attracts birds like the siskin during the winter months.

LIME TREE
The lime is very common in and around St Petersburg. In June and July the gardens are richly scented with its blooms.

HORNBEAM
Hornbeams, widely planted in Russia during the 19th century, supply generous shade and easily worked wood.

■ THE CARELIAN FOREST

WILLOW WARBLER
This long-distance migrant nests in large
numbers in the woods around St Petersburg,
where willows, rowans and birches predominate.

The forests of the St Petersburg region straddle a
transitional zone between the northern taiga, where conifers
proliferate, and the mixed woodlands of the temperate regions.
The latter, a blend of deciduous trees and
conifers, seem to have receded southward
following a very cold, wet period over four
thousand years ago. In the Carelian forest there
are fewer deciduous trees, and rowans
predominate. Numerous lakes, interspersed
with marshes and heather-covered peat bogs,
give this area a charm that is properly more
Scandinavian than Russian, yet this is the
quintessential "Russian forest" described
by novelists.

CHAFFINCH
Large numbers of
chaffinches populate the
St Petersburg region in
summer, migrating to
southern Europe in the
winter.

NORWAY PINE
Abundant on the sandy soils
around the northern rim of
the Gulf of the Neva.

BIRCH
One of the principal
hardwood trees in the
St Petersburg region; it often
grows with conifers.

SPRUCE
Typical of the Carelian forest.
Its fruits are a rich source of
food for woodland birdlife.

BEARBERRY
The *toloknyanka* is
very similar to the
bilberry and is widely
used in
pharmacology.

MILITARY ORCHID
The military orchid
flowers in May and
June on calcareous
sunny banks and along
the margins of woods.

SWAMP-BERRY
The deep blue fruit of
the swamp-berry is a
common sight in
marshy areas during
the autumn.

COTTON GRASS
In June, when the
puchitsa is in flower,
its fluffy seedballs
cover the ground like
newly-fallen snow.

ELK (MOOSE)
In the 1970's elk were still present in large
numbers up to the edge of the city. Stocks
have declined steeply in recent years.

GRAY WOLF
A small wolf population survives around
St Petersburg, but is now under severe
threat from hunters.

F. Desborder

■ CEMETERIES

The cemeteries of St Petersburg come as a surprise to most visitors to the city. From the outside they appear impenetrable, but those who persevere will be rewarded with the sight of an unkempt riot of graves, bushes and sprawling wild plants. During the Soviet era the cemeteries were not maintained, with the result that the growth of lush vegetation remained unchecked; this in turn attracted abundant wild creatures which took advantage of the near-natural conditions that prevailed there.

The tangle of plants and ruined tombstones offers a quiet refuge from the din of the surrounding city.

RED FOX
The parks and cemeteries of St Petersburg have made it possible for the red fox to survive in the heart of the city. Foxes may often be glimpsed by daylight, hunting for mice, rats and voles.

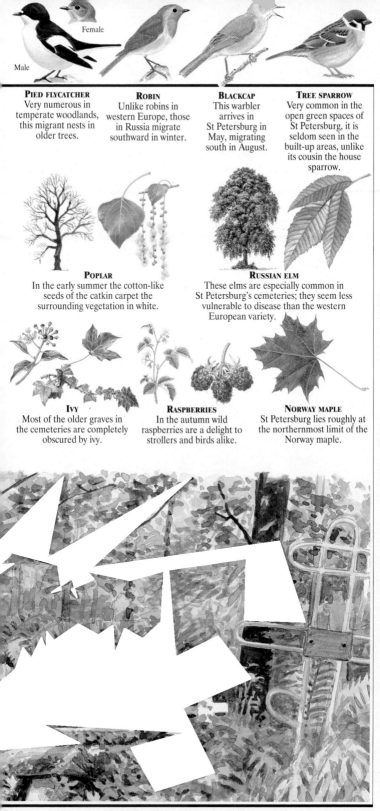

PIED FLYCATCHER
Very numerous in temperate woodlands, this migrant nests in older trees.

Female

Male

ROBIN
Unlike robins in western Europe, those in Russia migrate southward in winter.

BLACKCAP
This warbler arrives in St Petersburg in May, migrating south in August.

TREE SPARROW
Very common in the open green spaces of St Petersburg, it is seldom seen in the built-up areas, unlike its cousin the house sparrow.

POPLAR
In the early summer the cotton-like seeds of the catkin carpet the surrounding vegetation in white.

RUSSIAN ELM
These elms are especially common in St Petersburg's cemeteries; they seem less vulnerable to disease than the western European variety.

IVY
Most of the older graves in the cemeteries are completely obscured by ivy.

RASPBERRIES
In the autumn wild raspberries are a delight to strollers and birds alike.

NORWAY MAPLE
St Petersburg lies roughly at the northernmost limit of the Norway maple.

Light at Midnight

"Across the sky, gilded
By the sun's perpetual rays
Dawn hurries to relieve
The unconsummated dusk
And night endures for barely an hour."
Pushkin, *The Bronze Horseman*

As St Petersburg is not within the Arctic Circle, there is no midnight sun, but its latitude is sufficiently high (almost 60°N) to bring some light throughout the night. The sun only just dips below the horizon and the earth's atmosphere continues to diffuse its beams. Most plants are in full bloom at this time of year.

Northwest | North | Northeast
9am | Midnight | 3am

Toward the earth's poles, the sun rises less directly over the horizon, and the more the days vary in length over the year.

March 21
June 21 | December 21
September 21

The earth describes its elliptical orbit around the sun in 365 days and 6 hours. During this revolution the inclination of the earth varies in relation to the sun, determining the lengths of the days and seasons.

▼ **SUMMER SOLSTICE**
On June 21 the night, or rather twilight, lasts only five hours at St Petersburg. At midnight the sun lies only 6° beneath the horizon. In London at the same time of year the night lasts for seven hours and the sun drops 23° below the horizon. In New York the night lasts for nine hours and twenty minutes and the sun drops 25° below the horizon.

▲ **WINTER SOLSTICE**
On December 21 at noon the sun stands at slightly over 6° above St Petersburg. In London it is at 26° and in New York at 27°. From mid-afternoon onward the Gulf of Finland is under cover of night.

History
and language

1682–1725
Reign of Peter the Great, who
proclaimed himself Emperor

1700–21
Northern War: the Russians annex
Estonia, Latvia and Carelia

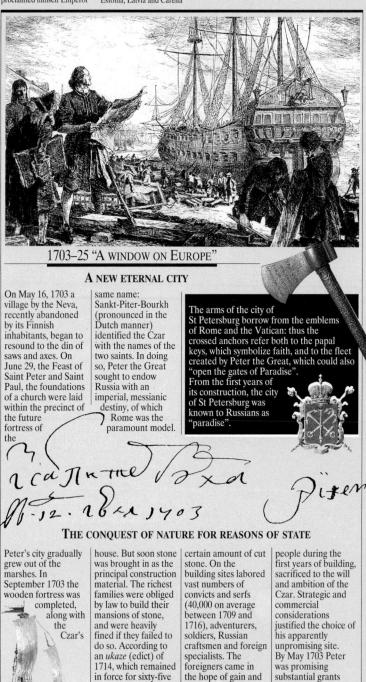

1703–25 "A WINDOW ON EUROPE"

A NEW ETERNAL CITY

On May 16, 1703 a village by the Neva, recently abandoned by its Finnish inhabitants, began to resound to the din of saws and axes. On June 29, the Feast of Saint Peter and Saint Paul, the foundations of a church were laid within the precinct of the future fortress of the same name: Sankt-Piter-Bourkh (pronounced in the Dutch manner) identified the Czar with the names of the two saints. In doing so, Peter the Great sought to endow Russia with an imperial, messianic destiny, of which Rome was the paramount model.

The arms of the city of St Petersburg borrow from the emblems of Rome and the Vatican: thus the crossed anchors refer both to the papal keys, which symbolize faith, and to the fleet created by Peter the Great, which could also "open the gates of Paradise". From the first years of its construction, the city of St Petersburg was known to Russians as "paradise".

THE CONQUEST OF NATURE FOR REASONS OF STATE

Peter's city gradually grew out of the marshes. In September 1703 the wooden fortress was completed, along with the Czar's house. But soon stone was brought in as the principal construction material. The richest families were obliged by law to build their mansions of stone, and were heavily fined if they failed to do so. According to an *ukaze* (edict) of 1714, which remained in force for sixty-five years, every boat, vessel or waggon entering the city had to bring with it a certain amount of cut stone. On the building sites labored vast numbers of convicts and serfs (40,000 on average between 1709 and 1716), adventurers, soldiers, Russian craftsmen and foreign specialists. The foreigners came in the hope of gain and were sometimes detained by force. Hunger and cold killed nearly 100,000 people during the first years of building, sacrificed to the will and ambition of the Czar. Strategic and commercial considerations justified the choice of his apparently unpromising site. By May 1703 Peter was promising substantial grants to the first three merchant vessels to drop anchor in the new port.

| 1795 | 1812 | June 18, 1815 | 1853–6: |
| Third partition of Poland between Austria, Prussia and Russia | Napoleon in Moscow | Battle of Waterloo | Crimean War |

1800

| | 1809 | September 26, 1815 |
| | Annexation of Finland | Foundation of the Holy Alliance |

1725–1856: ORIGINALITY AND IMITATION

THE "PALMYRA OF THE NORTH"

In a letter dated September 28, 1704, Czar Peter referred to the city under construction as his "new capital". The inauguration took place in 1712, at which time the Russian court, the Senate and the foreign embassies all moved to St Petersburg from Moscow; Peter was subsequently married there, to a Lithuanian peasant girl.

The first museums, a library, a theater, an observatory and the Academy of Sciences were quickly opened. In the vicinity of St Petersburg were built the palaces of Oranienbaum and Peterhof, while a road was built to Tsarskoe Selo, the future summer residence of the Czars.

foreign-born artists, St Petersburg "… became distinct from the other cities of Europe, precisely because it so nearly resembled each one of them". Travelers called it the "London", "Venice", "Rome", "Berlin" or "Paris" of Russia, as it struck them. But the city's new attractions obliged its inhabitants to adapt: some social groups to luxury and extravagance, the rest to the behavior of their superiors in the hierarchy. Poets and writers, meanwhile, became intrigued by the mystery of this seductive but far from traditional city.

THE DISAPPEARING CITY

After the death of Peter the Great, half the Russian court and at least half of the population of St Petersburg fled the city. The *ukaze* of 1729, which threatened fugitives with exile and the confiscation of their property, had little effect. New, harsher measures sparked a revolt, and in 1737 the city was burned down. Nevertheless the Empress Elizabeth I (right), Peter the Great's daughter, pressed on with the construction of the Winter and Anichkov palaces and the Gostiny Dvor, so realizing her father's dream. Catherine II ● *40* lifted the restrictions, enticed the population back with perquisites, and initiated major construction projects such as the Tauride Palace and Marble Palace, the Hermitage, the Smolny Institute, the bridges and the granite river embankment. Toward the mid-19th century, thanks to the talents of both Russian and

| **February 19, 1861** | **December 1865** | | **1889–92** |
| Abolition of serfdom in Russia | Abolition of slavery in the USA | | Counter-reforms |

| **1861** | | **1880** | |

| **1863–5** | **1864–76** | **March 1, 1881** | **1883** |
| Liberal reforms of Alexander II | Marx and Engels: the First International | Assassination of Czar Alexander | Marxist propaganda appears in Russia |

1856–1914 ST PETERSBURG IN THE FOREFRONT OF MODERNISM

THE INDUSTRIAL CENTER OF THE EMPIRE

The first steamships and the Moscow–St Petersburg railway line (1851) opened a new era in the city's history. By 1868 the Putilov factory was already a major producer of rails, locomotives and carriages. In 1900, 13,000 workers were employed there, with about a hundred more metallurgical factories developing in related sectors. Other factories, using modern British and German equipment (Nobel, Nevsky, Lessner) built ships and typographical machines and (in competition with Obukhov) supplied the needs of the Army. There was also a number of textile mills in and around St Petersburg. A new port, constructed in 1885, was added to that of Kronstadt, expanding the city's potential for international trade: corn and wood were exported in vast quantities, balancing imports of steel and machine tools. Banks, many of whose shareholders were foreigners, proliferated during the boom of the 1890's.

THE ST PETERSBURG CIVIL SERVANT

According to the poet Grigoriev, Russian civil servants – whose uniforms varied from one ministry to the next – were the "alpha and omega" of St Petersburg. Schoolboys, university students, soldiers, sailors, policemen and ecclesiastics completed the picture. Right from the time of its foundation, St Petersburg was a heavily regulated city: the aspect of the roofs and chimneys, the construction materials, the color and height of all buildings (which might on no account be taller than the Winter Palace), the width of the streets, the hours by which the gates had to be closed, and the arrangements for street cleaning were all carefully ordained by bureaucratic rules.

A CENTER FOR FREE THOUGHT

Paradoxically, it was in this tightly controlled environment that free thought blossomed – thanks to the culture of an intellectual elite, naturally, but also thanks to the special receptiveness of St Petersburgers. Seventy percent of the workers in the capital knew how to read and write, as opposed to an average of 21 percent in the rest of the Russian Empire. St Petersburgers spread the word on avant-garde art, along with technical innovation (airplanes) and new diversions (cinema, football).

1914–24: PETROGRAD: WAR AND REVOLUTION

THE COMING OF THE REVOLUTION

On July 20, 1914, from a balcony of the Winter Palace, Nicholas II read the declaration which brought Russia into the Great War. On August 18 the German name of the capital was changed to the more Russian-sounding Petrograd – much closer to "Pieter", as ordinary people had always called it. For the writer Solzhenitsyn, who described the war years practically from day to day (*The Red Wheel*, 4,000 pages), the declaration of war was the beginning of the greatest drama of the century, whilst for Lenin it represented a great gift offered by the Czar to the nascent Revolution.

According to Lenin, in an underdeveloped nation revolution could come about only as a consequence of war: while Karl Marx thought revolution improbable anywhere but within the most advanced capitalist systems. History began to prove Lenin right in February 1917.

On the night of October 24–5, insurgents attacked the Winter Palace, seat of the provisional government. With a roar that drowned the stutter of machine-gun fire, a wave of humanity swirled around the great building. The October Revolution was under way.

THE DESTRUCTION OF ST PETERSBURG

The October Revolution – so glorified for seventy-six years thereafter – led to many irreparable losses for St Petersburgers. The city was transformed in two ways. On the edge of the central area quantities of dilapidated buildings in which tens of thousands of workers lived were emptied and destroyed. Meantime the historic capital began to fall apart from the very first months of Soviet supremacy. Spacious apartments were divided up among working families, and the original décor, of two-headed eagles, crowns and statues, removed; a decree abolishing private ownership deprived houses and shops, fountains and gardens of ordinary maintenance; and railings, stained glass, stair carpets, bas-reliefs and weathercocks simply vanished. The campaigns against religion brought about the destruction or conversion into offices of a large number of churches. Much-needed capital was raised by the sale of works of art abroad. At the same time the names of streets and squares were altered, short-circuiting the collective memory: about 500 names were changed, including that of the Nevsky Prospekt, which became Avenue 25 October. About 400 names vanished altogether, along with the things they referred to. Finally, on Lenin's death in January 1924, the Soviet Congress, "at the request of the workers", abolished the name of the capital altogether.

1938	1939	1940	1941
Munich Agreements (September)	The Russo-German Pact (August). Partition of Poland (September)	Pact with Finland (March) Annexation of the Baltic States and Bessarabia (June)	The Germans invade Russia (June). They are halted outside Moscow (December)
1924		**1940**	

1929	1936	April 8–11, 1940	1949
First attempts at collectivization	The Anti-Komintern Pact (Germany and Russia)	Massacre of 1,400 Polish prisoners at Katyn by Russian security services	Creation of NATO (April)

1924–91: Leningrad, glory and calamity

A NEW IMAGE OF THE CITY

The houses of one and a half million emigrants and victims of war and revolution were occupied by workers and peasants fleeing collectivization (1928–33). These people became city workers and were distinct from the native St Petersburgers in their language and way of life. The atmosphere of the city, in which before the revolution the cream of the aristocracy and the intelligentsia had flourished, became envenomed as Leningrad found itself increasingly sidelined and provincialized. Nevertheless, the Soviet government in Moscow continued to regard Leningrad as a free-thinking potential rival. The Party's purges and wholesale arrests uprooted many recently arrived families, adding to the prevailing loss of identity in the city.

A new image was to emerge later, in consequence of the heroic resistance during the siege of Leningrad (1941–4), although the city's troubles did not come to an end until the 1960's and 1970's, with the stabilization of the population and an improvement in living conditions.

THE OPENING OF LENINGRAD TO TOURISM

The work of restoration which had continued ever since the end of the siege had taken on a different character by the end of the 1970's, the purpose of which was to recreate the city's former charm. After the opening of an initial underground railway in 1955, new lines were built on a regular basis; the length of the Neva embankment was tripled (nearly 100 miles of it were reinforced with granite); park space in the city was increased to 22,500 acres, and the number of bridges was increased to 310 by 1989. Meantime cheap high-rise housing began to make its mark on the various islands (42 new projects were completed in 1970). Soviet tourists arrived to visit the "glorious city", and with the new policy of detente toward the West even foreign visitors began to appear.

| March 5, 1953 | August 1, 1975 | | November 1989 | 1993 September 21: Supreme Soviet is |
Death of Stalin | Helsinki conference. Signature | | Fall of the Berlin | dissolved. December 12: Election of the |
	of the final act on Human		Wall	first Russian Duma; a new constitution
	Rights			is drawn up by referendum
1960		1980	1990	2005

February 1956   March 11, 1985   1991 June 12: First democratic election in Russia:
Khrushchev denounces   Gorbachev is elected First Secretary   Yeltsin elected President. December 25: The USSR
Stalin's personality cult   of the Soviet Communist Party   becomes the Commonwealth of Independent States

THE PALACES AROUND LENINGRAD

The environs of Leningrad suffered terribly from the German occupation, and after the Allied victory in World War Two the towns in the region were so badly damaged that they had to be reconstructed rather than restored. With their 18th-century palaces and parks, these museum-towns are very much a part of Leningrad and are well worth visiting. They are also highly functional: Petrodvorets, with its university campus, is populated by students; Tsarskoe Selo trains farmers from all over the country at its Agricultural Institute; Gatchina is a scientific research center with a number of different institutes. Oranienbaum, Pavlosk and the isthmus of Carelia are now popular summer resorts. The latter is well-known for its beach, Duny; it has become an upmarket resort for the people of St Petersburg. A sports complex is also being built there.

ST PETERSBURG SINCE 1991

REBIRTH OF THE CITY

On June 12, 1991, 54 percent of the city's inhabitants voted to restore its historic name. "St Petersburg" has come back, but with more difficulty than the Kirov Ballet experienced in readopting the name of Mariinsky, or the University in jettisoning the name of Zhdanov. For the 300th anniversary celebrations in 2003, St Petersburg was spruced up to reflect its past splendors. Some important restoration work was undertaken in the historic districts. The façades of the houses along the Nevsky Prospekt were repainted in brilliant colors. Another sign of a renaissance has been the resumption of literary works on and about the city, including a major collection entitled *The Petersburg Metaphysic*.

A SOLUTION TO THE PROBLEM OF FLOODING

On several buildings in the city are plaques indicating the levels of the worst floods among the 253 which have afflicted St Petersburg since 1703. One of these recalls the catastrophe of November 7, 1824, when the water rose 12 feet. Today, the reformist administrators of St Petersburg and their Finnish neighbors are committed to renewing the city's flood protection facilities, while respecting the ecology of the region.

GEDENKE
DES HOHEN WASSERS
AM 7 NOVEMBER
1824

35

Czar Alexander I
presents his army to
Napoleon.

MIKHAIL FYODOROVICH (1613–45)*. The first of the
Romanov Czars, son of Fyodor Nikitich, better known
as Filaret, patriarch of Tuchino and descendant of the
Riurik family (founder of the Kiev state, the first state
of Russia).

ALEXEI I (1645–76)*. The son of Mikhail Fyodorovich. In
the early years of his reign, the state was run by his tutor, the
boyar B. Morozov. This reign was marked by a major social
crisis and ecclesiastical reforms initiated by the Patriarch of
Moscow, Nikon.

SOPHIA (1682–9)*. In 1689 Sophia
Alexeyevna was assigned to the
monastery of Novodyvichy
(Moscow) and the regency
passed to Natasha Naryshkin
(second wife of Alexei I and
mother of Peter I).

FYODOR III (1676–82)*. The son
of Alexei I and Maria Ilinychna,
Fyodor was bored by affairs of
state and allowed his advisors to
run the country. He died at 21.

**CATHERINE
(1691–1733)**

ANNA YOANNOVNA (1730–40)*.
Niece of Peter I, Anna was
chosen by the supreme council
(over her daughters Anna and
Elizabeth) to succeed Peter II.
Hers was an arbitrary regime.

ALEXEI (1690–1718).
After joining the conspiracy
against his father, Alexei was
condemned by the Czar,
imprisoned and tortured.

PETER II (1727–30)*. Grandson
of Peter I. Peter's brief reign was
marked by the return of the court
to Moscow and the eviction of
Prince Menshikov.

IVAN VI (1740–1)*
Regency of Anna.

ALEXANDER I (1801–25)* (left).
The adored grandson of Catherine
II. Russia in his reign joined the
coalition against Napoleon; later,
Alexander instigated major reforms
and founded many new institutions.

ALEXANDER III (1881–94)*. Son of Alexander II.
The assassination of his father led him to bring
a halt to the reform movement and re-establish a
conservative regime.

NICHOLAS II ● *44* (1894–1917)*. Son of
Alexander III. The dynasty's last emperor.
His reign ended in the upheaval of the
Revolution in 1917, which cost Nicholas
and his family their lives (July 17, 1918).

IVAN V (1682–96)*
Brother of Fyodor III. Co-Czar with his half-brother Peter (the future Peter the Great), during the regency of Sophia Alexeyevna.

PETER I (1682–1725)*. ● 38. On the death of his mother, Peter the Great seized the reins of power. His second wife, **CATHERINE I (1725–7)*** was a Lithuanian peasant girl. On his death, she became the first Empress of Russia.

ANNA (1708–28)

ELIZABETH PETROVNA ● 31 (1741–61)*
Daughter of Peter the Great, she organized a coup d'etat in 1741, deposing Ivan IV, great-nephew of Anna Ivanovna.

PETER III (1761–2)*. Son of the Duke of Holstein-Gottorp. In 1745 he married Sophia of Anhalt-Zerbst (the future Catherine II).

CATHERINE II ● 40 (1762–96)*
Took power in a 1762 coup d'etat, supported by the officers who had assassinated her husband.

PAUL I (1796–1801)*. Son of Peter III and Catherine II, whom he loathed. Assassinated in the Engineer's Castle.

NICHOLAS I (1825–55)*. Brother of Alexander I. His reign was marked by the Decembrist uprising and the Crimean War.

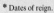

ALEXANDER II (1855–81)*
Son of Nicholas I. From the end of the Crimean War, he undertook a reform program (abolition of serfdom in 1861) but was assassinated by terrorists.

* Dates of reign.

RASPUTIN ▲ 202 (1872–1916)
Born a peasant (his real name was Grigor Novykh), Rasputin was introduced into the court of Nicholas II on account of his healing powers. Very quickly he gained huge influence over the Czar's political decisions. On December 16, 1916 he was assassinated by Prince Yusupov.

● PETER THE GREAT

By inviting Western technicians and military officers to Russia, Peter the Great was able to form a regular Army and Navy capable of defending his country's interests. As Czar, his principal objective was to make Russia a great military power, not to transplant European civilization into it. But a century after his death, Russian intelligentsia was divided between the Slavophiles, who wished to eradicate Peter from Russian history, and the Occidentalists, who recognized his openness to progress while acknowledging that civilization was beaten into Russia "by blows of the knout".

> "He sought first to make Germans and Englishmen, when he should have been making Russians."
> J.-J. Rousseau

SAILOR, SOLDIER AND CRAFTSMAN . . .
At the age of ten, and on his own initiative, Peter formed an army. This "child's game" led to the founding of the three elite regiments which later spearheaded Russia's victory over Napoleon. The Czar grew up far from the sea but was forever dreaming of it. An abandoned English ship in one of his grandfather's dry-docks sparked his longing for a great Russian fleet. He learnt about naval construction at Saardam, in 1697: the first frigate of Russia's fleet was partly built by his hands.

A "NOBLE SAVAGE"
In the European vogue, Peter had an African prince called Ibrahim brought to his court. The man who organized the kidnapping was an ancestor of Tolstoy's. Ibrahim became a general (Hannibal) in the Russian Army, and was the great-grandfather of the poet Pushkin ● 114.

ECCENTRIC VALUES

Culturally, Peter was an innovator; but many of his changes were frankly viewed as sacrilege. Beards had to be shaved; clothes were "teutonized" in styles that had formerly been regarded in Russia as carnival costumes. The Czar also instituted a Council of Drunkenness as a parody of the Ecclesiastical Council, and arranged elaborate marriages and funerals for dwarves, whom he pilloried to amuse his court. Russian culture somehow remained in place, but with its values knocked topsy-turvy.

THE DESPOT

Peter, as Czar, pitied no man and respected nothing. During his reign the nobles were forced to educate themselves; if they did not, they were forbidden to marry. They also had to "divert themselves": in other words, frequent cafés and drink vodka, and serve vodka on all occasions, on pain of forfeiting all their possessions. The Czar's son Alexei ▲ 147 was accused of plotting against him, arrested, condemned to death – and tortured by Peter's own hand.

BRONZE GROTESQUE ▲ 148

In 1991 Chemiakin, a Russian-French-American sculptor, offered to the city of St Petersburg a symbol of the fallen empire, in the form of a statue of Peter fixed in his chair. The head, sculpted after a mask done by Rastrelli in 1719, is completely disproportionate to the body.

On her arrival in Russia Sophia of Anhalt-Zerbst, Princess of Pomerania and fiancée of Peter III, noted in her journal: "I will reign alone over Russia." Shortly after, while Russophobia and disdain for the orthodoxy of her husband were causing outrage in St Petersburg, she converted to the Orthodox religion. In 1762 she acceded to the throne as Catherine II, supported by the officers who had assassinated her husband.

A CIVILIZING INFLUENCE

When Catherine acceded, the state of academic faculties in the city was such that there might be only one student per class; police had to recruit pupils on the day schools opened.

A PHILOSOPHER ON THE THRONE

Catherine wished her reforms to answer the desires and interests of her subjects. Quoting Montesquieu, Quesnay and Beccaria, she put forward her ideas in a treatise, the *Nakaz*, whose triumph is depicted in the allegory at right. In 1767 Catherine formed a legislative committee, but came up against deputies who were ignorant of both government and the mechanics of the modern state, and unanimously defended the right to possess serfs.

At the close of the 18th century Russia had nearly 300 schools, promoting the rise among ordinary Russians of an intelligentsia. The nobility was educated at home, but 200 of its daughters were taught at the Smolny Institute, which opened in 1764 ▲ *250*.

MILITARY GLORY

The victories of Marshal Alexander Suvarov over the Turks in 1790 and then over the French Army in the Alps in 1799 not only earned him the title of Prince of Italy but also gave Russia a decisive role on the European scene.

PUGACHOV'S REVOLT
In 1774, Pugachov, an illiterate cossack calling himself Peter III, threatened the throne of Catherine II.

People from the Volga regions, peasants working in the factories of the Urals and serfs flocked to Pugachov's banner.

"A WORSE REBEL THAN PUGACHOV"
This was Catherine's note on Radishchev's book *A Journey from St Petersburg to Moscow* (1790). Its author, a Russian noble who had studied at the University of Leipzig, was influenced by "half-baked scholars like Rousseau and Raynal". Observing the wretched state of the serfs in the two capitals, Radishchev condemned the regime of the "enthroned philosopher", who according to him was " . . . a deformed monster, impudent, obese, with a hundred yapping heads".

THE NOTES OF CATHERINE II
Kurakin, the Czar's best friend, secretly collected the only copy of the notes of Catherine II, sealed by Paul I. These notes did not appear until 1858, when they were published in French, in London, on the initiative of the revolutionary Herzen – who also published Radishchev.

MÉMOIRES

DE

L'IMPÉRATRICE CATHERINE

ÉCRITS PAR ELLE-MÊME,

ET PRÉCÉDÉS D'UNE PRÉFACE

PAR

A. HERZEN.

(ÉDITION DE N. TRÜBNER & Cⁱᵉ.)

LONDRES,
TRÜBNER & Cⁱᵉ, 60, PATERNOSTER ₁
1859.

1825: THE DECEMBRISTS

During the military campaigns against Napoleon (1813–14) aristocratic Russian officers, educated from an early age by foreign tutors and (later) professors, saw at first hand constitutional regimes which had rid themselves of serfdom, and whose masses were moved by revolutionary ideals. On their return to Russia they formed secret societies with the aim of transforming their own country along the same lines. From 1822 onward these societies had polarized into two opposing groups, the Northern and the Southern.

CONSTITUTIONAL MONARCHY OR REPUBLIC?
Lively debates pitted Pestel, republican leader of the Southern Society, against Nikita Muraviev, the Northern leader, who proposed a constitutional monarchy. Some of the conspirators saw Pestel as a new Robespierre.

THE SENATE SQUARE
The conspirators decided to act on December 14, 1825, when the regiments of St Petersburg were scheduled to swear their oath of loyalty to Nicholas I. While some caused a diversion among the soldiers drawn up on the Senate Square ▲ 194, others (including Prince Trubetskoy, the instigator of the coup) hesitated so long that the Czar's troops were able to foil the revolt, killing 1,271 people.

HANGED REBELS
The five leaders of the Decembrist insurrection were led to the gallows on July 14, 1826, with signs reading "Assassins of the Czar" hung around their necks. Three of the ropes broke, and the hangings had to be carried out again.

> "The public is right; in Russian writers it sees its only guides, its only defenders, and its only saviors against their country's autocracy, against orthodoxy, and against official nationalism."
>
> Bielinsky, Letter to Gogol, 1847

WOMEN OF COURAGE
"We, heroines? We are only such in the works of poets, for all we have done is follow our husbands . . ." wrote Alexandra Davidoff, wife of one of the Decembrist rebels condemned to exile in Siberia. With Alexandra went twenty-two other women, among them the princesses Trubetskoy, Volkonsky, and Shakhovskoy. All abandoned their children to go into voluntary exile.

FOR POSTERITY
Lost in the crowd, the fourteen-year-old Alexander Herzen witnessed the religious service ordered by Nicholas I at the Kremlin following the hanging of the Decembrists, which impressed him with a lasting horror. In 1855 the five martyrs featured on the cover of the review *Pole Star*, which Herzen published in London and which was aimed at the Russian intelligentsia.

THE EXILE OF THE DECEMBRISTS
The women and their servants found lodgings in the vicinity of the prisons where their husbands were detained. The 120 men were condemned to hard labor in the salt mines. Their shackles were removed in 1830, and rings made out of them for the men's wives to wear. Discussion, correspondence and clandestine visits helped the months to pass. Between 1832 and 1839, their sentences served, the Decembrists installed themselves in Siberia, where they contributed to cultural renewal and political debate.

THE 1905 REVOLUTION

Following a wave of political reforms, after 1890 the Russian economy had to cope with the industrial revolution and the expansion of the cities, in which only 13 percent of the population lived. The agrarian sector remained stagnant: the peasants, who made up 85 percent of the Russian population, were kept in a state of abject serfdom by local aristocrats, despite their official enfranchisement. Two percent of the population owned nearly all of Russia's land, and the autocratic government proved incapable of changing a steadily worsening situation for the better. Finally, a disastrous war with Japan revealed the depth of the crisis.

BLOODY SUNDAY
On January 9, 1905, 140,000 demonstrators stood before the Winter Palace, brandishing icons and chanting their grievances. The response of the imperial troops was to open fire. The nationwide wave of outrage at the massacre turned into full-blown revolution.

THE BATTLESHIP POTEMKIN
In the summer of 1905 a spoiled meat broth served to the seamen aboard the battleship *Potemkin*, docked in a Black Sea port, provoked a violent uprising which left Odessa in ruins.

THE OPENING OF PARLIAMENT

Faced with a general strike, on October 17, 1905 the Czar approved a manifesto introducing a constitutional order. The inauguration of the Duma (parliament) took place on April 27, 1906 in the throne room of the Winter Palace.

TROTSKY

In St Petersburg the Menshevik Leon Trotsky took an active part in creating a form of direct democracy. Through the soviets workers were enabled to organize themselves independently of the government.

AFTERMATH OF 1905

After the crushing of the revolution, gallows – known as "Stolypin cravats" – became a common sight. Officially the Russian state was a constitutional monarchy, but in reality laws were applied arbitrarily and agrarian problems remained unsolved.

THE AGRARIAN REFORM OF 1906

This reform, arranged by Piotr Stolypin, consigned to oblivion the peasant communes which had hitherto regulated daily life in the countryside. Instead, it proposed the creation of a new social category of independent landowners.

THE 1917 REVOLUTION

Nicholas II and his family, prisoners at Tsarskoe Selo.

Russia's problems were compounded by World War One. The economy was unable to accelerate its rate of production to meet the new needs. Prices rose and inflation attained alarming proportions. Nicholas II was no longer a credible monarch, being perceived as the protector of Rasputin, a debauched charlatan who had cured his son Alexei; and as he was commander-in-chief of the Army a series of military defeats were sufficient to destroy the Czar altogether. The 4th Duma, which had remained loyal to him until 1915, finally stiffened in its opposition and resolved to depose him.

THE FALL OF THE CZARIST SYSTEM

The Czarist regime collapsed in five days, between February 23 and 27. Two plots, one in the Czar's immediate entourage, the other fomented by deputies in the Duma, projected the Czar's replacement by his brother. But the conspirators were forestalled by a spontaneous uprising by workers and soldiers in Petrograd, who seized the Arsenal and proclaimed a republic.

TWO POWERS

A power struggle ensued between the members of the provisional government, led by Prince Lvov, who wished to install a parliamentary regime and thereafter maintain the status quo, and the Petrograd Soviet, which advocated radical change.

FRATERNITY

While the streets of Petrograd resounded to the strains of the "Varsovienne" in honor of the martyrs of international revolution, the April Crisis suddenly struck. The Soviet offered the allies a "peace without annexations or reparations", which the provisional government affected to ignore.

SOCIALIST POWER
The socialist Kerensky, who became Prime Minister in July, was unable to control the radicalization of the masses.

"ALL POWER TO THE SOVIETS"
From April onward this was the rallying cry of the Bolsheviks. Their role in crushing a *putsch* led by General Kornilov, a monarchist rival of Kerensky, enabled them to attract both revolutionary socialists and Mensheviks to their cause during August. The bolshevization of the soviets was then quickly accomplished.

THE BOLSHEVIK TRIUMPH
This poster, which has since become an icon, was at first little understood. The failure of the Kornilov *putsch* drew Western attention away from Russia. In France and England the fall of Kerensky and the October Revolution ▲ *248* were passed over almost without comment, even in well-informed socialist circles. The bolshevization of the soviets likewise went unnoticed.

The Terror, or Purge, is often explained in terms of the personal motivations of Stalin himself, who was bent on revenge against the older Bolsheviks and on gaining absolute power. In fact, Stalin's ambitions were quickly outstripped by the sheer enormity of the phenomenon he had instigated. After the assassination of Kirov the Purge reached a paroxysm, with over two million political prisoners between 1934 and 1938. The State-Party system never succeeded in overcoming the socio-economic difficulties stemming from violent collectivization and accelerated industrialization. Confronted with social tensions, officials at every level of Soviet society promoted the fear of Stalin, along with his virtual deification.

THE LENINGRAD OPPOSITION
In 1925 Zinoviev, the head of the Leningrad party, criticized the general party line represented by Stalin: the policy of concessions to the private sector (the NEP), inaugurated by Lenin, enriched new owners, while the workers' standard of living showed little improvement. Zinoviev changed his views at the 14th Congress in December 1925.

THE WHITE SEA–LAKE ONEGA CANAL
The canal linking the White Sea with Lake Onega, a giant construction project 140 miles long, was completed as part of the first Five Year Plan (1928–32). Mostly built by political prisoners, the canal gave its name to the tobacco brand Belomorkanal. The painting above illustrates the tribute in human lives which the Soviets had to pay to Stalin's planners.

THE ASSASSINATION OF KIROV

Kirov (below), the party chief, was very popular in Leningrad on account of his attempts to raise the workers' standard of living. On December 1, 1934 Kirov's assassination allowed those responsible for Russia's economic chaos to direct the popular fury against "spies", "saboteurs" and other "turncoats".

С. М. КИРОВ

ИСКОРЕНИМ ШПИОНОВ и ДИВЕРСАНТОВ!

"NIGHT TERROR"

The great show trials held in Moscow unleashed a widespread sense of insecurity, the "night terror". Arrests were invariably carried out at dawn.

THE PURGE OF COSMOPOLITANS

Leningrad artists and intellectuals were the first victims of a campaign led by Zhdanov, the ideological head of the Central Committee, who demanded "proletarian science and art".

1948: THE LENINGRAD AFFAIR

Popov, the party chief (below), was shot along with a number of other officials on a charge of seeking to turn Leningrad into the capital of a federal Russia.

ябрьской

THE SIEGE OF LENINGRAD

CONDEMNED TO DEATH
The three million inhabitants under siege by the Wehrmacht had fuel and provisions for only two months: their water and electricity supplies were cut by the bombardments. Only a quarter of the sixty-eight armaments factories supplying the defenders of Leningrad were operational.

Soviet agents and diplomats rapidly informed Stalin of alarming German troop movements along the frontier. Having underestimated the threat, Stalin found himself obliged to intervene personally when Nazi troops flooded into the USSR. The ensuing battle, as sudden as it was catastrophic, took a huge toll in Russian lives. The siege of Leningrad, which was to last nine hundred days, was one of the most tragic consequences of Stalin's giant error. On September 8, 1941 the front had come within 4 miles of the city's southwestern edge, and Leningrad was linked to the rest of the country only by air and by way of the frozen waters of Lake Ladoga.

FAMINE IN LENINGRAD
Famine took hold from the autumn of 1941 onward, and was sharpened by the loss by fire of most of the warehouses containing the city's meager reserves of food. By December over 53,000 people had died, and the daily bread ration was down to 9 oz for workers and 4½ oz for the unemployed and for children. During the siege over 800,000 people died of hunger, 17,000 were killed, and 35,000 were wounded in the fighting.

THE LIFELINE
One of the few ways out of besieged Leningrad lay across the frozen waters of Lake Ladoga. From November 1942 a track was made across the ice which allowed the city to be supplied with bread. In the summer a network of pipes and cables running across the bed of the lake carried electricity and gasoline to the beleaguered citizens.

> "We have no fear of bullets
> Nor do we grieve for our houses,
> But we are resolved to preserve our mother tongue
> In all its truth and force." Anna Akhmatova, Feb. 23, 1942

HOPE RETURNS

By the end of 1942 Leningrad was gradually coming back to life: factories reopened and the nightmare of famine faded. In January 1943 the Red Army succeeded in breaking the German blockade along the lake shore: a railway was constructed via Schlisselburg, known as the "Victory Line".

A SYMBOL OF LIFE

The composer Dmitry Shostakovich, who volunteered for military service, was assigned for his own safety to sentry duty on the roof of the Conservatoire and ordered to compose a special work for the People's Theater. Evacuated from Moscow at the age of 35, he completed his work in the Urals: the 7th ("Leningrad") Symphony ▲ 228 was performed at Kubichev and Leningrad in 1942.

IMPERISHABLE GLORY

The celebratory fireworks of January 27, 1944 clothed the city in a lasting aura of heroism. After the war a million citizens were decorated for their part in the siege.

At the coming of *perestroika*, the Museum of the Defense of Leningrad (instituted 1946–9), reopened its doors; an association of survivors was founded, and September 8 was declared a day of national mourning.

● The Russian Language

Russian belongs to the Eastern Slavic family of languages. This family is further subdivided into three main groups: the Occidental Slavic languages (Sorb, Czech and Slovak), the southern Slavic languages (Serbian, Macedonian and Bulgarian), and the oriental Slavic languages (Ukrainian, Byelorussian and Russian). The second and third groups are all written with the cyrillic alphabet, with very slight variations.

The Cyrillic Alphabet

The monk Cyril and his brother Methodus perfected the glagolitic alphabet in 863. This alphabet was soon supplanted by a simplified equivalent, the cyrillic. The cyrillic alphabet includes several characters taken from both the Greek and Roman alphabets. In 1710 Peter the Great, with his *grajdnka* (civil alphabet), suppressed the graphic survivals of nasal vowels, and simplified the forms of certain letters. The orthographic reform of 1917 replaced the Ѣ by e, and almost did away with the use of the hard sign Ъ. The cyrillic alphabet in its present form contains thirty-two letters.

The Slavic Language

Common Slavic was the only language spoken in the plains of Northern Europe toward the middle of the first millennium AD. Old Slav as spoken in the 9th century (at the beginning of the differentiation between the Slavic languages and peoples) is still understood by most Slavs. From it came Slavonic, a literary and religious language still used in the liturgy of Orthodox Slavs.

52

FOREIGN CONTRIBUTIONS

Cyril and Methodus were sent to Moravia by the Byzantine Emperor Michael III to evangelize the Slavs. Their new alphabet allowed them to translate the New Testament into the old Slav language. For centuries thereafter the Psalter was to be the principal reading matter of Russians. Their many contacts with Byzantium, both peaceful and belligerent, eventually led to the conversion of the Kiev prince Vladimir in 988, followed by that of his people; this event marked the entry of the pagan Slavs into Christendom. Later Western influences contributed to the development of oral and folk art, in addition to an original and precocious body of literature, notably *The Sayings of Prince Igor*.

After the 11th century, old Russian texts, such as the Ostromir New Testament, were written in a mixture of authentic Russian and Slavonic, the proportions of which varied from period to period and genre to genre. The interraction of these two languages eventually determined the form of what we know as literary Russian.

LOMONOSOV
In his *Russian Grammar* (1755) Lomonosov, a brilliant self-taught scholar, historian and philologist, purged the written language of obsolete Slavonic expressions, then reordered the lexicon into three categories: Slavonic, mixed and Russian terms. Three styles emerged from the combination of these elements: low, medium and high. This rigid classification had the merit of giving spoken Russian the place it deserved in literature (including song, epigram, private correspondence, comedy), the Slavonic terms being relegated to a more abstract, elevated linguistic register.

THE AWAKENING NATION

The Mongol invasion (13th century) and the domination of the "Golden Horde" (Tartar state) condemned the Russian language to centuries of isolation, which was eventually shaken off by a new religious and national awareness. This turning inward, at first forced but later deliberate, was generally damaging, but after a period of difficulty, in 1613 the Romanovs took over: intellectual inquiry again appeared along with literature. The Slavonic, Greek and Latin Academy, founded in Moscow in 1682, used a ponderous, artificial, heavily russified Slavonic language which stifled poetic creativity; yet it laid the groundwork for the blossoming of Russian literature in the following century, by bringing *belles-lettres* to the forefront of Russian life.

LITERATURE AND THE RUSSIAN LANGUAGE

THE LANGUAGE OF POETS

Even more than grammarians, writers like Sumarokov, Derzhavin and Karamzin (left) were the architects of the modern Russian language. At the turn of the 18th into the 19th century they prepared the ground for the great works of Pushkin. Under Catherine the Great intellectual and artistic life intensified in richness and was marked by a desire to imitate French classicism as well as scrupulously to respect the hierarchy of genres and styles established by Lomonosov. Karamzin rejected all distinctions between the spoken language and the written one: his ambition was to elevate spoken Russian to the status of a literary language.

MODERN RUSSIAN

Thus modern literary Russian emerged by stages, enriched by the language spoken by ordinary people. Russian songs and *bylines* (song epics) passed into print and, thanks to the discovery of *The Sayings of Prince Igor*, the master story-writer Ivan Krylov was able to contribute to a synthesis between popular and academic Russian. Nevertheless, it was Alexander Pushkin who perfected literary expression in the Russian language, with his motto: "When things are simple, say them simply."

THE SPREAD OF THE RUSSIAN LANGUAGE

With the creation of the Soviet Union and its fifteen republics, twelve of which were non-Slav, Russian became the official language of the Federation.

Learning the language was made compulsory, not only for Soviet youth but also for the youth of the other Eastern countries. Many Africans, Asians and Latin Americans went to study in the Soviet Union and learned to speak fluent Russian.

Under the cultural influence of the West the language has borrowed heavily (and sometimes inelegantly) from foreign tongues, absorbing words which have often supplanted Russian ones. Yet Russian is also acquiring new home-grown terms to describe the political, economic, social and moral upheavals of the era.

oday Russian one of the five fficial languages of he United Nations, even though Russia's current difficulties impede its spread.

Arts and traditions

Today, as in the past, foreign visitors to Russia are amazed by the magnificence of the Orthodox liturgy, the gold of its icons and its polyphonic choral music. The Russians themselves cherish the beauty and symbolism of their Byzantine rite; a beauty which, according to the old chronicles, originally motivated their conversion to Christianity. Beyond their esthetic value these rites embody theological and spiritual teachings which remain unaltered since the 17th-century schism of the traditionalist "Old Believers". The Orthodox liturgy was the sole vehicle of faith permitted by the Soviet regime.

THE LITURGY
The length and the sheer splendor of Orthodox services tend to reinforce the idea of eternity and holiness, while its informality seems to welcome all comers.

The Orthodox year, with its round of feasts and fasts, is extremely rich and varied. The Russian Church still observes the Julian Calendar, which is thirteen days out of step with the Gregorian Calendar. The linchpin of church life is the Sunday Eucharist, during which clergy and congregation, including young children, take Communion.

RUSSIAN CLERGY
Parish priests (often married men) form the "white" clergy, while the "black" clergy are monks who have taken vows. Formerly the color of their vestments showed the difference between them. The bishops are appointed from among the monks and celibate or widowed priests; the principal of these bishops, the Patriarch of Moscow, is the titular head of the Russian Orthodox Church.

THE ICONOSTASIS
Covered with five rows of icons ● *58* and topped by a cross, the iconostasis is a central element in every Russian Orthodox church. It depicts the prophets, the feasts of the liturgical year and the dëesis (prayer) of the saints in company with Christ. The larger lower row is made up of the icons of Christ, the Virgin and the various saints. It has three doors, used by the clergy: the central one (the "royal door"), reserved for the most solemn rites of the Orthodox Church, symbolizes the entrance to the kingdom of God.

ORTHODOX CHURCHES
As the meeting point of God and mankind, the church signifies heaven on earth. Orthodox churches can be square or cruciform, and have a central dome; important churches have five domes, symbolizing Christ and the four Evangelists.

THE SEVEN SACRAMENTS
The Orthodox rite of baptism is followed by Chrismation (or Confirmation). The other sacraments are the Eucharist, marriage, ordination of the clergy, penitence, and the anointing of the sick.

ORTHODOX EASTER
Called the "feast of feasts", Easter is the climax of the Orthodox year. After the forty-day Lenten fast and the ceremonies of Holy Week, the celebration rite begins with a candlelit procession, followed by the announcement of Christ's Resurrection. At Matins the victory of life over death is exalted; later, friends and relatives gather round the Easter table, with its Easter eggs and cakes blessed at church.

● ICONS

The Orthodox Church, which rejected the charge of idolatry made during the iconoclastic controversy in Byzantium (8th century), defines the icon as bearing witness to divine revelation, and thus justifiable in terms of the dogma of incarnation (God may not be represented in a picture but Christ, who was made man, can be). The icon is neither a work of art nor a pious image: it has a clear liturgical function, as well as a teaching role.

THE ORIGINS
Icons, which came to Russia with Christianity from Byzantium, reached a degree of perfection following the iconoclastic crisis. The Greek mosaic artists who decorated the churches of Kiev in the 11th century trained the first Russian iconographers. In the *Head of Christ* below the influence of mosaic is clearly discernible, notably in the golden lines traced through the hair.

A PAINTED SCRIPT
The technique of icon-making has not changed for centuries. It employs only natural materials. The wooden panel is first covered with a fine layer of plaster, and the image is painted on the wet surface; the powdered mineral colors are blended with an egg-based emulsion. The painting is then embellished with gold leaf and varnished, and the title is inscribed in vermilion lettering. In the Slavonic language a single word is used for the functions of writing and painting; therefore the artist does not merely paint his icon but he "writes" it too.
Above: *Life of Saint Serge of Radonega* (16th century).

A WINDOW ON ETERNITY
This *Christ in Majesty* (16th century) shows all the symbolism and sanctity of the icon, through the use of concentric circles and inverted perspective to express a relationship between time and space which is very different to that of the world in which we live. In this way the icon becomes a kind of window on eternity. Such rules were codified in manuals, which also laid out guidelines for icon composition, the ordering of themes and use of color.

ANONYMOUS WORKS
Novgorod, Pskov, Suzdal and later Moscow succeeded one another as schools of iconography, each with its own tradition. The icon was never signed by an individual, but the fine rendering of the *Presentation of Christ* (right) is probably the work of Andrei Rublev, the great Muscovite icon-painter of the 15th century.

DECADENCE
From the 17th century onward the art of the icon was affected by excessive symbolism and borrowings from the West. The detailed and naturalistic *Trinity* (1671) by Simeon Ushakov, the official Kremlin painter, differs greatly from the icon by Rublev which inspired it.

REDISCOVERY OF THE ICON
In the 16th century a tradition arose of covering almost the entire work with precious metals. In the *Virgin of Kazan* (above, late 19th century) only the faces are visible. In the early 20th century the icon regained its original esthetic and theological aspects.

In the 18th century gold and silver work made in St Petersburg differed little from that of the rest of northern Europe, because the craft was essentially the preserve of foreigners who had moved to Russia's new capital. Even so, while the second half of that century was strongly marked by the influence of France, St Petersburg gained a high reputation for the sheer quantity and refinement of the objects produced by its jewelers. Although luxury items they were often in everyday use at court and in the houses of the rich. As a result this specifically Russian taste for enamel and precious stones had a strong influence on local production.

Part of a harness (1730).

JEWELRY AND GEMSTONES

Jérémie Pauzié, who made the gemstone flowers above, was born in Switzerland in 1716. At the age of thirteen he was apprenticed to a St Petersburg jeweler and, although he belonged to no special guild, was made court jeweler in 1740. This bouquet, mounted in a vase in the 19th century, was originally made to be worn at the shoulder or on a belt. It is typical of the court's pronounced taste in gems, which Pauzié used in profusion.

STEEL WORK

The Tula works, founded in 1712, produced a wide variety of objects. Although its specialty was weapons it was also famous for its domestic products; later it turned to the manufacture of furniture, the finest examples of which may be seen at Pavlovsk. The technique used was that of "blueing" the steel, and subsequently decorating it with gold, silver or copper. The cutting of the steel to resemble facetted pearls, as well as its polish, produced an effect which is still highly valued by collectors.

MASTERWORKS

This gilded silver platter, decorated by the *repoussé* technique, resembles the work being done at the same period in Germany. There is no hallmark on the piece but the dedication to Peter the Great dates it to between 1721 and 1725.

Chessmen, Tula, late 18th century.

TOBACCO BOX

Tobacco boxes of this type were very much the fashion at the Russian court; they were frequently presented by monarchs as diplomatic gifts, and were also given as lovers' pledges. Pauzié made scores of them for the Empress Elizabeth I.

Cigarette box, gold and enamel (1908).

"If you compare my creations to those of Tiffany, Boucheron and Cartier you will conclude that they are of lesser value ... but what, in fact, are these companies? They are sellers of jewelry, they are not artists. Hugely valuable objects interest me little, if their value resides in nothing more than an infinity of diamonds and pearls." This remark by Fabergé neatly expresses the spirit of his world-famous firm.

CARL FABERGÉ
Born in St Petersburg in 1846, the son of a modest jeweler of Huguenot stock, Peter Carl Fabergé took over the family business in 1870 and began by producing jewelry to conform with the prevailing taste for all things French. The arrival of his brother Agathon, an imaginative artist, contributed to the blossoming of the business after 1882.

THE FLOWERS
Fabergé's naturalist compositions are executed with astonishing skill: oatgrass and cornflowers on golden stalks rise from a translucent vase of rock crystal.

THE EGGS
Fabergé's eggs are marvels of inventiveness and delicacy. They are still copied today.

ENAMELS

Worked in *champlevé* or applied in successive layers on a checkered background, enamelwork was produced in over a hundred different hues.

PRECIOUS METALS

Fabergé's metals were also very finely worked: up to four shades of gold might be blended to produce the desired effect. Silver was deliberately left in its original state.

SEMI-PRECIOUS STONES

Pink and black rhodonite, mouse-gray Kalkan jasper and pale green nephrite (mined in the Urals) gave Fabergé's designers all the imaginative scope they needed to create their confectionery dishes, figurines and quaint animal sculptures.

IMPERIAL COMMISSIONS

Under the aegis of the master Mikhail Perkhin, in the 1890's Fabergé's workshops produced large quantities of objects and gems, many of them commissioned by the Czar's family. Fabergé Easter eggs were given by Nicholas II to his mother and his wife.

1749

Peter the Great had tried to reproduce Delft and Meissen "porcelain" (in fact it was faience) in Russia, without success. It was not until the appearance of Dmitry Vinogradov (1720–58), a friend of the famous savant Lomonosov, that the technique was achieved with any degree of success. Later, in the reign of Elizabeth I, the process of manufacture was perfected, a fact mentioned in a contemporary publication. The first imperial porcelain works on the banks of the Neva produced buttons, cane tops and knife handles (1745–50). Then, as technical skills improved, complete table services were manufactured for the court, along with statuettes whose imperfections were often masked by lavish gilding.

MADE-TO-ORDER TABLE SERVICES
Private factories soon made their appearance, competing directly with the imperial works; they created made-to-order table services, some commissioned by Catherine II. These services, which might include up to a thousand pieces, reflect the growing luxury of the imperial table, particularly in the 19th century.

FIGURINES
The production of figurines, typically Russian, has never ceased in St Petersburg. The only changes brought to it by the Revolution were in the types of figures portrayed.

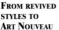

GUREEV TABLE SERVICE (1807)
This service bears the name of the head of Alexander I's Imperial Cabinet. The various pieces are remarkably diverse, with beautifully defined figures.

FROM REVIVED STYLES TO ART NOUVEAU
Following its approximation to the Sèvres style in the late 18th century, Russian porcelain went through a historicist period in the first quarter of the 19th century. Later it regressed into a multicolored, richly gilded Rococo style. At the close of the 19th century the imperial porcelain works came under the influence of Copenhagen, adopting modern simplified forms and new colors and designs in the Art Nouveau style.

CONSTRUCTIVIST PORCELAIN
Porcelain manufacture was a domain in which the modernization of designs and ideas could immediately be applied. This meant that propaganda themes coexisted with Constructivist work, often produced by such renowned artists as Malevich and Kandinsky, who in no way disdained this unusual medium. Above, a tea-service in porcelain designed by Malevich; the link with his paintings
● *109*, *110* is evident.

● FURNITURE

As a rule the palaces of St Petersburg were decorated with furniture designed on French, English and German models, when these pieces were not directly imported from Western Europe. Furniture made in Russia remained simple and massive until the reign of Peter I, but its quality developed rapidly throughout the second half of the 18th century. The extensive building projects of Catherine II and her court stimulated a marked increase in demand, which eventually could be satisfied only by locally made products.

In the time of Peter the Great, the furniture trade specialized in marquetry as well as carved, painted and gilded pieces.

FREEDOM OF MOVEMENT
In the 18th century the work of cabinet-making in Russia was shared between the master-craftsmen of St Petersburg and trained serfs on aristocratic estates. Their virtuosity proved the innate skills of Russian woodworkers: the materials they used were many and varied, and they did not hesitate to blend indigenous wood species, which had an undeserved reputation for poor quality, with more exotic ones.

CARELIAN BIRCHWOOD
In the early 19th century new types of furniture – tiered consoles, serpent-shaped elbow rests and claw-foot armchairs – were introduced. Between 1820 and 1840 the use of natural woods became generalized, emphasizing the ornate aspect of Carelian birchwood.

NEW MATERIALS
An instinct for variety in materials is characteristic of this aspect of Russian decorative art. Already in the reigns of Elizabeth I and Catherine II steel-based furniture manufactured at the Tula works had made its appearance ● *60* near Moscow.

SCHOOL OF TALACHKINO
At the close of the 19th century the predominant furniture style still had its roots in Russian culture. Furniture of the Talachkino School reflected the carved geometrical shapes of the empire's Byzantine origins.

"RUSSIAN JACOB"
Another exclusive style of the late 18th century was "Russian Jacob" (strips of brass inlaid in mahogany, in geometrical patterns).

GILT AND SEMI-PRECIOUS STONES
In the 19th century Russia produced remarkable pieces of furniture (such as tables and monumental candelabra) incorporating colored crystal and stones mined in the Urals, which added to the exoticism of the new Italianate palaces then being built.

In their own way the theaters of St Petersburg bear witness to Russian political history, since their names invariably changed to reflect the party in power. As the custodians of Russia's great dramatic, lyrical and choreographical works the imperial Mariinsky and Alexandrinsky theaters mounted the masquerades of the early 20th century, which are evoked in Anna Akhmatova's "Poem without a Hero". These illustrated the dreams of a society in crisis; they included Lermontov's legendary *Masked Ball*, with lavish décor by Alexander Golovine. With *perestroika*, new theaters emerged; and innovative productions directed by Lev Dodin have demonstrated the enduring vitality of the Russian theater.

ALEXANDRINSKY THEATER ▲ 230. As the Academy of Drama in 1920, renamed the Pushkin Theater in 1937, the Alexandrinsky was, along with the Maly Theater in Moscow, one of the two great centers of 19th-century Russian culture. Between 1908 and 1918 it was profoundly influenced by the work of the great reformer Vsevolod Meyerhold (below).

MARIINSKY THEATER ▲ 202
This great institution was inaugurated in 1860, with the purpose of presenting the classical repertoire. Renamed the Kirov Theater in 1935, it later became the mecca of the Russian Ballet ▲ 200. It reverted to its original name in 1993.

LITTLE THEATER OF OPERA AND BALLET ▲ 225
Also known as the Maly or Mussorgsky Theater, at one time this was named the Mikhailovsky Theater. As the third of the former imperial playhouses it was the home of a French company from 1879 to 1917. Renamed the Little (*maly*) Theater, it was one of the few experimental institutions for opera and ballet in Russia during the 1930's.

BDT (TOVSTONOGOV THEATER)

"Theater of tragedy, romantic drama and high comedy" – or so its original purpose was described.

The theater was known as the Gorky Theater between 1932 and 1993. For thirty years it mounted the classic plays of G.A. Tovstonogov (below right, during a rehearsal), after whom it was renamed in 1993.

BDT poster for Shakespeare's Henry IV (right)

В. Шекспир

Король
Генрих IV

THEATER OF MUSICAL COMEDY (1929)

The director and satirical artist Nicholas Akimov (left) worked here from 1930 to 1950. This theater is known for its original repertoire.

LITTLE (MALY) DRAMATIC THEATER ▲ 238

This repertory theater, founded in 1944, acquired a wider reputation in the 1980's under its director Lev Dodin. The Maly Theater Company gained worldwide fame with new plays like *Brothers and Sisters* (1985, from a novel by F. Abramov) and *Gaudeamus* (1990, by Sergei Kaledin, left). In 1998 the Maly Theater won the accolade of Theater of Europe, the third to do so after the Odeon in Paris and the Piccolo Teatro in Milan.

St Petersburg, where the first school of Russian dance opened in 1738, well in advance of Moscow, is the cradle of ballet. The entire history of classical dance is marked by Russian emotion and poetry, which enriched a technique originally imported from Europe. This enabled Russian dancers, while mastering both Italian virtuosity and French academic rigor, to apply themselves to the expression of the inner life of their roles. From the *divertissements* and interludes devised by 18th-century ballet masters such as Landé and Fossano to the worldwide phenomenon of the Diaghilev ballets, Russia has raised this particular art to the highest level of her cultural heritage.

BALLETS RUSSES (1908–29)
The success of the Ballets Russes gave a new stimulus to European ballet, as dance in Russia became the focus of a wide variety of artistic movements and interests. The research of the choreographer Fokine and the painters Bakst and Benois resurrected images of antiquity, the Orient, Old Russia and traditional festivals.

LEON BAKST (1866–1924)
As a scene-painter and decorator working for Serge Diaghilev, Leon Bakst moved to Paris in 1909. Above, a costume design for *Narcisse*, Saisons Russes, Paris 1911.
Baskt's sketches are on show at the Theater Museum, Ostrovsky Square ▲ 231.

SERGE DIAGHILEV (1872–1929)
As the founder of the World of Art association Diaghilev masterminded the successful Saisons Russes tours abroad. He brought together the most brilliant and innovative artistic talents of his time: Bakst and Picasso, Fokine and Nijinsky, Karsavina and Pavlova, Rimsky-Korsakov, Stravinsky, Prokofiev and many more.

MARIA TAGLIONI (1804–84)

The romantic inspiration of this dancer continued to be influential until the emergence of authentic Russian dance in the 20th century. Her greatest achievement was the title role in *La Sylphide*, still a classic of the ballet.

HIGHLY COLORED MINIATURES

Fokine's Impressionist ballets broke with the epic compositions of Marius Petipa ▲ *200*.

VASLAV NIJINSKY (1889–1950)

The legendary *Après-midi d'un Faune* (1912), Nijinsky's first creation, along with *Jeux* and *Le Sacre du Printemps* (1913), shattered academic canons and broadened the artistic range of dance. These productions also foreshadowed the development of ballet in the second half of the 20th century.

CHARLES DIDELOT (1767–1837)

The French director of the St Petersburg Ballet School, who brought Russian dance to the fore in Europe.

The Capella, the Conservatoire and the Philharmonia, as the centers of St Petersburg's musical establishment, made it their business to encourage artistic creativity and the expression of musical talent. In the 20th century the musical traditions of the St Petersburg School are associated with the esthetic of the Group of Five, which included the composers Balakirev, Borodin, Cui, Mussorgsky and Rimsky-Korsakov. While the historic past and folktales of Russia were the main sources of inspiration, the music itself remained thoroughly European.

THE CAPELLA

Founded in 1479 in the reign of Ivan III, the original purpose of the Capella was to train church choirs. In the 18th century, at St Petersburg, it became an imperial chapel, with the most talented musicians serving as its directors. Later it offered a wide variety of musical training, from directing of choirs (1846) to folk music (1918). In 1920 the Capella introduced women's voices into Russian choirs for the first time.

THE CONSERVATOIRE

The fame of the Conservatoire, founded in 1862, rests on the extraordinary creative activity which at one time was centered upon it. The musicologist and art historian Stasov was the catalyst for the Group of Five composers, who were inspired by folktales and historical legends such as Boris Godunov; these were very different from the Moscow School, represented by Tchaikovsky and Rachmaninov, whose musical inspiration was more European in style.

THE PHILHARMONIA
This institution was named after Shostakovich in 1974. Dmitry Shostakovich (1906–75), although a quasi-official Soviet composer, fell out of favor with the authorities in 1947. Encouraged by Zhdanov, he belonged to the tradition of Bach and Mussorgsky. His work includes fifteen symphonies, among them the famous *7th ("Leningrad") Symphony* ● *51.*

SERGEI PROKOFIEV (1891–1953)
Trained as a pianist and composer at the St Petersburg Conservatoire, Prokofiev began his career as a concert artist. Between 1918 and 1932 he lived outside Russia; on his return to the Soviet Union he suffered political persecution. His work sums up the finest achievements of Russian music, from Glinka through to Rachmaninov (*Romeo and Juliet*, 1938).

IGOR STRAVINSKY (1882–1971)
A pupil of Rimsky-Korsakov, Stravinsky lived in Russia until 1914. He was later a permanent member of the Saisons Russes in Paris, where his ballets *The Firebird* (1910), *Petrushka* (1911) and *The Rite of Spring* (1913) were performed. The themes of these ballets were inspired by Russian folklore.

● RECIPE: "BLINIS"

Blinis, made from one of the oldest of flour-based recipes, were originally eaten "in communion" with the souls of deceased loved ones in Russia: at Christmas with *koutia* (broth made with cracked wheat), at funerals and during Carnival. Following the 1917 Revolution *blinis* became everyday fare in Russia, unconnected with the Orthodox calendar.

PREPARING THE MIXTURE
Ingredients
(for six people):
2lb 3 oz/10 cups flour
1½ oz yeast
½ tsp salt
1 tsp caster sugar
10 fl. oz lukewarm water
1 pint lukewarm milk
3 tbsp oil
3 eggs

1. Prepare in advance: in a warm bowl dissolve the yeast, salt and sugar in the lukewarm water. Pour the mixture into a mixing bowl.

2. Mixing well with a whisk, add the flour, milk and egg yolks, working till smooth.

3. Allow the mixture to rise in a warm place for 40 minutes. Cover the bowl. Then whip the egg whites until stiff.

4. Gently fold the egg whites into the mixture with a spatula.

6. Pour a little of the mixture into the heated frying pan, turning the pan to make the mixture spread as thinly as possible.

5. Lightly grease a 5-inch frying pan with a half-potato dipped in melted butter.

7. Cook at medium heat, as with pancakes (the first is often a disaster).

8. The *blinis* are then covered with melted butter and thick cream (*smetana*), and eaten with *zakuski* (hors d'oeuvres): smoked salmon, tarama, herring, salmon eggs, or similar tasty accompaniments. Traditionally, Russians serve *blinis* with an assortment of chilled red and black caviar and ice-cold vodka.

● RUSSIAN SPECIALTIES

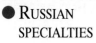

SHAWLS
Light and warm, Russian shawls come in many colors, usually with bright flower patterns. They are available in most department stores in St Petersburg.

ZEFIRS
Sweets resembling meringues coated in chocolate.

RUSSIAN VODKA
The best place to buy good-quality vodka is in shops specializing in the national drink. The most highly recommended brands are Sankt Petersburg, Diplomat, Piatizvezdnaya, and Sinopskaya.

RUSSIAN VODKA MUSEUM
The displays here trace the history of distilling in Russia from the 10th century. Guided visits include the opportunity to taste some of the best vodkas, along with a suitable selection of zakouski.

MATRYOSHKAS
These little dolls, usually made by Muscovite craftsmen, are very popular with tourists. The quality of the painted design may vary considerably.

CRAFTS
Handpainted wooden toys (above); objects made of amber or semi-precious stones (green malachite box, far right); lacquered Palekh boxes (right) echo the art of this former school of iconography.

Architecture

THE TOWN PLAN: THE FOUNDING OF ST PETERSBURG

In May 1703 Peter I, then at war with the Swedes, captured a stronghold at the mouth of the Neva river. To consolidate his victory he began building a new fortress 4 miles downstream dedicated to saints Peter and Paul, later adding the Admiralty and shipyards on the left bank. The site was unhealthy and ill-protected; nevertheless, by 1712 the Czar was determined to build his new capital there. St Petersburg, ". . . the window through which Russia looked out on Europe", evolved into a huge experiment, whereby patterns borrowed from Western cities were assimilated into Russian tradition.

HISTORY AND LEGEND
The legend of this city, which was born of the will of a single man, has left an indelible mark on history. Built "on the corpses of thousands of men", popular tradition has it that St Petersburg will one day return to the waves from which it rose.

THE MOUTH OF THE NEVA IN 1698
Apart from one or two settlements of Carelians, the flat, sea-level islands of St Petersburg were uninhabited and clothed with forest. They were subject to floods made even more fearsome by the current flowing out of Lake Ladoga where it meets the powerful waves of the Gulf of Finland.

THE PETER AND PAUL FORTRESS (1703)

A symbol of autocratic military power, the Peter and Paul Fortress stands directly opposite the Imperial Palace. The gilded spires of the Peter and Paul Cathedral, the Admiralty and Mikhail Palace add bright verticals to the flat, gray urban landscape.

THE DEVELOPMENT OF THE CITY

The plans drawn up by Jean-Baptiste Leblond, the chief architect for St Petersburg, were remarkable for a system of Dutch-style canals, supposed to absorb the flood waters and facilitate communications. Other features were an arrangement of the various districts to suit different sections of the population, and an attempt (eventually abandoned) to surround the city with ramparts.

● St Petersburg in 1725

Although in 1725 St Petersburg was far from completed, the planning options governing its later construction were already fixed. There were two fortresses to guard the mouth of the Neva (Peter and Paul on the right bank and the Admiralty on the left); the Menshikov Palace and the Kunstkammer endowed Vasilyevsky Island with its first architectural features; the Summer Palace and the gardens bounded the city to eastward; the river's tributaries had been channeled; and the Nevsky Prospekt had been laid out.

WAREHOUSES
The first constructions in the city were of wood, always abundant in Russia.

STANDARD HOUSES

In the interest of stylistic unity, the Italian architect Domenico Trezzini designed standard houses "... adapted to every class of society". With its Corinthian pilasters and central flight of steps, the House of the Ambassadors (above, 1710) was the most elegant building in St Petersburg, although it was constructed of wood and puddled clay. At left, the standard "economy" house.

In his haste to jettison Muscovite traditions Peter the Great engaged foreigners to build his modern city, naval installations and cultural center. Dutch engineers and Italian and German architects succeeded one another, until the arrival in 1716 of the French master builder Leblond. Leblond and his team were commissioned both to build, and to train the Russians in contemporary Western architectural concepts. "Naryshkin Baroque", characteristic of late 17th-century Moscow, gave way to Dutch pediments cheek by jowl with Italianate superimposed orders, German staircases and French curb-roofing.

THE KIKIN PALACE
▲ 250
Built around 1714 in the Dutch style (with gables and perron) for a senior commissariat officer of the Admiralty, the palace was never occupied by its owner, who was executed for his part in a plot against Peter I.

THE MENSHIKOV PALACE ▲ 161
The construction of this building (1710) began under the direction of Giovanni Maria Fontana, who was succeeded by the German Gottfried Schädell; but in effect every foreign architect in Petersburg seems to have made some contribution to it. The lateral projections were topped by gables in the Dutch style, while the main part of the building was covered by steel curb-roofing. The rooms of the upper floors were decorated with faience tiles, hangings and paintings. The first floor servants' quarters were vaulted, and glass was used for the principal windows, a novelty for Russia.

Plan of the Menshikov Palace

THE SUMMER PALACE
Built in 1710 by Trezzini along the lines of the "standard"
St Petersburg house for "notables", the Summer Palace was enlarged
and redecorated by Andreas Schlüter in 1714.

**EUROPEAN-STYLE
WINDOW, SUMMER
PALACE**
Light is admitted to
the palace by two
levels of rectangular
windows. Between
these levels, exactly
aligned with the
windows, are
terracotta reliefs
illustrating Russian
naval triumphs.

CABIN OF PETER THE GREAT ▲ *151*
The last surviving example of the first period
of construction at St Petersburg, this little
building is in the classic form of the *isba*. It
comprises two small rooms on either side of
an entryway. The wooden walls are painted
red in imitation of brick on the outside, and
hung with fabric on the inside. The window-
panes are of mica.

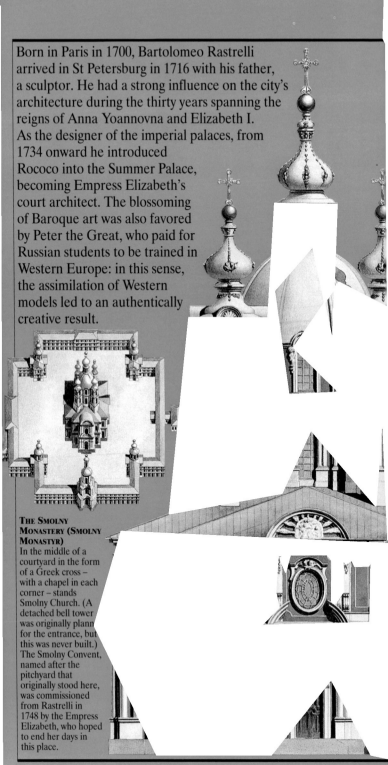

Born in Paris in 1700, Bartolomeo Rastrelli arrived in St Petersburg in 1716 with his father, a sculptor. He had a strong influence on the city's architecture during the thirty years spanning the reigns of Anna Yoannovna and Elizabeth I. As the designer of the imperial palaces, from 1734 onward he introduced Rococo into the Summer Palace, becoming Empress Elizabeth's court architect. The blossoming of Baroque art was also favored by Peter the Great, who paid for Russian students to be trained in Western Europe: in this sense, the assimilation of Western models led to an authentically creative result.

THE SMOLNY MONASTERY (SMOLNY MONASTYR)
In the middle of a courtyard in the form of a Greek cross – with a chapel in each corner – stands Smolny Church. (A detached bell tower was originally plann[ed] for the entrance, but this was never built.) The Smolny Convent, named after the pitchyard that originally stood here, was commissioned from Rastrelli in 1748 by the Empress Elizabeth, who hoped to end her days in this place.

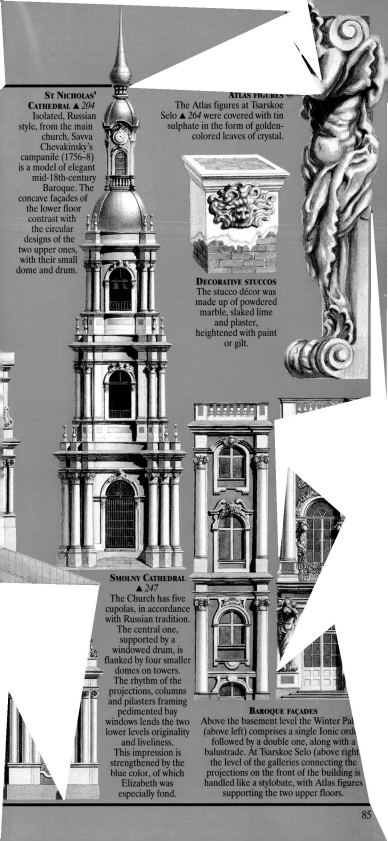

**ST NICHOLAS'
CATHEDRAL ▲ 204**
Isolated, Russian
style, from the main
church, Savva
Chevakinsky's
campanile (1756–8)
is a model of elegant
mid-18th-century
Baroque. The
concave façades of
the lower floor
contrast with
the circular
designs of the
two upper ones,
with their small
dome and drum.

ATLAS FIGURES ◁
The Atlas figures at Tsarskoe
Selo ▲ 264 were covered with tin
sulphate in the form of golden-
colored leaves of crystal.

DECORATIVE STUCCOS
The stucco décor was
made up of powdered
marble, slaked
lime
and plaster,
heightened with paint
or gilt.

SMOLNY CATHEDRAL
▲ 247
The Church has five
cupolas, in accordance
with Russian tradition.
The central one,
supported by a
windowed drum, is
flanked by four smaller
domes on towers.
The rhythm of the
projections, columns
and pilasters framing
pedimented bay
windows lends the two
lower levels originality
and liveliness.
This impression is
strengthened by the
blue color, of which
Elizabeth was
especially fond.

BAROQUE FAÇADES
Above the basement level the Winter Pal
(above left) comprises a single Ionic orde
followed by a double one, along with a
balustrade. At Tsarskoe Selo (above right
the level of the galleries connecting the
projections on the front of the building is
handled like a stylobate, with Atlas figures
supporting the two upper floors.

The New Holland Arch

On the accession of Catherine II, Bartolomeo Rastrelli was no longer in favor. The Czarina, who preferred sober lines, imposed a return to the canons of antiquity and the 17th century, surrounding herself with European architects such as Vallin de la Mothe, Antonio Rinaldi, the Scottish court architect Charles Cameron, Yuri Velten and Giacomo Quarenghi. Later, Alexander I brought the Empire style to St Petersburg (known in Russia, as the "classic" style), as a statement of imperial power. After the accession of Nicholas I in 1825 the major town planning review of the capital was entrusted to the Italian Carlo Rossi. It was Rossi who conceived the great colonnaded squares, so strong   a feature of the city today.

THE TAURIDE PALACE ▲ 251
Built between 1783 and 1789 by Ivan Starov for Prince Potemkin, the Tauride Palace is austere to a fault, with smooth walls, rectangular unadorned bays, an upper level topped by a frieze of alternating triglyphs and bare metopes, and a Doric portico.

PLAN OF THE TAURIDE PALACE
The central axis leading to the main gallery is flanked by pavilions linked to the main body of the building by wings; one of these contains the theater, the other the private apartments.

A DECORATIVE PROJECT
Devised for the state bedroom of the Grand Duchess Maria Fyodorovna, the wife of the future Paul I, in the Catherine Palace of Tsarskoe Selo ▲ 264. The designer was Charles Cameron.

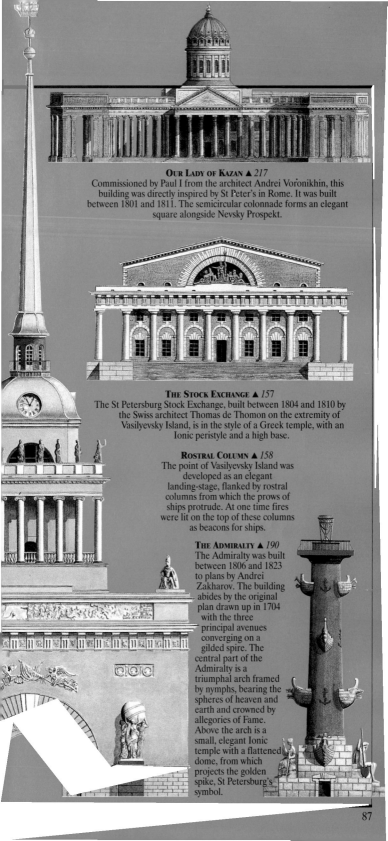

Our Lady of Kazan ▲ 217
Commissioned by Paul I from the architect Andrei Voronikhin, this
building was directly inspired by St Peter's in Rome. It was built
between 1801 and 1811. The semicircular colonnade forms an elegant
square alongside Nevsky Prospekt.

The Stock Exchange ▲ 157
The St Petersburg Stock Exchange, built between 1804 and 1810 by
the Swiss architect Thomas de Thomon on the extremity of
Vasilyevsky Island, is in the style of a Greek temple, with an
Ionic peristyle and a high base.

Rostral Column ▲ 158
The point of Vasilyevsky Island was
developed as an elegant
landing-stage, flanked by rostral
columns from which the prows of
ships protrude. At one time fires
were lit on the top of these columns
as beacons for ships.

The Admiralty ▲ 190
The Admiralty was built
between 1806 and 1823
to plans by Andrei
Zakharov. The building
abides by the original
plan drawn up in 1704
with the three
principal avenues
converging on a
gilded spire. The
central part of the
Admiralty is a
triumphal arch framed
by nymphs, bearing the
spheres of heaven and
earth and crowned by
allegories of Fame.
Above the arch is a
small, elegant Ionic
temple with a flattened
dome, from which
projects the golden
spike, St Petersburg's
symbol.

HISTORICISM AND ECLECTICISM

Western Europe's fascination with the past was reflected in St Petersburg, where neo-Baroque, neoclassicism, neo-Gothic and neo-Renaissance vied for precedence. The architecture of St Isaac's Cathedral is reminiscent of St Paul's in London, while the lavish décor of its interior borrows from every conceivable style. The Church of the Resurrection (also known as the Church of the Redeemer, or the Church of the Spilt Blood) is an example of a specifically Russian form of historicism, which had its origin in Moscow. It was built on the spot where Alexander II was assassinated, and has magnificent mosaics.

ATLAS AT THE BELOSELSKY-BELOZERSKY PALACE
This was the first palace in St Petersburg built with specific reference to the Russian Baroque style created by Rastrelli a century earlier.

THE CHESME CHURCH
Built between 1777 and 1780 by Yuri Velten, in honor of Orlov's 1770 naval victory against the Turks, this church and the palace in front of it are the earliest examples of neo-Gothic in Russia.

ECLECTIC DÉCOR
Behind the classical exterior of St Isaac's is a lavish interior: here painted frescos have been supplanted by mosaics (right) and marble wall-surfaces. The columns of the iconostasis are covered with lapis lazuli and malachite.

A HOMAGE TO TRADITIONAL RUSSIAN ART
Built between 1883 and 1907 by Alfred
Parland on the site of Alexander II's
assassination, this church was
intended as a celebration of Russian
art's enduring values. The aim was
not so much to imitate traditional
construction methods as to draw
on the decorative repertoire of
medieval Russia and 12th-century
mosaic techniques.

THE PEDIMENTS
The décor of the exterior pediments was
executed from cartoons by the greatest
Russian painters of the time, among them
V.M. Vaznetsov.

CHURCH OF THE
RESURRECTION ▲ *228*
The building was
directly inspired by
St Basil's Cathedral
in Moscow (1555–60).
Its main features
include a variety of
onion domes,
central tower with
a pyramidal roof,
kokoshniki or
halo-like decorated
arches, and tall
drums supported
by columns. It is
now open to the
public and
contains some
magnificent
restored
mosaics.

The brick exterior
heightens the overall
impression of
lavishness.

THE PORCHES
With their stout balusters and
hanging arches the porches at
ground level are built to a pattern
common in Russia until the late
17th century.

● BRIDGES

Trophies of empire on the
Panteleimon Bridge.

St Petersburg, eternally confronted with the
need to tame the flooding Neva and maintain
communications between its various islands, is
a veritable museum of bridge-building with a
wide variety of construction techniques. Until
the mid-18th century the only bridges here were of wood; later,
toward 1760, this was changed by new techniques of
construction in stone. Steel and cast-iron bridges arrived
at the turn of the 19th century, with the Industrial
Revolution. Toward 1850 the floating bridges spanning
the Neva were finally supplanted by steel bridges;
today these are still raised
to admit the larger
seagoing vessels.

THE NEPTUNE SCALE
Along the Moika Canal,
near the Blue (Sini) Bridge,
an obelisk was raised in 1971
to commemorate the
worst floods experienced
by the city.

CROSS-SECTION OF BRIDGE-ANCHORING SYSTEM
(Post Office Bridge across the Moika Canal.) Here decoration is
subordinated to the structure itself. The stay (steel chain) is buried in
a core of mortar, while beds of stone are angled into the ground to
bear the vertical load.

STONE SWING BRIDGE (LOMONOSOV BRIDGE)
The central bay was lifted with chains hauled by
winches, which were set in the granite towers at
either end of the bridge. Only two bridges in
St Petersburg (one being the Lomonosov
Bridge) have retained their original towers.
Toward 1780 seven identical arched stone
bridges were built,
each with a movable
central bay.

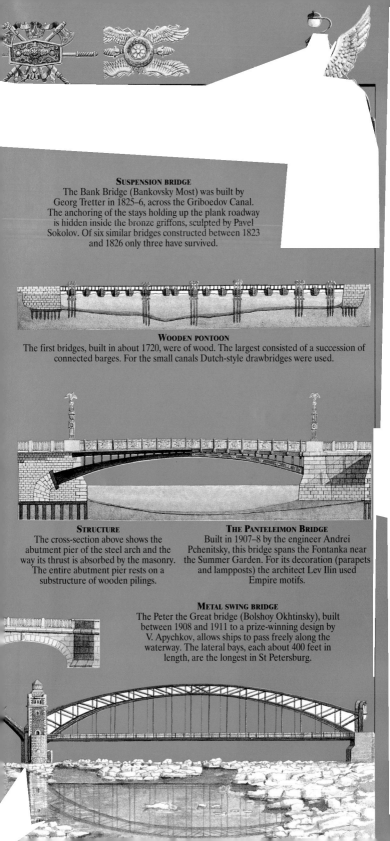

SUSPENSION BRIDGE

The Bank Bridge (Bankovsky Most) was built by Georg Tretter in 1825–6, across the Griboedov Canal. The anchoring of the stays holding up the plank roadway is hidden inside the bronze griffons, sculpted by Pavel Sokolov. Of six similar bridges constructed between 1823 and 1826 only three have survived.

WOODEN PONTOON

The first bridges, built in about 1720, were of wood. The largest consisted of a succession of connected barges. For the small canals Dutch-style drawbridges were used.

STRUCTURE

The cross-section above shows the abutment pier of the steel arch and the way its thrust is absorbed by the masonry. The entire abutment pier rests on a substructure of wooden pilings.

THE PANTELEIMON BRIDGE

Built in 1907–8 by the engineer Andrei Pchenitsky, this bridge spans the Fontanka near the Summer Garden. For its decoration (parapets and lampposts) the architect Lev Ilin used Empire motifs.

METAL SWING BRIDGE

The Peter the Great bridge (Bolshoy Okhtinsky), built between 1908 and 1911 to a prize-winning design by V. Apychkov, allows ships to pass freely along the waterway. The lateral bays, each about 400 feet in length, are the longest in St Petersburg.

Wrought-iron "entrelac" design.

In the early 20th century St Petersburg, like other European capitals, was affected by modernist trends. The Art Nouveau style, popular almost everywhere, seems to have acquired certain typically regional characteristics when it reached the banks of the Neva. The majestic architecture of the classical age, the exuberance of Baroque and the innovations of Art Nouveau in Europe and Scandinavia were metamorphosed in a highly original manner in St Petersburg.

RESIDENTIAL BLOCKS
In the Petrograd district a number of Art Nouveau buildings were constructed, notably that of no. 28 Bolshaya Zelenina (19th century), which included both artists' studios and ordinary apartments. The façade is varied by two oriels, and crowned by an extensive mosaic.

THE PRIVATE TOWNHOUSE
The townhouse of the ballerina Mathilda Kshesinskaya, on Kronversky Avenue, is a typical example of a picturesque yet elegant European-style Art Nouveau structure. It was built (1904–6) by the architect A.I. Hogen.

THE COMMERCIAL BUILDING

The Azovsko-Donskoy bank was built (1908–9) by the architect F.I. Lidval and the sculptor V.V. Kuznetsov. Designed in every way to reflect the grand scale of the capital, this building was inspired by the classicism of Catherine II's reign.

BAS-RELIEFS

Neoclassical Art Nouveau also had its place, in the bas-reliefs, decorative friezes and medallions of the bank's façade.

MATERIALS OF ART NOUVEAU

The door of the Zimmerman Building, built in 1906 on Avenue Kamennoostrovsky, shows the diversity of the materials and construction techniques used in Art Nouveau. Rough-hewn projecting stones, bricks and mortar surfaces combine for a colorful yet formal effect.

BLUE CERAMIC AND WROUGHT IRON

These supply the decorative motif for the cornice, which is handled in the classical manner. Note the foliated ribbon pattern on the flambeaux, with their pine-cone tops.

PROFILING

The profusion of glass, wrought iron, natural stone and vegetable ornamentation in the details of the surrounding balustrade and the projecting window show that the architect has fully mastered the new style without succumbing to eclecticism.

● CONSTRUCTIVISM

The Revolution of October 1917 marked a turning point in the development of Russian architecture. Thereafter the vogue was for the "Soviet style", or Constructivism, which could suitably represent the new ideology and exonerate architects from the charge of Formalism. Soon enough, Russian architects accomplished a stylistic transition, assimilating their classical heritage into a relatively human brand of Constructivism. This style, which developed in the 1940's and 1950's, was later baptized "Stalinist Empire".

RATIONALISM AND FUNCTIONALISM
This 1929 project, with its extensive glass and its concrete-covered walls, is typical of Constructivism.

ABSENCE OF DECORATION
Constructivism sought to respond to the needs of society, and condemned all embellishments as "bourgeois" and superfluous. Nevertheless, the residential building above (Karpovka Embankment, 1930) displays an example of Constructivist sculpture.

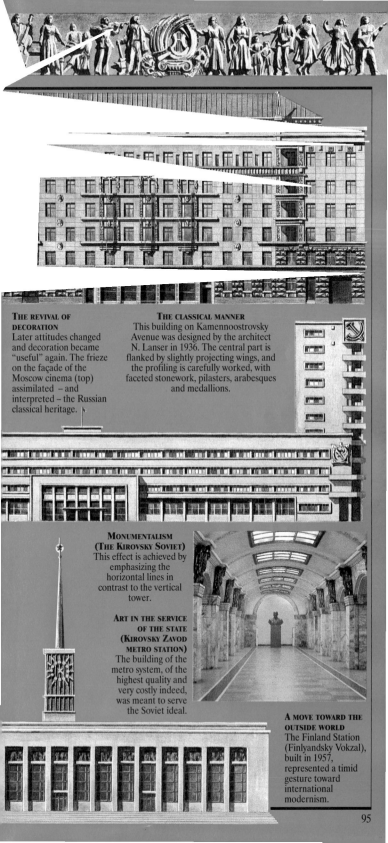

THE REVIVAL OF DECORATION
Later attitudes changed and decoration became "useful" again. The frieze on the façade of the Moscow cinema (top) assimilated – and interpreted – the Russian classical heritage.

THE CLASSICAL MANNER
This building on Kamennoostrovsky Avenue was designed by the architect N. Lanser in 1936. The central part is flanked by slightly projecting wings, and the profiling is carefully worked, with faceted stonework, pilasters, arabesques and medallions.

MONUMENTALISM (THE KIROVSKY SOVIET)
This effect is achieved by emphasizing the horizontal lines in contrast to the vertical tower.

ART IN THE SERVICE OF THE STATE (KIROVSKY ZAVOD METRO STATION)
The building of the metro system, of the highest quality and very costly indeed, was meant to serve the Soviet ideal.

A MOVE TOWARD THE OUTSIDE WORLD
The Finland Station (Finlyandsky Vokzal), built in 1957, represented a timid gesture toward international modernism.

95

Moscow Square, like so many others in St Petersburg, is regular and symmetrical. Government offices (right) and residential blocks (left), in the Stalinist Empire style, frame an area which dwarfs its human occupants.

STATUARY
The Soviet regime glorified its heroes by immortalizing them in the centers of city squares. The greatest of these, Lenin himself, dominates Moscow Square, while the heroes of the defense of Leningrad in 1941 (left) occupy Victory Square (both are the work of Mikhail Konstantinovich Anikushin, the People's Sculptor of the Soviet Union).

St Petersburg
as seen by painters

Like many of his Swedish compatriots Benjamin Patterssen (1750–1815) came to seek his fortune in St Petersburg. His arrival coincided with an important moment in the history of the city. The avenues were under construction and the people were impatient to see how their town would look once they were completed; above all, they had become acutely planning-conscious and were fascinated by major architectural ensembles. Profiting from this vogue, Patterssen began painting detailed views of St Petersburg in 1793; these were very popular on account of their refined technique and architectural exactitude. Patterssen also excelled as an engraver and draftsman; but his paintings of the city's monuments belong in the realm of poetry. His *View of the Kutuzov and Palace Embankment* (opposite) is remarkable for its rendering of the atmosphere and luminosity of springtime.

F yodor Alexeyev (1753–1824) was launched by the Fine Arts Academy as a painter of theater décors and a master of perspective. The result was that he was unable to give free rein to his own brand of classicism until 1790, at which time his views of St Petersburg had become so successful that Czar Paul I commissioned Alexeyev to paint several other cities in the empire, most notably Moscow.

Below, his *View of the Palace Embankment from the Peter and Paul Fortress.*

G rigory Chernetsov (1801–65) shifted the artistic focus from topography to portraiture. As a former pupil at the Fine Arts Academy, he followed his master Maxim Vorobiov (1787–1855) on the path of Romanticism. His *Neva Embankment in Front* *of the Fine Arts Academy: Night* **(2)** (about 1830) is a subject also treated by Vorobiov. This picture is not so much a representation of the city but more a picture of the river itself, and of the dreamlike atmosphere investing it during the hours of darkness, while *Parade on the* *Marsovo Pole (Field of Mars)* (1831–7) **(3)**, commissioned by Czar Nicholas I is a veritable portrait of St Petersburg society. The main interest of this huge painting lies in the figures that people it, which include, most notably, literary lions such as Krylov, Pushkin, Griboedov and Zhukovsky **(1)**.

At the St Petersburg Fine Arts Academy the art of interior painting reached its apogee in the mid-19th century. The teaching of perspective was revived by the efforts of Maxim Vorobiov (1787–1855). One of his pupils, Constantin Ukhtomsky (1818–81), along with two St Petersburg-based foreign painters (Edward Hau, 1807–87, and Luigi Premazzi, 1814–91), were chosen to paint the Winter Palace and the rooms of the New Hermitage (Novy Ermitazh) designed for the imperial collections. The three artists faced an identical challenge: to paint as much space as possible with the maximum number of details, juggling angles of view from perspectives that were impossible in real life. The commission was brilliantly carried out, as attested by Ukhtomsky's *Cimmerian Bosphorus Antiquities Room* (**2**), Hau's *Italian School Gallery* (**3**) and *History of Painting Gallery* (**4**), and Premazzi's *Artist's Apartment, Winter Palace* (**1**). The three artists' talents as watercolorists and their mastery of trompe l'oeil were also much admired by contemporaries, who followed the Czar's example in having the interiors of their palaces and houses similarly recorded.

1	
2	4
3	

From the time of their arrival in Russia in the late 18th century until the October Revolution of 1917 the Benois family remained implacably French. Nevertheless the painter Alexander Benois (1870–1960) was able to make the connection between the culture of his origins and that of St Petersburg, which he always considered his home. An avid historian, he maintained that his feelings about the past were "... more tender and affectionate" than his feelings about the present. As leader of the World of Art movement Benois created a completely new genre, the historical landscape, which allowed him to bring the 18th century back to life. His city of St Petersburg, whose image he held so clearly in his mind that he tirelessly painted it from memory, is peopled by courtesans and more or less enlightened monarchs. In much of his work St Petersburg is the background for ballet and theater décors. Real landscapes, personal memories and Benois' own deep knowledge allowed him to fill these décors with childlike innocence and freshness, as in *Holy Week Fair on Admiralty Square, about 1830* (right).

Anna Ostrumova-Lebedeva (1871–1955) illustrated another aspect of the historical landscape, with St Petersburg as the central theme. For her the only significant epoch was that of classicism, whose architecture and ambiance she painted in preference to people, as seen in *Columns of Our Lady of Kazan* (1903) **(2)**. Until her death, she continued to perfect her art, using watercolors and xylographs to depict the four elements and above all the waters of the Neva, which she viewed as the fountainhead of the city's poetry. *The Fontanka and the Summer Garden* (1922) **(1)**.

The Russian Avant-Garde

In the early 20th century the intellectual and artistic catalyst of St Petersburg (renamed Petrograd in 1914 and Leningrad in 1924) produced several avant-garde movements, led by creative talents of the first rank. Russian artists felt themselves on a par with their European counterparts, notably the French Cubists and Italian Futurists. They also expressed themselves within the context of various trends dominated by the new painting.

The Young Movement (1910–14), which generated most of the avant-garde's initiatives, attracted artists as different as Matiushin, Rozanova, Malevich, Tatlin and Filonov. Their links with Parisian Cubists and the Expressionists of Munich (Kandinsky) eventually produced a conceptual structure (Rozanova, 1913) which led to the blossoming of Cubo-Futurism and the abstract art associated with Malevich. The movement which was to reverberate through the rest of the 20th century came to the forefront in December 1915 with the "Last Futurist Exhibition: 0, 10", at which Tatlin's "counter-reliefs" firmly established the trend toward Constructivism. Thus the dialectic of the decades that followed was inaugurated in St Petersburg. The 1917 Revolution led many of the most prominent artists to migrate to Moscow, but after 1921 the focus of modern art, now subordinated to Productivism, again shifted to Petrograd. Artists met at the Institute of Artistic Culture (GINHUK), by whose agency their works were assembled in the Russian

Museum ▲ 226 and the Zubov Art History Institute. The latter, which was opened in 1912, was intended to give St Petersburg's art an international dimension. Formalist (or Abstract) art, as championed by the Institute, fell into disfavor in the later 1920's, and eventually disappeared altogether.

MIKHAIL LARIONOV
Autumn (1912), a Primitivist work

In the years leading up to World War One St Petersburg attracted artists who had a powerful influence on the development of the plastic arts in the 20th century. Expressionist and Cubist exhibitions were held in the city, as were Futurist shows and other activities organized by Marinetti, Mayakovsky and others.

OLGA ROZANOVA, *Suprematist Composition* (1916–17)

Goncharova (1881–1962) and Larionov (1881–1964), the leaders of Futurism in Moscow, featured strongly in the exhibitions of 1910–14.

KASIMIR MALEVICH *Portrait of Ivan Klium* (1913)

NATALIA GONCHAROVA *Peasants Carrying Fruit* (1911–12)

KASIMIR MALEVICH
Supremus no. 55 (1916)

KASIMIR MALEVICH
The Carpenter (1930–1)

The brilliant Cubo-Futurist theories of Matvejs (1877–1914) were championed by Olga Rozanova (1886–1918). This artist, whose notions of color emerged in the form of Futurist-Expressionist paintings between 1911 and 1913, went on to produce striking "trans-rational" compositions (1915) in which the figurative element was used as a metaphor rather than an object. The Cubist work of Pavel Filonov (1883–1941) was inspired by Russian folklore and mystical aspirations, while the Suprematism of Malevich (1879–1935) took its cue from European culture. With its intuitive, abstract construction, Malevich's work moved away from material reality to celebrate "pure sensibility" (Suprematism, or "pure non-objectivity" as he himself defined it). Malevich's approach, inspired by Cubism but refined by him, demonstrates a basic unity; and it was this above all which characterized his first Suprematist constructions.

MIKHAIL MATIUSHIN
Movement in Space
(1919–22)

"his passage to the third dimension" d to a theorization f his thought and n individual pproach to spatial eality, to which the rtist applied imself in the 1920's. Mikhail Matiushin 1861–1934), a riend of Malevich, vas one of the most riginal artists uturist group a musician, painter, culptor and theorist f the plastic arts, e developed n original view f the multi- imensional space evealed by upra-sensorial xperience. According to his heory of "enlarged sion" our erception of the vorld can go eyond the real to different level of

subjective and intuitive experience. His work as a teacher and publisher established the literary and theoretical validity of the Russian Avant-Garde.

OLGA ROZANOVA
Office (1915)

THE RUSSIAN AVANT-GARDE

VLADIMIR TATLI
*Project for the
Monument to the
Third Internation*
(1920)

It is also in St Petersburg that the most famous work of Vladimir Tatlin (1885–1953), the model for his monument to the Third International, was created in 1919–20. This emblematic Constructivist piece, inspired by the Eiffel Tower, was supposed to ally the "logic of materials", which had fascinated Tatlin since 1914, with the Functionalist demands of the dawning technical age. The fame of the monument eclipsed the purely pictorial decline of this artist, who embraced the ideology of "renunciation of painting" in 1920–21. After the brief Formalist (Abstract) period epitomized by the work of Altman and Lebedev (now in the Russian Museum), the Avant-Garde period was supplanted by Socialist Realism, which faithfully reflected the new "restrictive" ideology.

Relief, 1914

● ALEXANDER PUSHKIN

"An extraordinary phemonemon and a unique expression of the Russian spirit," said Nikolai Gogol ● 122 of Alexander Sergeivich Pushkin (1799–1837). One of Russia's greatest poets, he was born into ancient Russian gentry on his father's side and, on his mother's, was descended from the Ethiopian Ibrahim Hannibal. After a rebellious childhood and the restrictive life of a courtier in St Petersburg, he lived through censorship, exile, close surveillance . . . and complete isolation. Revered as a national genius and a liberator of the Russian language, he is still considered to be a major figure in world literature. At his funeral a distraught elderly man, asked if he was close to the poet, replied "No, but I am a Russian."

A CLASSICAL EDUCATION
At an early age Pushkin discovered the major classical writers in the extensive family library. His taste for French writers (Voltaire especially) earned him the nickname of "Frenchman" at the Tsarskoe Selo Lyceum ▲ 267 (1811) where he was a pupil. It was here, at this famous school for the sons of nobility, that Pushkin first began writing poetry at the age of fifteen.

FIRST JOB, FIRST WRITING
In October 1817, Pushkin entered government service but was more interested in launching himself into a literary career and a rowdy lifestyle. He completed his first work, the Romantic epic poem *Ruslan and Ludmilla* (1817–20), which earned him a position at the forefront of the literary world.

"DEAR FRIEND HAVE FAITH . . . RUSSIA SHALL FROM HER AGE-OLD SLEEP ARISE"
In 1819, Pushkin belonged to a circle known as "The Green Lamp"; the Tsar's discovery of his revolutionary writings led to his exile (1820–4) in the south, followed by a period under close surveillance in Mikhailovskoe. The Decembrists' rising ● 42 changed his life. In a letter to the Tsar, he swore he had had nothing to do with this plot and requested permission to leave Mikhailovskoe. In exchange, Nicolas I offered his protection . . . and his own personal censorship.

"ₒRIS GODUNOV"
"lowing publication
the historical drama
ris Godunov, Nicolas I
cided to make Pushkin
ourt poet insisting
e must write a novel
the style of Walter
ₒtt."

AN UNHAPPY BUT CREATIVE EXILE
During his exile in the south of
Russia, Pushkin was given
subaltern duties under the
governor of Bessarabia. He
was allowed, however, to
visit the Caucasus and the
Crimea, where he was introduced to
Eastern and Greek
culture. Pushkin's
Southern Poems: "The
Prisoner of the
Caucasus", "The
Fountain of
Bakhchisarai" (1823)
and "The Gypsies" (1824)
bear witness to these new
and exotic influences
and also
demonstrate his
admiration for the
poetry of his
contemporary,
Lord Byron.

"EUGENE ONEGIN"
A mirror of 19th-
century Russian
society, *Eugene
Onegin* (1823–30) is
considered by some
to be the first
Russian novel
worthy of that title.
Its eponymous hero
is a frivolous dandy
based in
St Petersburg,
leading a life of
excess. He
eventually wearies
of the tedious
merry-go-round
and retreats to
the provinces, a
reflection of
Pushkin's own fate.

Les Grands-Croix, Commandeurs et Chevaliers du Sérénissime Ordre des Cocus réunis en grand Chapitre sous la présidence du vénérable grand-Maître de l'Ordre, S.E.O.L. Narychkine, ont nommé à l'unanimité Mr Alexandre Pouchkine coadjuteur du grand Maître de l'Ordre des Cocus et historiographe de l'Ordre.

Le secrétaire perpétuel: Cte J. Bor...

"THE BRONZE HORSEMAN" AND "THE QUEEN OF SPADES"

"I earn money from my work and my work demands solitude . . ." Despite feeling oppressed by a difficult and turbulent life during his enforced stay at the family home of Boldino in 1833, Pushkin wrote two of his most celebrated works: "The Bronze Horseman" ● 118 and *The Queen of Spades*. The latter is the story of an obsession which turns into a nightmare: it tells of the secret of three cards the last of which, the Queen of Spades, brings about the downfall of the protagonist.

A LIBELOUS LETTER

On November 4, 1836, Pushkin received an unsigned letter dishonoring him and his wife. The writer was Baron Haeckeren, the adopted father of George d'Anthès, a French emigrant who was devoted to Pushkin's wife. The last thing that Pushkin wrote was a letter of reply to Baron Haeckeren.

СРЕДА. ТОМ I. №. 8. ФЕВРАЛЯ 9.

ЛИТЕРАТУРНАЯ ГАЗЕТА.

1830 ГОДЪ.

LITERARY CRITICISM
Pushkin was one of the first Russian writers to make a living almost entirely from writing. Following his return from exile, he became involved with his friend Delvig's *Literary Gazette*. In 1836, he obtained permission to start his own literary review, *Contemporary Life*, a collection of articles and critical studies on contemporary Russian and foreign literature. Only four editions were published during Pushkin's lifetime.

СОВРЕМЕННИКЪ,

ЛИТТЕРАТУРНЫЙ ЖУРНАЛЪ,

ИЗДАВАЕМЫЙ

АЛЕКСАНДРОМЪ ПУШКИНЫМЪ.

"VENUS AND THE VULCAN"
On February 18, 1831, Pushkin and Natalia Goncharova were married in Moscow. The poet was then caught up in a whirl of celebrations (and growing debts). In 1831 at Tsarkoe Selo, Natalia was officially presented to the Empress . . . and was soon after courted by the Emperor.

THE DUEL
On January 26, 1837, George d'Anthès challenged the poet to a duel. On January 27, on the banks of the Moika Canal, Pushkin was mortally wounded and carried back to his home at 12, Moika Quay ● *82*. He died on January 29. Several days later the young Lermontov hurled these vengeful lines: "All of your vile blood can never wash away/The fair blood of the poet!"

MAJESTY

PETER'S CREATION

"The Bronze Horseman" (1833) is an epic poem in which Etienne-Maurice Falconet's statue of Peter the Great, erected by Catherine the Great, comes to life and chases a clerk through the city during the 1824 flood. In this poem Alexander Pushkin (1799–1837) ● 114 uses the contrast between the menacing equestrian statue and the hero Eugene to symbolize the destructive effect of Peter the Great's imperialist Russia upon the ordinary man.

❝I love you, Peter's creation, I love your stern
Harmonious look, the Neva's majestic flow,
Her granite banks, the iron tracery
Of your railings, the transparent twilight and
The moonless glitter of your pensive nights,
When in my room I write or read without
A lamp, and slumbering masses of deserted
Streets shine clearly, and the Admiralty spire
Is luminous, and, without letting in
The dark of night to golden skies, one dawn
Hastens to relieve another, granting
a mere half-hour to night. I love
The motionless air and frost of your harsh winter,
The sledges coursing along the solid Neva,
Girls' faces brighter than roses, and the sparkle
And noise and sound of voices at the balls,
And, at the hour of the bachelor's feast, the hiss
Of foaming goblets and the pale-blue flame
Of punch. I love the warlike energy
Of Mars' Field, the uniform beauty of the troops
Of infantry and of the horses, tattered
Remnants of those victorious banners in array
Harmoniously swaying, the gleam of those
Bronze helmets, shot through in battle. O martial
Capital, I love the smoke and thunder
Of your fortress, when the empress of the north
Presents a son to the royal house, or when
Russia celebrates another victory
Over the foe, or when the Neva, breaking
Her blue ice, bears it to the seas, exulting,
Scenting spring days.❞

"THE BRONZE HORSEMAN",
SELECTED POEMS OF ALEXANDER PUSHKIN,
TRANS. D.M. THOMAS, PUB. SECKER & WARBURG, LONDON 1982

ST PETERSBURG MORNING

Vladimir Nabokov (1899–1977) and his family left Russia for Germany in 1919, and he lived thereafter in Berlin, Paris, the US and finally Switzerland. He wrote mainly in Russian until he moved to the US in 1940.

❝How utterly foreign to the troubles of the night
were those exciting St. Petersburg mornings when
the fierce and tender, damp and dazzling arctic spring
bundled away broken ice down the sea-bright Neva!
It made the roofs shine. It painted the slush in the
streets a rich purplish-blue shade which I have never
seen anywhere since. On those glorious days *on aller se*

promener en équipage – the old-world expression current in our set. I can easily refeel the exhilarating change from the thickly padded, knee-length *polushubok*, with the hot beaver collar, to the short navy-blue coat with its anchor-patterned brass buttons. In the open landau I am joined by the valley of a lap rug to the occupants of the more interesting back seat, majestic Mademoiselle, and triumphant, tear-bedabbled Sergey, with whom I have just had a row at home. I am kicking him slightly, now and then, under our common cover, until Mademoiselle sternly tells me to stop. We drift past the shop windows of Fabergé whose mineral monstrosities, jeweled troykas poised on marble ostrich eggs, and the like, highly appreciated by the imperial family, were emblems of grotesque garishness to ours. Church bells are ringing, the first Brimstone flies up over the Palace Arch, in another month we shall return to the country; and as I look up I can see, strung on ropes from housefront to housefront high above the street, great, tensely smooth, semitransparent banners billowing, their three wide bands – pale red, pale blue, and merely pale – deprived by the sun and the flying cloud-shadows of any too blunt connection with a national holiday, but undoubtedly celebrating now, in the city of memory, the essence of that spring day, the swish of the mud, the beginning of mumps, the ruffled exotic bird with one blood-shot eye on Mademoiselle's hat.❞

❝When museums and movie houses failed us and the night was young, we were reduced to exploring the wilderness of the world's most gaunt and enigmatic city. Solitary street lamps were metamorphosed into sea creatures with prismatic spines by the icy moisture on our eyelashes. As we crossed the vast squares, various architectural phantoms arose with silent suddenness right before us. We felt a cold thrill, generally associated not with height but with depth – with an abyss opening at one's feet – when great, monolithic pillars of polished granite (polished by slaves, repolished by the moon, and rotating smoothly in the

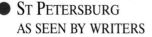

polished vacuum of the night) zoomed above us to support the mysterious rotundities of St. Isaac's cathedral. We stopped on the brink, as it were, of these perilous motifs of stone and metal, and with linked hands, in Lilliputian awe, craned our heads to watch new colossal visions rise in our way – the ten glossy-gray atlantes of a palace portico, or a giant vase of porphyry near the iron gate of a garden, or that enormous column with a black angel on its summit that obsessed, rather than adorned, the moon-flooded Palace Square, and went up and up, trying in vain to reach the subbase of Pushkin's *'Exegi monumentum'.* **"**

VLADIMIR NABOKOV, *SPEAK, MEMORY:*
AN AUTOBIOGRAPHY REVISITED,
WEIDENFELD AND NICOLSON, LONDON 1960

AMONG FRIENDS?
In which Dostoyevsky makes arrangements. . . .

"At the end of the Nevsky Prospekt is Alexander Nevsky Square . . . with the great convent and the church . . . and two ancient cemeteries, in one of which, Tikhvin, rests Dostoyevski, who had begged his wife not to bury him in the Volkovskoye cemetery among the literati. ('I do not want to lie in the middle of my enemies.') Around Dostoyevski are Glinka, Mussorgsky, Rimsky-Korsakov, Borodin, Tchaikovsky. Dostoyevski had never shown a particular inclination toward music; he appreciated Beethoven, Mendelssohn, and Rossini and could not bear Wagner. Destiny wished him to have as neighbors in death, besides his friend Nekrasov, the greatest musicians of Russia. After our companions in school, in military service, in hospital or prison, these are our final companions.**"**

ALDO BURGYS, "CHEKHOV IN SONDRIO",
TRANS. ANN GOLDSTEIN, PUB. *NEW YORKER,*
SEPT. 14, 1992

THE WINTER PALACE
After the great fire of 1837, the Winter Palace was rebuilt in a year.

"Under the Empress Elizabeth the palace had taken eight years to build; Kleinmichael completed it in one. True it is that almost the whole of the masonry resisted the fire, but the whole of the interior had to be reconstructed, and what a task that was! The work went on literally day and night; there was no pause for meals; the gangs of workmen relieved each other. Festivals were unheeded; the seasons themselves were overcome. To accelerate the work, the building was kept, the winter through, artificially heated to the excessive temperature of twenty-four to twenty-six degrees Réaumur. Many workmen sank under the heat, and were carried out dead or dying; a painter, who was decorating a ceiling, fell from his ladder struck with apoplexy. Neither money, health, nor life, was spared. The Emperor, who, at the time of the conflagration, had risked his own life by penetrating into the innermost apartments to save the lives of others, knew nothing of the means employed to carry out his will. In the December of the following year, and in proud consciousness of his power, he entered the resuscitated palace and rejoiced over his work. The whole was constructed on the previous plan, but with some improvements and many embellishments. With the Empress on his arm, and followed by his whole family, he traversed the apartments of this immense building, completed, in one year's time, by the labour of thousands of men. He reached the saloon of St. George, the largest and most beautiful of all, and the royal family remained there longer than anywhere else, examining the costly gold mouldings of the ceiling, the five colossal bronze chandeliers, and the beautiful relievo over the throne, which represents St. George slaying the dragon. The Empress was tired, and would have sat down; – the patron spirit of Russia prevented her: as yet there was no furniture in the hall so she leaned on the Emperor's arm and walked into the next room, followed by the entire retinue. The last of these had scarcely passed through the door when a thundering crash resounded through the palace, which trembled to its very foundations, and the air was darkened by clouds of dust. The timbers of the ceiling of the saloon of St. George had yielded to the weight of the chandeliers; and the whole had fallen in, crushing everything beneath its enormous mass. The saloon, a moment before so brilliant, was a heap of ruins. The splendid palace was again partly destroyed, but the genius of Russia had watched over her destiny – the imperial family were saved. **99**

EDWARD JERRMANN, *PICTURES OF ST PETERSBURG,*
TRANS. BY FREDERICK HARDMANN, LONDON 1852

COLORS

The poet and novelist Andrey Biely (1880–1935) describes a walk along the Moika Canal.

66Below, to one side of them, the Moika Canal appeared blue; on the other side stood the familiar three-story colonnaded building with the same familiar series of modeled ornaments: ring after ring, and inside each ring a coat of arms – a Roman helmet between two crossed swords.

Before them, where the canal took a turn to the left of a stone projection, loomed the dazzling dome of St. Isaac's Cathedral against a background of exquisite turquoise.

They had reached the Embankment: the deep waters of the Neva looked green-blue. Far, far away, appearing ever so remote, the islands looked incredibly flat and low; and their buildings seemed so flat too that the deep green-blue waters threatened suddenly to wash over and submerge them. A pitiless sunset hovered above this green blue surface, scattering its gleams here and there: the Troitsky Bridge and the Winter Palace glowed purple.

Suddenly, a clearly defined silhouette appeared above these green-blue waters and against the background of the red sky; the flaps of a coat cape beat in the breeze like a pair of wings; carelessly, a waxen face with protruding lips came into view; the eyes seemed to search for something in the blue expanse of the Neva and, unable to find what they sought, took refuge under the visor of a modest cap; the eyes saw neither Sofya Petrovna nor Varvara Evgrafovna: they saw only the green-blue depths; they rose and fell – beyond the Neva, where the buildings glowed purple on the sunken banks of the island. A bulldog, carrying in his mouth a whip with a silver handle, ran snorting ahead of the silhouette. As he passed them, the young man barely blinked his eyes, touched the band of his cap with his fingers, and walked on without a word. The buildings glowed purple.**99**

ANDREY BIELY, *ST PETERSBURG*, TRANS. BY JOHN COURNOS, PUB. GROVE PRESS INC., NEW YORK, 1959

PETERSBURG SOCIETY

WORKING PEOPLE

Dramatist and prose writer Nikolai Gogol (1809–52) was born in the Ukraine but moved to St Petersburg in 1828. He wrote a series of short stories set in the city in the mid 1830's, which are satirical and exaggerated in tone yet brilliantly descriptive.

66Let us begin with earliest morning when all Petersburg smells of hot, freshly-baked bread and is filled with old women in ragged gowns and pelisses who are making their raids on the churches and on compassionate passers-by. Then the Nevsky Prospect is empty: the stout shopkeepers and their assistants are still asleep in their linen shirts or washing their genteel cheeks and drinking their coffee; beggars gather near the doors of the confectioners' shops where the drowsy Ganymede who the day before flew round like a fly with chocolate, crawls out with no cravat on, broom in hand, and thrusts stale pies and scraps upon them. Working people move to and fro about the streets: sometimes peasants cross it, hurrying to their work, in high boots caked with mortar which even the Ekaterinsky canal, famous for its cleanness, could not wash off. At this hour it is not proper for ladies to walk out, because Russian people like to explain their meaning in rude expressions such as they would not hear even in a theatre. Sometimes a drowsy government clerk trudges along with a portfolio under his arm, if the way to his department lies through the Nevsky Prospect. It may be confidently stated that at this period, that is, up to twelve o'clock, the Nevsky Prospect is for no man the goal, but simply the means of reaching it: it is filled with people who have their occupations, their anxieties, and their annoyances, and are thinking nothing about it. Peasants talk about ten kopecks or seven coppers, old men and women wave their hands or talk to themselves, sometimes with very striking gesticulations, but no one listens to them or laughs at them with the exception perhaps of street boys in homespun smocks, darting like lightning along the Nevsky Prospect with empty bottles or pairs of boots from the cobblers in their arms. At that hour you may put on what you like, and even if you wear a cap instead of a hat, or the ends of your collar stick out too far from your cravat, no one notices it.**99**

NIKOLAI GOGOL, "THE NEVSKY PROSPECT", FROM *THE OVERCOAT & OTHER STORIES*, TRANS. BY CONSTANCE GARNETT, PUB. CHATTO & WINDUS, LONDON, 1923

EXODUS

Born in Moscow, Fyodor Dostoevsky (1821–81) first moved to St Petersburg in 1838 to study at the St Petersburg Engineering Academy. During the 20th century, Dostoevsky has become the most widely read and influential of Russian writers in Britain and the US. He was a powerful thinker, influenced by Socialism and liberal ideas in the first half of his life, and then by the Russian Orthodox Church. In this extract from his short story "White Nights", written in 1848, is Dostoevsky's description of what he considered to be an alarming trend in St Petersburg society.

"It was only this morning that at last I discovered the real cause of my unhappiness. Oh, so they are all running away from me to the country, are they? I'm afraid I must apologise for the use of this rather homely word, but I'm not in the mood now for the more exquisite refinements of style, for everybody in Petersburg has either left or is about to leave for the country; for every worthy gentleman of a solidly-prosperous and dignified position who hails a cab in the street is at once transformed in my mind into a worthy parent of a family who, after his usual office duties, immediately leaves town and, unencumbered by luggage, hastens to the bosom of his family – to the country; for every passer-by now wears quite a different look, a look which almost seems to say to every person he meets, 'As a matter of fact, sir, I'm here by sheer chance, just passing through, you understand, and in a few hours I shall be on the way to the country.' If a window is thrown open and a most ravishing young girl, who a moment ago had been drumming on it with her lovely white fingers, pokes out her pretty head and calls to the man selling pots of plants in the street, I immediately jump to the conclusion that the flowers are bought not for the purpose of enjoying the spring and the flowers in a stuffy old flat in town, for very soon everybody will anyway be leaving for the country and will take even the flowers with them. Why, I've got so far in my new discovery (quite a unique discovery, you must admit) that I can tell at once, just by looking at a man, in what sort of a cottage he lives in the country. The residents of the Stone and Apothecary Islands can be recognised by their studied exquisiteness of manners, their smart summer clothes, and their wonderful carriages in which they come to town. The inhabitants of Pargolov and places beyond 'inspire' your confidence at the first glance by their solidly prosperous position and their general air of sobriety and common sense; while the householder of Krestovsky Island is distinguished by his imperturbably cheerful look. Whether I happen to come across a long procession of carters, each walking leisurely, reins in hand, beside his cart, laden with whole mountains of furniture of every description – tables, chairs, Turkish and non-Turkish divans, and other household chattels – and, moreover, often presided over by a frail-looking cook who, perched on the

very top of the cart, guards the property of her master as though it were the apple of her eye; or whether I look at the barges, heavily laden with all sorts of domestic junk, sailing on the Neva or the Fontanka, as far as the Black River or the Islands – both carts and barges multiply tenfold, nay, a hundredfold in my eyes. It really seems as though everything had arisen and set off on a journey, as though everything were moving off in caravan after caravan into the country; it seems as though the whole of Petersburg were about to turn into a desert, and it is hardly surprising that in the end I am overwhelmed with shame, humiliation, and sadness."

DOSTOEVSKY, "WHITE NIGHTS",
FROM *THE BEST SHORT STORIES OF DOSTOEVSKY*,
TRANS. BY DAVID MAGARSHACK,
PUB. THE MODERN LIBRARY, NEW YORK, 1955

ENTRANCE TO A BALL

It took Count Lev Nikolaevich Tolstoy (1828–1910) almost seven years to write "War and Peace", an epic novel following the fortunes of three aristocratic families through the Napoleonic invasion.

66Natasha had not had a moment free since early morning and had not once had time to think of what lay before her.

In the damp chill air and crowded closeness of the swaying carriage, she for the first time vividly imagined what was in store for her there at the ball, in those brightly lighted rooms – with music, flowers, dances, the Emperor, and all the brilliant young people of Petersburg. The prospect was so splendid that she hardly believed it would come true, so out of keeping was it with the chill darkness and closeness of the carriage. She understood all that awaited her only when, after stepping over the red baize at the entrance, she entered the hall, took off her fur cloak and, beside Sonya and in front of her mother, mounted the brightly illuminated stairs between the flowers. Only then did she remember how she must behave at a ball, and tried to assume the majestic air she considered indispensable for a girl on such an occasion. But, fortunately for her, she felt her eyes growing misty, she saw nothing clearly, her pulse beat a hundred to the minute and the blood throbbed at her heart. She could not assume that pose, which would have made her ridiculous, and she moved on almost fainting from excitement and trying with all her might to conceal it. And this was the very attitude that became her best. Before and behind them other visitors were entering, also talking in low tones and wearing ball-dresses. The mirrors on the landing reflected ladies in white, pale-blue, and pink dresses, with diamonds and pearls on their bare necks and arms.

Natasha looked in the mirrors and could not distinguish her reflection from the others. All was blent into one brilliant procession. On entering the ball-room the regular hum of voices, footsteps, and greetings deafened Natasha, and the light and glitter dazzled her still more. The host and hostess, who had already been standing at the door for half an hour repeating the same words to the various arrivals, '*Charmé de vous voir,*' greeted the Rostovs and Peronskaya in the same manner.

The two girls in their white dresses, each with a rose in her black hair, both curtsied in the same way, but the hostess's eye involuntarily rested longer on the slim Natasha. She looked at her and gave her alone a special smile, in addition to her usual smile as hostess. Looking at her she may have recalled the golden, irrevocable days of her own girlhood and her own first ball. The host also followed Natasha with his eyes and asked the count which was his daughter.

'Charming!' said he, kissing the tips of his fingers.

In the ball-room guests stood crowding at the entrance doors awaiting the Emperor. The countess took up a position in one of the front rows of that crowd. Natasha heard and felt that several people were asking about her and looking at her. She realized that those noticing her liked her, and this observation helped to calm her.

'There are some like ourselves and some worse,' she thought.99

LEO TOLSTOY, *WAR AND PEACE*,
TRANS. BY LOUISE AND AYLMER MAUDE,
PUB. EVERYMAN'S LIBRARY, LONDON,
AND ALFRED A. KNOPF, NEW YORK, 1992

BACKSTABBING

Anton Chekhov (1860–1904) deplored theatrical society in St Petersburg. The premiere of "The Sea Gull" at the State Theatre in 1896 was disastrous yet it was later a great success when staged at the Moscow Arts Theatre, and he took all his subsequent plays to the latter.

66I am tired out, like a ballerina after five acts and eight tableaux. Banquets, letters which one is too lazy to answer, conversations and all sorts of bosh. Right now I've got to take a cab to Vasilievsky Island, to dine there, yet I am bored and I have to work. I will stay here for three days more and see: if this ballet continues I'll either go home or to Ivan in Sudoroga.

I am enveloped by a dense atmosphere of ill will, extremely vague, and to me inexplicable. They are tendering me dinners and chanting banal dithyrambs to me and at the same time are all set to devour me. Why? The devil knows. If I had shot myself I would have afforded great pleasure to nine-tenths of my friends and admirers. And in what petty ways people express their pettiness! Burenin berates me in a *feuilleton*, even though it is not customary for newpapers to berate their own contributors; Maslov (Bezhetsky) no longer goes to dine with the Suvorins; Shcheglov tells all the gossip current about me, and so on. All this is dreadfully foolish and boring. They're not people, but some sort of mold.**"**

LETTER TO M.P. CHEKHOVA, ST PETERSBURG, JANUARY 14, 1891,
IN *LETTERS OF ANTON CHEKHOV*, TRANS. BERNARD GUILBERT GUERNEY,
PUB. VIKING PRESS, NEW YORK, 1968

"There is in Petersburg a species of men whose speciality it is to jeer at every aspect of life; they cannot even pass by a starving man or a suicide without saying something vulgar. But Orlov and his friends did not jeer or make jokes, they talked ironically. They used to say that there was no God, and personality was completely lost at death; the immortals only existed in the French Academy. Real good did not and could not possibly exist, as its existence was conditional upon human perfection, which was a logical absurdity. Russia was a country as poor and dull as Persia. The intellectual class was hopeless; in Pekarsky's opinion the overwhelming majority in it were incompetent persons, good for nothing. The people were drunken, lazy, thievish, and degenerate. We had no science, our literature was uncouth, our commerce rested on swindling – 'No selling without cheating.' And everything was in that style, and everything was a subject for laughter.**"**

ANTON CHEKHOV, "AN ANONYMOUS STORY",
FROM *THE LADY WITH THE DOG*, TRANS. CONSTANCE GARNETT,
PUB. CHATTO & WINDUS, LONDON, 1919

LERMONTOV

The writings of Ivan Turgenev (1818–83) were the first by a major Russian author to find success in Europe. Here he describes a meeting with the Romantic poet and novelist Mikhail Lermontov (1814–41), just over a year before the latter was killed in a duel.

❝Lermontov, too, I saw only twice: at the house of Princess Sh[akhovskoy], a Petersburg high society woman, and a few days later at a New Year's fancy dress ball at the Noblemen's Club on the eve of 1840. At Princess Sh[akhovskoy]'s I, a very rare and unaccustomed visitor at high society parties, saw him only from a distance, observing the poet, who had become famous in so short a time, from a corner where I had secreted myself. Lermontov sat down on a low stool in front of a sofa on which, wearing a black gown, was sitting one of the society beauties of those days, the fair-haired Countess [Emilia] Mussin-Pushkin, who died young and who really was a strikingly beautiful girl. Lermontov wore the uniform of the Life Guards Hussar Regiment. He had removed neither his sword nor his gloves and, frowning and hunching his shoulders, gazed sullenly at the Countess. She only exchanged a few words with him, talking mostly to Count Sh[akhovskoy], also a Hussar officer, who was sitting beside him. There was something ominous and tragic in Lermontov's appearance: his swarthy face and large, motionless dark eyes exuded a sort of sombre and evil strength, a sort of pensive scornfulness and passion. His hard gaze was strangely out of keeping with the expression of his almost childishly tender, protruding lips. His whole figure, thick-set, bow-legged, with a large head on broad, stooping shoulders, aroused an unpleasant feeling; but everyone had at once to acknowledge its immense inherent strength. It is, of course, a well-known fact that he had to some extent portrayed himself in Pechorin. The words: 'His eyes did not laugh when he laughed,' from *A Hero of Our Time*, etc., could really have been applied to himself. I remember that Count Sh[akhovskoy] and the young Countess suddenly burst out laughing at something and went on laughing for some time; Lermontov, too, laughed, but at the same time he kept looking at them with a sort of offensive astonishment. For all that I could not help feeling that he was fond of Count Sh[akhovskoy] as a fellow-officer and that he was also well-disposed towards the Countess. There could be no doubt that, following the fashion of those days, he was trying to assume a Byronic air together with a number of other even worse eccentricities and whimsicalities. And he paid dearly for them! At heart Lermontov was probably terribly bored; he felt stifled in the airless atmosphere where fate had forced him to live.❞

IVAN TURGENEV, *LITERARY REMINISCENCES AND AUTOBIOGRAPHICAL FRAGMENTS*, TRANS. BY DAVID MAGARSHACK, PUB. FABER & FABER, LONDON, 1959

FASHION

Russian revolutionary Alexander Herzen (1812–70) combined his personal life and his opinions with political views in his autobiography published in 1885.

❝The Petersburghers laugh at the costumes seen in Moscow; they are outraged by the caps and Hungarian jackets, the long hair and civilian moustaches. Moscow certainly is a non-military city, rather careless and unaccustomed to discipline, but whether that is a good quality or a defect is a matter of opinion. The harmony of uniformity, the absence of variety, of what is personal and whimsical, a traditional obligatory dress and external discipline are all found on the largest scale in the most inhuman condition in which men live – in barracks. The uniform and a complete absence of variety are passionately loved by despotism. Nowhere are fashions followed so respectfully as in Petersburg, and that shows the immaturity of our culture; our clothes are alien. In Europe people dress, but we dress up, and so are terrified if a sleeve is too full, or a collar too narrow. In Paris all that people are afraid of is being dressed without taste; in London all that they are afraid of is catching cold; in Italy every one dresses as he likes best. If one were to show an Englishman the battalions of fops on the Nevsky Prospect, all wearing exactly similar, tightly buttoned coats, he would take them for a squad of 'policemen'.❞

ALEXANDER HERZEN, *MY PAST AND THOUGHTS*, TRANS. BY CONSTANCE GARNETT, PUB. CHATTO & WINDUS, LONDON, 1924

FESTIVITIES

English tutor William Coxe (1747–1828) witnessed an enormous and ultimately rather dangerous party in St Petersburg.

❝On the 6th of December we were witness to a very singular entertainment given to the public by a Russian, who had acquired a large fortune by farming, during four years only, the right of vending spirituous liquors. On surrendering his contract, he gave, as proof of his gratitude to the lower class of people, by whom he had enriched himself, a feast near the garden of the summer-palace . . . announced by hand-bills distributed throughout the city . . . which commenced at two o'clock in the afternoon. A large semicircular table was covered with all kinds of provision, piled in different shapes, and in the greatest profusion. Large slices of bread and caviare, dried sturgeon, carp, and other fish, were ranged to a great height, in the form of pent-houses and pyramids, and garnished with craw-fish, onions, and pickles. In different parts of the grounds were rows of casks full of spirituous liquors, and still larger vessels of wine, beer, and quass. Among the decorations, I observed the representation of an immense whale in pasteboard, covered with cloth and gold or silver brocade, and filled in the inside with bread, dried fish, and other provisions.

All sorts of games and diversions were exhibited for the amusement of the populace. At the extremity of the grounds was a large square of ice well swept for the scaters; near which were two machines like the swinging vehicles at Bartholomew Fair. One of these machines consisted of two cross-beams fixed horizontally to a pole in the center by means of a pivot; from the ends of the beams hung four sledges, in which people seated themselves, and were turned round with great velocity; the other had four wooden horses suspended from the beams, and the riders were whirled round in like manner. . . . Beyond these were two ice-hills. . . . Two poles, above twenty feet in height, were also erected, with colours flying; and at the top of each was placed a piece of money, as a prize for those who could swarm up and seize it. The poles, being rubbed with oil, soon froze in this severe climate; many and tedious were the attempts of the various competitors in this slippery ascent to fame. The scene was lively and gay; for about 40,000 persons of both sexes were assembled on the occasion. . . .

It was preconcerted, that, on firing a rocket, the people were to drink a glass of spirituous liquor, and, on the discharge of a second, to begin the repast. But the impatience of the populace anticipated the necessity of a second signal; and the whole multitude was soon and at once in motion. The whale was the chief object of contention; within the space of a few minutes he was entirely divested of his gaudy trappings, which became the spoils of his successful invaders. . . . They rend him into a thousand pieces, to seize the provision with which his inside was stored. The remaining people . . . were employed in uncovering the pent-houses, and pulling down the pyramids. . . . Others crowded around the casks and hogsheads; and with great wooden ladles lapped incessantly wine, beer, and spirits. The confusion and riot, which soon succeeded, is better conceived than described; and we thought it expedient to retire. . . .

But the consequences of this feast were indeed dreadful. The cold had suddenly increased with such violence, that Fahrenheit's thermometer, which at mid-day stood only at 4, sunk towards the close of the evening to 15 below freezing point. Many intoxicated persons were frozen to death; not a few fell a sacrifice to drunken quarrels; and others were robbed and murdered in the more retired parts of the city, as they were returning late to their homes. From a comparison of various reports, we had reason to conclude, that at least 400 persons lost their lives upon this melancholy occasion. (The following day I counted myself no less than forty bodies, collected in two sheds near the place of entertainment.)**

WILLIAM COXE, "TRAVELS IN RUSSIA",
SEVEN BRITONS IN IMPERIAL RUSSIA 1698–1812,
ED. PETER PUTNAM,
PUB. PRINCETON UNIVERSITY PRESS, 1952

CATHERINE THE GREAT
The first of the two following extracts tells of the beginnings of the Hermitage picture collection; the second, a love letter, tells of Catherine's difficulties in communicating with Prince Grigory Potemkin in the Winter Palace.

[Catherine] entered into negotiations with the dealer Gotskowski. This gentleman also regularly supplied pictures to Frederick II of Prussia, who had done so much to further Catherine's marriage (which, incidentally, in no way inhibited her from calling him her mortal enemy once she was on the throne, nor yet from subsequently signing a Treaty of Alliance with him: she had, in fact, lost no time in mastering the rules of politics). Gotskowski was in debt and Catherine was delighted to strike a bargain with him and thus secure for herself in Berlin itself 225 pictures which should normally have gone to Sans Souci to delight the eyes of Frederick. Spite may, indeed, have been the mainspring of Catherine's love of art collecting.

PIERRE DESCARGUES,
THE HERMITAGE, TRANS.
K. DELAVENAY, LONDON, 1961

My little darling, good morning! As so often happens, I could not enter your apartments as the Palace is full of human cattle, wandering about in the passages. I greet you from afar and pray for your good health.

LETTRES D'AMOUR DE CATHERINE II À POTEMKIN,
ED. G OUDARD,
PARIS 1934, TRANS. FROM THE FRENCH BY
MARIE NOÊLE KELLY

A COMIC WEDDING

In 1740 Empress Anne, displaying an extraordinary sense of humour, organized Prince Galitzine's bizarre wedding to Avdotaya Ivanovna.

❝The winter of 1739–40 was unusually cold, and the scientists of the Academy embarked on a programme of experiments to test the properties of ice that was available in such abundance. Knowing this, a court Chamberlain called Alexander Tatishchev thought of combining it with a new entertainment for the court – building a palace of ice on which artists and artisans as well as scientists could exercise their skills. In the end it turned out to be a setting for another of the Empress's macabre jokes for which poor Golitsyn was again the butt. . . . One morning a huge and astonishing procession formed up in the streets. Goats, pigs, cows, camels, dogs and reindeer were seen harnessed to various vehicles each of which contained a representative pair from each of the 'Barbarous Races' in the Empire. There were Lapps and Kirghiz, Tunguses and Tatars, Bashkirs and Finns – each couple in 'national dress'. But the centrepiece was an elephant with an iron cage on its back. The cage contained Golitsyn and his unlovely bride. To the accompaniment of cymbals, bells and the occasional roaring of an angry beast, the procession passed the Palace and eventually arrived at Ernest Biron's covered riding school, where a banquet had been prepared for the captive bridal pair and their guests. By the Empress's express command each couple was served with its own traditional dishes – including such culinary delights as reindeer meat, horse-flesh and fermented mare's milk. There was entertainment too. A poet named

Tredyakovski declaimed an ode composed specially for the occasion entitled: 'Greetings to the Bridal Pair of Fools', and each pair of guests was made to dance its own 'national dance' for the amusement of onlookers. Then the procession formed up again to accompany the bride and groom to their home for the night – the palace made of ice. No other material had been used in its construction – walls and steps, baroque bald columns, even the decorative figurines and window-panes were made of ice. So was the furniture – a huge four-poster bridal bed, chairs, tables, chandleliers, a clock, a commode, a set of playing cards, with the markings coloured in, and a statue of a Cupid. Outside there were other marvels of engineering and the sculptor's art – flowers and trees complete with perching birds, ice cannon which fired real charges, a pair of dolphins which breathed out flames of fire (thanks to a device inside which pumped out naptha), and a life-sized model of an elephant equipped with a machine to squirt out water to a height of two hundred and fifty feet. Everything had been done to excite the eye and astonish the imagination – and all at a cost of only thirty thousand roubles. The Empress accompanied the bridal pair inside, saw them undressed and laid upon their bed of ice. Then she withdrew. From her bedroom she had an excellent view of the Ice Palace, and next morning she saw Golitsyn and his wife emerge apparently none the worse for their experience. The stove installed inside their chilly bedroom, as the scientists of the Academy took careful note, had proved effective.❞

PHILIP LONGWORTH, *THE THREE EMPRESSES*, LONDON, 1972

HISTORY

ASSASSINATIONS

"Under Western Eyes" by Joseph Conrad (1857–1924) describes the fate of a student who is caught up in the Russian Revolution.

❝Mr. de P– was being driven towards the railway station in a two-horse uncovered sleigh with footman and coachman on the box. Snow had been falling all night, making the roadway, uncleared as yet at this early hour, very heavy for the horses. It was still falling thickly. But the sleigh must have been observed and marked down. As it drew over to the left before taking a turn, the footman noticed a peasant walking slowly on the edge of the pavement with his hands in the pockets of his sheepskin coat and his shoulders hunched up to his ears under the falling snow. On being overtaken this peasant suddenly faced about and swung his arm. In an instant there was a terrible shock, a detonation muffled in the multitude of snowflakes; both horses lay dead and mangled on the ground and the coachman, with a shrill cry, had fallen off the box mortally wounded. The footman (who survived) had no time to see the face of the man in the sheepskin coat. After throwing the bomb this last got away, but it is supposed that, seeing a lot of people surging up on all sides of him in the falling snow, and all running towards the scene of the explosion, he thought it safer to turn back with them. In an incredibly short time an excited crowd assembled round the sledge. The Minister-President, getting out unhurt into the deep snow, stood near the groaning coachman and addressed the people repeatedly in his weak, colourless voice. 'I beg of you to keep off. For the love of God, I beg of you good people to keep off.' It was then that a tall young man who had remained perfectly still within a carriage gateway, two houses lower down, stepped out into the street and walking up rapidly flung another bomb over the heads of the crowd. It actually struck the Minister-President on the shoulder as he stooped over his dying servant, then falling between his feet exploded with a terrific concentrated violence, striking him dead to the ground, finishing the wounded man and practically annihilating the empty sledge in the twinkling of an eye. With a yell of horror the crowd broke up and fled in all directions, except for those who fell dead or dying where they stood nearest to the Minister-President, and one or two others who did not fall till they had run a little way. The first explosion had brought together a crowd as if by enchantment, the second made as swiftly a solitude in the street for hundreds of yards in each direction. Through the falling snow people looked from afar at the small heap of dead bodies lying upon each other near the carcases of the two horses. Nobody dared to approach till some Cossacks of a street-patrol galloped up and, dismounting, began to turn over the dead. Amongst the innocent victims of the second explosion laid out on the pavement there was a body dressed in peasant's sheepskin coat; but the face was unrecognizable, there was absolutely nothing found in the pockets of its poor clothing, and it was the only one whose identity was never established.❞

JOSEPH CONRAD, *UNDER WESTERN EYES*,
EVERYMAN'S LIBRARY, LONDON, AND
ALFRED A. KNOPF, NEW YORK, 1992

REVOLUTION

English writer William Gerhardie
(1895–1977 was born in St Petersburg and later served in the British Embassy there.

❝One morning, as I was about to cross the Troitski Bridge to meet the Admiral, I was stopped by the police and was compelled to go home and change into uniform. When I returned the revolution had already broken out. The Admiral had just witnessed the sacking of the Arsenal by a disorderly crowd. Regiment after regiment was going over to the revolution. Solitary shots, and now and then machine-gun fire, were heared from varius quarters of the city. The Admiral and I stood at the window and watched. Lorry after lorry packed with armed soldiery and workmen, some lying in a 'ready' attidtude along the mudguards, went past us in a kind of wild and dazzling joy ride, waving red flags and revolutionary banners to shouts of 'Hurrah!' from the crowds in the street. The Admiral stood with his hands folded on the window-sill, unable to withhold his enthusiasm. It was a clear, bright day, I think and very cold.

That evening following the outbreak of the revolution was vividly impressed upon my memory. During the day I had listened to innumerable speeches, some of a Liberal loftiness; others of a menacingly proletarian character, threatening death to capital and revolution to the world at large. There was a tendency to flamboyant extravagance and exaggeration. 'Down with Armies and Navies!' shouted one speaker hysterically. 'Down with militarism! Through red terror to peace, freedom and brotherhood!' Therewere placards and banners and processions. 'Land and Liberty!' was a popular watchword. Red was the dominant colour, and the opening bars of the Marseillaise were a kind of recurring *Leitmotiv* in the tumult. Crossing a bridge I passed a company of soldiers newly revolted. They marched alert and joyous to the sound of some old familiar marching song till they came to the words 'for the Czar.' Having sung these words they stopped somewhat abruptly and perplexed. '*How* for the Czar?' one of them asked. '*How* for the Czar?' they repeated, looking at each other sheepishly. Then they marched on without singing. There were peasants who did not know the 'revolution' and thought it was a woman who would supersede the Czar. Others wanted a republic with a czar. And there were others still who interpreted the word republic as 'rezshpublicoo,' thinking that it meant 'cut up the public'.

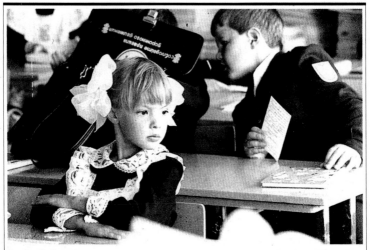

In the Troitski Square I was stopped by a young enthusiastic Russian officer, who attracted by my British uniform, spoke to me in English, his eyes glittering with excitement. 'Sir,' he said, 'you now will have more vigorous Allies.' And then in the Nevski I passed a procession of Anarchists who are regarded by the Bolsheviks with about the same degree of unmitigated horror as the Bolsheviks are regarded by the *Morning Post*. They marched with a gruesome look about their faces, bearing their horrible colours of black, crested with a human skull and cross-bones. **99**

WILLIAM GERHARDIE, *FUTILITY*,
PUB. DUCKWORTH, LONDON, 1927

AN ARISTOCRATIC REVOLUTIONARY

Prince Peter Kropotkin (1842–1921) was born into the Russian aristocracy but his political beliefs were left-wing extremist. He left the army in 1872 to work for the International Working Man's Association. Arrested and imprisoned in 1874, he escaped to England in 1876, and spent the next forty years in exile, not returning to Russia until the 1917 Revolution.

66One day I received a quite unexpected visit. The Grand Duke Nicholas, brother of Alexander II, who was inspecting the fortress, entered my cell, followed only by his aide-de-camp. The door was shut behind him. He rapidly approached me, saying 'Good-day, Kropótkin.' He knew me personally, and spoke in a familiar, good-natured tone, as to an old acquaintance. 'How is it possible, Kropótkin, that you, a page de chambre, a sergeant of the corps of pages, should be mixed up in this business, and now be here in this horrible casemate?'

'Every one has his own opinions,' was my reply.

'Opinions! So your opinions were that you must stir up a revolution?'

What was I to reply? Yes? Then the construction which would be put upon my answer would be that I, who had refused to give any answers to the gendarmes, 'avowed everything' before the brother of the Tsar. His tone was that of a commander of a military school when trying to obtain 'avowals' from a cadet. Yet I could not say No: it would have been a lie. I did not know what to say, and stood without saying anything.

'You see! You feel ashamed of it now' –

This remark angered me, and I at once said in a rather sharp way, 'I have given my replies to the examining magistrate, and have nothing to add.'

'But understand, Kropótkin, please,' he said then, in the most familiar tone, 'that I don't speak to you as an examining magistrate. I speak quite as a private person, – quite as a private man,' he repeated, lowering his voice.

Thoughts went whirling in my head. To play the part of Marquis Posa? To tell the

Emperor through the grand duke of the desolation of Russia, the ruin of the peasantry, the arbitrariness of the officials, the terrible famines in prospect? To say that we wanted to help the peasants out of their desperate condition, to make them raise their heads, and by all this try to influence Alexander II? These thoughts followed one another in rapid succession, till at last I said to myself: 'Never! Nonsense! They know all that. They are enemies of the nation, and such talk would not change them.'

I replied that he always remained an official person, and that I could not look upon him as a private man.

He then began to ask me indifferent questions. 'Was it not in Siberia, with the Decembrists, that you began to entertain such ideas?'

'No; I knew only one Decembrist, and with him I had no talks worth speaking of.'

'Was it then at St. Petersburg that you got them?'

'I was always the same.'

'Why! Were you such in the corps of pages?' he asked me with terror.

'In the corps I was a boy, and what is indefinite in boyhood grows definite in manhood.'

He asked me some other similar questions, and as he spoke I distinctly saw what he was driving at. He was trying to obtain avowals, and my imagination vividly pictured him saying to his brother: 'All these examining magistrates are imbeciles. He gave them no replies, but I talked to him ten minutes, and he told me everything.' That began to annoy me; and when he said to me something to this effect, 'How could you have anything to do with all these people – peasants and people with no names?' – I sharply turned upon him and said, 'I have told you already that I have given my replies to the examining magistrate.' Then he abruptly left the cell.

Later, the soldiers of the guard made quite a legend of that visit. The person who came in a carriage to carry me away at the time of my escape wore a military cap, and, having sandy whiskers, bore a faint resemblance to the Grand Duke Nicholas. So a tradition grew up amongst the soldiers of the St. Petersburg garrison that it was the grand duke himself who came to rescue me and kidnapped me. Thus are legends created even in times of newspapers and biographical dictionaries.**

PETER KROPOTKIN, *MEMOIRS OF A REVOLUTIONIST*,
PUB. DOVER PUBLICATIONS, INC., NEW YORK, 1971

CAFÉ LIFE

American novelist John Dos Passos (1896–1970) visited St Petersburg in 1928.

In the evening the café under the Europskaya Hotel seems a great relief. Here's something a guy doesn't have to cudgel his wits to understand. It's like Europe, it's like the East Side of New York. Beer, jingly music, white tablecloths, shoddy whores. You can give your order to the waiter and he politely brings you a breaded cutlet. There are businessmen at the tables, tricky-looking articles who will assist you to buy a genuine antique ikon or a young lady's recumbent halfhour. There are speculators who will change your dollars for rubles in the black market. It's the kingdom of money again, the blessed land of valuta. After a while the nightlife begins to get a stale look, the beer begins to taste sour; best thing to do's to go to bed. It's too drearily obvious that the café's a grimy microcosm of the capitalist world across the Frontier, too obvious to be funny even. I'm no Y.M.C.A. secretary, but Red Putilov has somehow taken the edge off it. When I ask my Russian friends about it they laugh and say, 'That's the underworld. The police let that place stay open so that they can always know where the criminals are when they want to put their hands on them.'

JOHN DOS PASSOS, *JOURNEYS BETWEEN WARS*,
PUB. HARCOURT BRACE & COMPANY, NEW YORK, 1938

SEASONS

SNOW

English traveler E.D. Clarke (1769–1822) found Russian snow extraordinary.

**The season began to change before we left Petersburg. The cold became daily less intense; and the inhabitants were busied in moving from the Neva large blocks of ice into their cellars. A most interesting and remarkable phænomenon took place the day before our departure, – the thermometer of *Fahrenheit* indicating only nine degrees of temperature below the freezing point; and there was no wind. At this time, snow, in the most regular and beautiful crystals, fell gently upon our clothes, and upon the sledge, as we were driving through the streets. All of these crystals possessed exactly the same figure, and the same dimensions. Every one of them consisted of a wheel or star, with six equal rays, bounded by circumferences of equal diameters; having all the same number of rays branching from a common centre. The size of each of those little stars was equal to the circle presented by the section of a pea, into two equal parts. This appearance continued during three hours, in which time no other snow fell.❞

E.D. CLARKE, *TRAVELS IN VARIOUS COUNTRIES OF EUROPE, ASIA AND AFRICA,*
PUB. T. CADELL & W. DAVIES, LONDON, 1816

NEVA

Now regarded as one of the major poets of the 20th century, Osip Mandelstam (1891–1938?) fell out of favor with the Soviet regime and died of a heart attack after his second arrest in 1938.

❝I'm feeling cold. Transparent springtime is
clothing Petropolis in a green down.
But still the Neva's wave, like a medusa,
inspires in me a slight sense of aversion.
On the embankment of the northern river
the fireflies of the automobiles whirl,
steel dragon-flies and beetles rush along,
the gold pins of the stars are flickering,
but no stars, no stars whatever, will kill
the weightly emerald of the sea's waves.❞

OSIP MANDELSTAM, "TRISTIA", FROM *POEMS FROM MANDELSTAM,*
TRANS. BY R.H. MORRISON,
PUB. ASSOCIATED UNIVERSITY PRESSES, LONDON, 1990

EARLY MORNING

Russian poet and essayist Joseph Brodsky was born in St Petersburg in 1940.

❝Once upon a time there was a little boy. He lived in the most unjust country in the world. Which was ruled by creatures who by all human accounts should be considered degenerates. Which never happened.

ALEXANDRE DUMAS
ILLUSTRÉ

IMPRESSIONS DE VOYAGE
—

En Russie

ILLUSTRATIONS
DE
DE LA CHARLERIE, GUSTAVE DORÉ, GERLIER, PHILIPPOTEAUX,
RAFFET, ETC.

And there was a city. The most beautiful city on the face of the earth. With an immense gray river that hung over its distant bottom like the immense gray sky over that river. Along that river there stood magnificent palaces with such beautifully elaborated façades that if the little boy was standing on the right bank, the left bank looked like the imprint of a giant mollusk called civilization. Which ceased to exist.

Early in the morning when the sky was still full of stars the little boy would rise and, after having a cup of tea and an egg, accompanied by a radio announcement of a new record in smelted steel, followed by the army choir singing a hymn to the Leader, whose picture was pinned to the wall over the little boy's still warm bed, he would run along the snow-covered granite embankment to school.

The wide river lay white and frozen like a continent's tongue lapsed into silence, and the big bridge arched against the dark blue sky like an iron palate. If the little boy had two extra minutes, he would slide down on the ice and take twenty or thirty steps to the middle. All this time he would be thinking about what the fish were doing under such heavy ice. Then he would stop, turn 180 degrees, and run back, nonstop, right up to the entrance of the school. He would burst into the hall, throw his hat and coat off onto a hook, and fly up the staircase and into his classroom.

It is a big room with three rows of desks, a portrait of the Leader on the wall behind the teacher's chair, a map with two hemispheres, of which only one is legal. The little boy takes his seat, opens his briefcase, puts his pen and notebook on the desk, lifts his face, and prepares himself to hear drivel. **99**

JOSEPH BRODSKY, *LESS THAN ONE*,
PUB. FARRAR, STRAUS, GIROUX, NEW YORK, 1966

THE TSAR'S MANIFESTO

The ambassador Maurice Paléogue was the only foreigner present at the ceremony, in St George's Gallery in the Winter Palace, when the Tsar proclaimed Russia's entry into the 1914 War.

66After the final prayer the court chaplain read the Tsar's manifesto to his people – a simple recital of the events which have made war inevitable, an eloquent appeal to all the national energies, an invocation to the Most High, and so forth. Then the Tsar went up to the altar and raised his right hand toward the gospel held out to him. He was even more grave and composed, as if he were about to receive the sacrament. In a slow, low voice, which dwelt on every word he made the following declaration.

'Officers of my guard, here present, I greet in you my whole army and give it my blessing. I solemnly swear that I will never make peace so long as one of the enemy is on the soil of the fatherland.'

A wild outburst of cheering was the answer to this declaration which was copied from the oath taken by the Emperor Alexander I in 1812. For nearly ten minutes there was a frantic tumult in the gallery and it was soon intensified by the cheers of the crowd massed along the Neva. **99**

MAURICE PALÉOGUE, "AN AMBASSADOR'S MEMOIRS 1914–1917"
FROM *ST PETERSBURG, A TRAVELLERS' COMPANION*,
SELECTED AND INTRODUCED BY LAURENCE KELLY,
PUB. CONSTABLE, LONDON, 1981

Itineraries in St Petersburg

Palace of Pavlovsk ▲   Palace of Tsarskoe Selo and detail of Atlas figure (right) ▼

Winter Palace, Hermitage Museum ▼

By the Fortress in winter ▲

The Moika Canal ▲   The Sphinx landing stage, University Embankment ▼

Vasilyevsky Island, from the Admiralty Embankment ▲   Palace Embankment and the Hermitage ▼

The frozen Neva and the Peter and Paul Fortress ▼

Palace Bridge ▲   Trinity Bridge (also called Troitsky Bridge) ▼

From the
Peter and Paul Fortress
to the islands of the delta

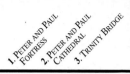

🕐 **Half a day**

◆ A-B-C

FROM THE BASTION TO THE MAUSOLEUM CHAPEL
The Peter and Paul Fortress has never been a residential area. Its only inhabitants were the garrison and the clergy attached to the Cathedral. It was, however, the symbolic center of the Russian Empire because successive sovereigns from Peter the Great onward (including the executed Czarevich Alexei ● 36) are buried there.

FORTIFICATIONS

With the coming of the age of artillery a Vauban-style fortress with bastions was planned for the defense of the island. It is likely that Peter the Great was inspired in this by what he had seen in the West (1696–8). After the first earthworks had been raised the walls were continued in stone under the supervision of the architect Trezzini. The bastions bore the name of the princes who were given responsibility for each military sector. Thus, from Peter's (Petrovsky) Gate these are known as the CZAR, NARYSHKIN, TRUBETSKOY, ZOTOV, GULUKIN AND MENSHIKOV BASTIONS. In about 1740 the initial fortifications were doubled around each gate leading to the mainland by a curtain wall with moats; the latter were filled in during the 19th century. As a result it is necessary to pass through St John's Gate in order to reach Peter's Gate. When she built up the Neva embankment Catherine II added a granite dressing to the fortifications in 1779. Although it stands on the Petrograd Side the Arsenal, or Kronverk, complements the ramparts of the fortress and is an integral part of them. In the event, the Peter and Paul Fortress never had to play the defensive role for which it was designed.

THE GATES

PETER'S GATE. The decoration of this gate, with its imperial eagle and wooden bas-relief, refers to the victories of Peter the Great. On either side statues of the goddesses Bellona and Minerva serve as reminders of Peter's military prowess and political sagacity.

NEVA GATE. Built by Lvov between 1784 and 1787, this gate leads to the Fortress' only deep-water landing stage. It is crowned by a triangular pediment and framed by two groups of twin columns, joined by two blocks of facetted stone. The image of SAINT NICHOLAS guards this gate, which serves as the fortress exit toward Vasilyevsky Island, while SAINT BASIL stands sentry over the gate between the Trubetskoy and Zotov bastions.

"The fortress of St Petersburg was built, like all fortresses, to be a visible symbol of the antagonism between the people and its sovereign. No doubt it defends the city, but it threatens it to a far greater extent; no doubt it was built to repel the Swedes, but in practice it has been a prison for Russians."

Alexandre Dumas,
Voyage en Russie

After the annexation by Russia of the mouth of the Neva during the Northern War the first fortress was built, in May 1703. This structure was close to the sea and naturally defended by the Neva itself. The island of Petersburg on which it stood was small enough to be entirely enclosed, leaving no room for enemy forces to gain a foothold. It was the last upstream island of the delta, and no ship could enter the waterway without passing it.

PETER'S GATE
The wooden relief shows the fall of Simon Magus, a reference to the Russian victory over Sweden.

1. ST JOHN'S BRIDGE
2. ST JOHN'S GATE
3. PETER'S GATE
4. CZAR'S BASTION
5. MENSHIKOV BASTION
6. ENGINEERS' BUILDING
7. COMMANDANT'S HOUSE
8. NEVA GATE
9. NARYSHKIN BASTION
10. PETER AND PAUL CATHEDRAL
11. BOAT HOUSE
12. MINT
13. PRISON
14. TRUBETSKOY BASTION
15. ST BASIL'S GATE
16. ZOTOV BASTION
17. ST NICHOLAS' GATE
18. GULUKIN BASTION

A LANDMARK AND DEPARTURE POINT
The Fortress is one of St Petersburg's great historical and architectural landmarks, and also a departure point for tourists. The ramparts overlooking the Neva offer a splendid panoramic view of the city. St Petersburg can also be explored from the air: helicopter trips depart from Vasilyevski Gate, the exit from the fortress.

THE CANNON
The cannon-shot which is still fired at noon is the last vestige of the Fortress' military past.

147

PETER AND PAUL CATHEDRAL ★

The first church inside the fortress was built of wood. Its construction began on June 29, 1703, the feast day of Saint Peter and Saint Paul. The construction of the present cathedral (PETROPAVLOVSKY SOBOR; Петропавловский собор) was undertaken in 1712 under the direction of the architect Trezzini, who opted for the Western style of the period. The tower has been struck by lightning and rebuilt several times, and the cathedral was reconstructed following a fire in 1753. Its nave is conventional European Baroque, both in its floor plan and its elevation. There is also a pulpit, which is unusual for a Russian Orthodox cathedral.

ICONOSTASIS ● 56. The architectural framework, which is ill-adapted to the Russian ritual, imposed an original solution for the iconostasis; in effect it occupies the entire breadth of the cathedral, and its royal doorway runs the width of the central nave.

CHIMING CLOCK. After 1724 the cathedral was equipped with a Dutch clock, presented by Peter the Great. Its bells originally sounded a carillon in honor of the Czar. Later, with the change of political regime, it sounded the Soviet anthem. Today every six hours it chimes *God Save the Czar*, a tune by the 18th-century composer Bortniansky and every hour the Orthodox *Alleluya*.

THE GOVERNOR'S MAUSOLEUM. Against the east wall of the cathedral is the mausoleum reserved for governors of the Fortress who died during their tenure. Among other duties the governors had to alert the sovereign to the fact that the Neva was once again navigable at winter's end, by bringing him a goblet of water from the river.

THE BOAT HOUSE

THE PAVILION. The Boat House (Botny Dom/Ботный дом), built by the architect Alexander Wist (1761–5) in the Baroque style, is crowned by an allegory of navigation sculpted by David Jensen (1891). Today it is occupied by a luxury souvenir shop.

ST PETERSBURG HISTORY MUSEUM

ENGINEERS' BUILDING. The whole Fortress precinct houses the St Petersburg History Museum; the collections in the Engineers' Building demonstrate certain aspects of daily life, in particular through a series of highly colored shop signs painted in a naive style. On the way through to the Commandant's House stands Mikhail Shemyakin's statue of Peter I (1990).

THE COMMANDANT'S HOUSE. This building, which dates from the 1740's, contains an exhibition documenting the history of the Fortress, from the first human occupation of the site to the fall of the monarchy. The naval aspect of its history is especially well represented.

THE OLD ARSENAL

Between 1705 and 1708 the Fortress was protected on the Petrograd Side by the construction of the original Kronverk. Of this auxiliary earthwork nothing remains today except ruins, with a stream running at their foot.

MONUMENT TO THE DECEMBRISTS. The execution of the Decembrists ● 42 took place at the Arsenal. The obelisk commemorating the five victims bears a medallion showing their profiles.

ARTILLERY MUSEUM. The Arsenal building is a brick-built construction with a façade regulated by pilasters; each segment includes a carriage gateway and twinned bays on the second floor. In 1856 the military collections assembled since 1776 were installed in the arsenals of the Kronverk, where they may still be seen today.

THE PRISON
Outside is the sauna bath which the prisoners were allowed to visit once a week. The cells were furnished with an iron bed and a table, both sealed to the wall, and a stool: they were heated one by one by a stove kept in the corridor. In the old days, one corner of the prison was known as the Dance Floor, in reference to a punishment inflicted on malingering soldiers, who were lashed to a stake with their bare feet resting on pointed sticks. The pain forced them to constantly shift their weight from one foot to the other, so that they looked as though they were dancing.

THE ANCESTOR OF THE RUSSIAN FLEET
For Peter I a powerful war fleet was the guarantor of Russia's opening up to the rest of the world. He personally sailed a large Dutch sloop from Moscow, his admirals plying the oars while he himself held the tiller. This vessel, known to this day as the "Grandfather of the Russian Fleet", was placed in the Boat House in 1761; since 1940 it has been in the Naval Museum (Stock Exchange) ▲ 157.

THE PETROGRAD SIDE

PETERSBURG ISLAND. In the early days of the city this island (known today as the Petrograd Side) was important because it was close to the Fortress. All commercial and social life was concentrated around the old Revolution Square, now renamed TROITSKAYA. It suffered decline with the development of the left bank; by the second half of the 19th century wooden houses without gas or running water were in evidence, just as they were on the right bank.

RAPID MODERNIZATION. At the turn of the 20th century land was cheap and the influx of money into St Petersburg gave a powerful incentive to construction. The Petrograd Side was quickly built up, almost uniformly in the Art Nouveau style ● 92. The construction of the TRINITY BRIDGE (1897–1903) (Troitsky Most) gave the district further cachet by linking it to the grander quarters of the far bank. This bridge replaced a floating one ● 91, which had to be dismantled each year when the Neva swept away all the ice from Lake Ladoga.
MUSEUM OF POLITICAL HISTORY. In 1904, the architect A.I. Hogen built a townhouse ● 92 for Mathilda Kshesinskaya, favorite ballerina of Nicholas II. It was commandeered by the Bolsheviks in March 1917, and later became the Museum of the Great October Socialist Revolution. Now the Museum of Political History, it also incorporates a display devoted to the life of Mathilda Kshesinskaya and is the venue for musical evenings.

ALEXANDER PARK

The Gorkovskaya metro station (Горьковская) is surrounded by an immense park, until recently named after Lenin but now with its old title of Alexander Park restored. It occupies the old military training grounds around the Kronverk ▲ *149* and is a favorite place for St Petersburgers.

THE ZOOLOGICAL GARDENS. West of the Kronverk is the zoo, converted from a 19th-century private menagerie. It has seen better days; nevertheless, although giraffes and elephants are currently absent, the zoo does have a comprehensive collection of northern animal species, some of them virtually unknown to the Western public. Children visiting this zoo will discover that minks, sables and martens exist in other forms than coats and stoles; they will also be interested by rare animals from Siberia, such as the long-eared hedgehog and the Przewalsky horse. In addition, there is a large aviary of birds of prey, and a number of bears, the emblem of Russia.

CABIN OF PETER THE GREAT ★

A WOODEN LODGE ● *83*. Facing the Neva is the small cabin occupied by Peter the Great (DOMIK PETRA; домик Петра) in the summer of 1703. The roof is made of wooden slats in the shape of tiles, while the brick imitation of the exterior is reminiscent of a Dutch cottage. One of the two rooms was made into a chapel under Nicholas I; dismantled in 1930, this was replaced by an 18th-century style interior. The stone house built around the cabin also encloses a boat built by Peter the Great himself, along with an exhibition of engravings.

THE MOSQUE
(МЕСНЕТ; мечеть)
Islam is the second most popular religion in Russia, with about 20 million adherents. Although Muslims were present in St Petersburg from the earliest years, the city had no mosque until 1910. Designed by Vasilyev, who took as his model the Gour Emir Mausoleum at Samarkand (15th century), the mosque is thoroughly oriental in style, with an entry porch and two minarets covered in polychrome tiles.

The Cabin of Peter the Great was the first building in St Petersburg; it was said to have been built in three days.

The banner reads: ...РАСТЬ СОВЕТАМ

THE CRUISER "AURORA" ★

The cruiser *Aurora* (KREISER AVRORA; крейсер Аврора) of the Baltic Fleet was launched in 1903; it became a cadet training vessel after the war with Japan in 1904. The crew, many of whom had progressive ideas, played a key role at the start of the Revolution ● *46*; at a signal given from the Fortress, one of the *Aurora*'s guns opened the people's attack on the Winter Palace. It is open to the public as part of the Naval Museum (Stock Exchange).

LENIN SQUARE

In the middle of Lenin Square (PLOSHCHAD LENINA; пл.Ленина) stands a bronze effigy of the great revolutionary sculpted by Sergei Yevseyev. The statue, unveiled in 1926, shows Lenin standing on the turret of an armored vehicle, his right arm thrust out and left thumb grasping his waistcoat. An inscription reads "Long Live the Socialist Revolution throughout the World".

FINLAND STATION. This station, rebuilt in the 1960s, is the boarding point for trains to Finland, Vyborg and the Isthmus of Carelia between Lake Ladoga and the Baltic Sea, and to resorts such as Zelenogorsk, Sosnovo, Repino and Komarovo (the burial place of the poet Anna Akhmatova). At weekends the station is packed with city families heading out of town to their garden plots, returning later with flowers, vegetables, mushrooms and blueberries. A sculpted frieze on the station front depicts the Revolution; Lenin ▲ *248* arrived here on his journey from Finland on April 3, 1917. Locomotive no. 293, which brought him secretly to Finland, was presented to the Soviet Union by the Finnish Railway Company in 1957; it still stands by the platform here, behind glass.

APOTHECARIES' ISLAND

BOTANICAL GARDENS (BOTANICHESKY SAD; Ботанический сад). Apothecaries' Island (APTEKARSKI OSTROV; Аптекарский остров), separated from the island of Petrograd by the river Karpovka, is named after the Botanical Gardens at no. 2 Professor Popov Street. As the successor of the medicinal garden founded by Peter I in 1714, this institution became the Imperial Botanical Garden in 1823. Its collections were enriched over the years by contributions from explorers in Asia, Siberia and Central and South America. At the close of the 19th century, it became a center for agricultural research. The species from temperate climates are distributed around an English-style park (top right) while the greenhouses are reserved for tropical and subtropical plants. This garden is closely associated with the Botanical Museum built up around the vegetable samples collected by Peter the Great for his *cabinet de curiosités* in the Kunstkammer ▲ *160*.

SHALYAPIN HOUSE. The Apartment-Museum of Fyodor Shalyapin (Chaliapin) is at no. 2B Heinrich Graftio Street, in what used to be his private residence. Here the great singer received the artistic elite of St Petersburg. The building houses an exhibition that describes his work and includes recordings of his incomparable voice.

FYODOR SHALYAPIN (1873–1938)
Shalyapin was one of the great figures of Russian opera. He had a remarkable bass-baritone voice, and became especially famous for his interpretation of the role of Boris Godunov in Mussorgsky's eponymous opera.

THE ISLANDS OF THE DELTA

KAMMENY ISLAND (KAMENNY OSTROV; Каменный остров). This island has retained its old name, translated from a Finnish word meaning "stone". Several princely palaces were built here in the late 18th century, among them the Stone Island Palace (Kamennoostrovsky Dvorets), built (1776–81) by Yuri Felten, with the exception of its façade, attributed to Quarenghi. The Stone Island Palace was commissioned by Catherine II for her son Paul I. It was built on the point of the island, where the Neva divides into two. Its central part has a pediment supported by columns, with roof eaves enhanced by

Polovtsev's dacha.

CHURCH OF ST JOHN THE BAPTIST
This church was built on Kamenny Island in 1778 by Velten, to celebrate Catherine II's victory over the Turks.

ELAGIN PARK
The entire island is laid out in the English style, complete with pavilions, stables, landing stage, bandstands and orangeries. Today Elagin Island is St Petersburg's best-loved park.

a long balustrade. Today the palace is surrounded by barracks, and is used as a military sanitarium; efforts are being made to restore it to its original splendor. In the early 20th century a number of dachas were built on Kammeny Island; many of these are now abandoned, but others have been restored for the use of Russian dignitaries and distinguished guests from abroad. POLOVTSEV'S DACHA is an old neoclassical palace with a façade of Ionic columns; it was built (1911–16) by Fomin, who modeled it on Russian gentlemen's residences of the 18th century. After the October Revolution Polovtsev's dacha was used as a rest home for workers. It now contains offices. By the road out to Elagin Island stands the Summer Theater,

which was built in 1827 by Shustov and altered later by Cavos, in 1844. This theater is entirely constructed of wood, including its frontal colonnade, which gives it the air of a Greek temple. The Ballroom Dancing Company puts on performances here.

ELAGIN ISLAND (OSTROV YELAGIN; остров Елагин). This island was a present to Ivan Elagin by Catherine the Great in 1770. In 1794 it passed to Count Orlov and in 1817 was purchased by Alexander I ● *36*, for his mother Maria Fyodorovna, the widow of Paul I. The transformation of ELAGIN PALACE was Carlo Rossi's ▲ *181* first project in St Petersburg (1818–22). The central feature of the façade overlooking the river is a colonnaded half-rotunda topped by a flat dome, whose upper floor gives access to a roof terrace more appropriate to the climate of Italy than to that of St Petersburg. The interior décor reflects the taste of the time, with a large amount of white and pastel-toned painted stucco as well as much sculpture. This palace was seriously damaged during World War Two, since when it has been carefully restored. It now contains a museum of decorative arts of the 19th and early 20th centuries.

KRESTOVSKY ISLAND (KRESTOVSKY OSTROV; Крестовский остров). As they always have done, St Petersburgers still go to the island of Krestovsky to bathe in the waters of the Neva and breathe the sea air, all for the price of a tram ticket. The island is also the location for a number of important sporting facilities, among them an Olympic Training Institute, and the KIROV STADIUM, which is the largest sporting complex in St Petersburg, having a capacity of 73,000 people.

✪ "THE ISLANDS"
Collectively known as "the islands" by St Petersburgers, Kammeny Island, Elagin Island and Krevstovsky Island were the favorite holiday spots for the gilded youth of the 19th century. Wealthy young people would come here to be entertained by gypsies and cabaret dancers, and to watch the sun go down over the Gulf of Finland. Although the islands are now part of St Petersburg, they are an oasis of greenery. Opposite Elagin Island (91 Primorski Prospekt) the largest Buddhist temple in Europe, built in 1915 and reestablished as a centre of worship in 1990, is worth a visit.

Vasilyevsky Island

1. MINING INSTITUTE
2. LIEUTENANT SCHMIDT BRIDGE
3. STATUE OF ADMIRAL KRUSENSTERN
4. SPHINX PIER
5. PASSENGER PORT
6. ACADEMY OF ARTS
7. MENSHIKOV PALACE
8. PALACE BRIDGE

⊡ Half a day ◆ B-D

Vasilyevsky Island (VASILYEVSKY OSTROV; Васильевский остров) is the largest of the various islands in the Neva Delta. Its street plan was laid out by the architect Jean-Baptiste Leblond ● 82, whose project was approved by Peter I on January 1, 1716. Leblond's idea was to divide the island into a network of streets and canals meeting at right angles. He also envisaged the excavation of a broad navigable canal, which would follow the line of the present Bolshoy Prospekt. Each side of the streets running at right angles to the canal was called a "line" and bore a number; this system still operates today. Shortly after Peter I's death the island was relegated to a secondary role in the development of St Petersburg, being too frequently subject to flooding, and the project for a canal network was shelved indefinitely.

THE POINT (STRELKA)

One of the finest vantage points on Vasilyevsky Island is the Strelka, meaning Arrow or Point. Peter I intended this site to be the prestigious center of his capital, with a broad square and magnificent government buildings.

NAVAL MUSEUM (TSENTRALNY VOENNO-MORSKOY MUZEY; центральный Военно-морской музей). The heart of this architectural ensemble is the old Stock Exchange building ● 87, rebuilt between 1804 and 1810 by Thomas de Thomon. The Exchange, with its massive granite base, was the place of business to which merchants came on their arrival at the port of St Petersburg ▲ 192. Since 1940 the building has been allocated to the Naval Museum.

HISTORY OF THE RUSSIAN FLEET
The collections of the Naval Museum include over 1,700 model ships, from the oldest (Peter I's small vessel) to the most modern, along with designs and maquettes.

ЦЕНТРАЛЬНЫЙ
ВОЕННО-МОРСКОЙ
ОРДЕНА
КРАСНОЙ ЗВЕЗДЫ
МУЗЕЙ

RARE SPECIES
The St Petersburg Zoological Museum is one of the largest of its kind in the world. It has examples of over forty thousand different animal species, with about fifteen million specimens in reserve.

ROSTRAL COLUMNS ★
● 87. On the square in front of the Exchange are the two rostral columns (the term is derived from the Latin *rostrum*, the bows of a vessel), to which are attached metal ships' prows. These are flanked by colossal statues, allegories of the four great rivers of Russia – the Volga, the Dnieper, the Volkhov and the Neva – sculpted in stone from studies by I. Chamberlain and J. Thibaut. For some time beacons, fueled by hemp oil, burned on the top of the columns, and these functioned as lighthouses at the entrance to the port.

OLD PORT WAREHOUSES. On either side of the Exchange are port warehouses, built between 1826 and 1832 by the architect Giovanni Luchini. The south building is now the ZOOLOGICAL MUSEUM (ZOOLOGICHESKY MUZEY; Зоологический музей), founded in 1896. This was the former site of the palace of Czarina Prascovia Fyodorovna (1664–1723), the wife of Peter I's half-brother, Czar Ivan Alexeyvich (1666–96) and mother of the future Empress Anna Yoannovna ● 36. The north warehouse is now the DOKUCHAYEV MUSEUM OF SOIL SCIENCE (TSENTRALNY MUZEY POCHVOVEDENIYA IM. V. DOKUCHAYEV; центральный музей Почвоведения им. V. Докучаева),

MUSEUM OF LITERATURE (LITERATURNY MUZEY; Литературный музей). The old Customs House was built between 1829 and 1832 under the supervision of Luchini. Since 1927 this building has served as the Institute of Russian Literature (or Pushkin House) and the Museum of Literature. Both establishments were founded after the 1899 exhibition in honor of Pushkin's centenary ● 114. Their archives include over two thousand manuscripts from the 13th to the 18th centuries, along with a number of texts by Tolstoy and Dostoevsky ▲ 207. The museum houses an extraordinary collection of original oil paintings and watercolors.

opened in 1904. This museum is devoted to the study and protection of Russia's soils and to increasing their productivity.

MAKAROV EMBANKMENT

The embankment is named for Stepan Makarov (1849–1904), the famous Russian Navy Admiral. The granite facing of the embankment was built between 1806 and 1809, as were the buildings by the Customs House pier (note the broad stairway with its sculpted lions).

LIBRARY OF THE ACADEMY OF SCIENCES (BIBLIOTEKA AKADEMII NAUK; библиотека Академии наук). The main façade completes the view from the main Neva waterway along the Mendeleev "line", named for the chemist Mendeleev (1834–1907). Founded in 1714, the Library of the Academy of Sciences (1912–25, architect R. Marfeld) is one of the oldest scientific establishments in the city. It contains over twenty million volumes, as well as engravings, drawings, watercolors, manuscripts, maps and charts.

THE TWELVE COLLEGES (DVENADTSAT KOLLEGI; Двенадцать Коллегий). Constructed between 1722 and 1742 by Domenico Trezzini ● 83 and Theodore Schwertfeger, and now attached to the University of St Petersburg, this complex is made up of twelve identical buildings in an unbroken line, intended for the various government bodies: the Senate, the Synod and the ten "colleges" or ministries. The glazed second floor is now the corridor of the University and is famed for its length. In 1835 all these buildings were handed over to the University authorities, by whom they were partially reconstructed. Visitors are admitted to the museum named after the chemist Mendeleev, who devised the periodic table of chemical elements, and lived and worked here from 1866 to 1890.

UNIVERSITY EMBANKMENT

At the beginning of the University Embankment
(UNIVERSITETSKAYA NAB.; Университетская наб.) are a
number of buildings which are linked to the history of the
Academy of Sciences.

THE KUNSTKAMMER ★ ▲ *250*. The Kunstkammer, Peter the
Great's gallery of curiosities, is an interesting example of early
Russian Baroque. Built between 1718 and 1734 by the
architects G. Mattarnovy, N. Herbel, G. Ciaveri and
M. Zemtsov, the Kunstkammer has wings of two stories with
a tower between. The Kunstkammer was the first Natural
Science Museum in Russia, and it included a library and
an observatory. From 1783 to 1796 the Academy was
directed by E. Dashkova, a friend of Catherine II and
one of the most cultivated women of her time. In 1878 it
became the Museum of Anthropology and Ethnology
(MUZEY ANTROPOLOGII I ETNOGRAFII IM. PETRA
VELIKOVO; музей Антропологии и Этнографии им.
Петра Великого). The museum's displays include items
which illustrate the daily lives and cultures of many
different countries, along with their weapons, clothes
and religious objects.

M. LOMONOSOV MUSEUM (MUZEY M. LOMONOSOVA;
музей М. Ломоносова). In 1949 the M. Lomonosov
Museum ● *53* was installed inside the Kunstkammer, in
memory of the great scientist. Among its attractions are
Lomonosov's scientific instruments and his writings, in
addition to a reconstitution of the Academy of
Sciences' conference hall.

ACADEMY OF SCIENCES (AKADEMIYA NAUK; Академия наук).
Beside the Kunstkammer, also on the embankment at no. 5 is
the main Academy of Sciences building, which was
constructed between 1783 and 1789 by Giacomo Quarenghi
● *86*. In 1925 the main staircase in the vestibule was
embellished with a mosaic panel by Lomonosov, which was
entitled *The Battle of Poltava*. In the same year the Academy
became known as the
Academy of
Sciences of the
Soviet Union,
before its
headquarters
were
transferred to
Moscow nine
years later, in
1934.

THE GLOBE
At the Lomonosov
Museum is a
reconstruction of the
huge terrestrial globe
of the Academy of
Sciences. Made in the
1600's for the Duke
of Holstein-Gottorp,
it was presented as a
gift to Peter the Great
in 1713.

**CABINET OF
CURIOSITIES**
The collections of
monstrosities and
curiosities in the Kikin
Palace ▲ *250* were
amassed by Peter I
and transferred to the
Kunstkammer in
1727.

ALEXANDER MENSHIKOV (1672–1729)
The son of a baker, Menshikov was a childhood friend of Peter the Great. He wielded immense influence on affairs of state, and distinguished himself in a number of military campaigns (he was promoted to general in 1705). He later directed part of the construction of St Petersburg. Following the death of Peter the Great, Menshikov, who had become a member of the Secret Supreme Council and had married off his daughter to the future Peter II, was sole master of Russia for over two years. But he aroused the hostility of the nobility and his grip on power ended with his arrest in 1727. All his property was confiscated and he was deported with his family to Siberia, where he died two years later.

MENSHIKOV PALACE (DVORETS MENSHIKOVA; дворец Меншикова) ★ ● *82*. At no. 15 on the embankment stands the architectural ensemble of the Menshikov Palace. In the early years of the 18th century Prince Menshikov, who was a close friend of Peter the Great, had his private mansion here. The building has two floors and a mansard roof; it was designed by the architects Giovanni Maria Fontana and Gottfried Schädell. It was here that Peter I held lavish assemblies and celebrations of Russian victories, and received foreign embassies. In 1781, two years after Menshikov's death, the palace was the barracks of an elite regiment, the Foot Guards, before it was passed on to the Army's First Cadet Corps. The left wing of the palace was enlarged by the addition of a new building, which was itself enlarged during the 1770s. Works initiated in 1966–81 restored the palace's original aspect, which was remarkable for its famously splendid interiors. A spacious vestibule leads to the formal oak staircase, with wrought-iron banisters struck with the monograms of Peter the Great and Menshikov himself. The stairs go up to the apartments of Prince Menshikov and his sister-in-law Varvara Arseneva (who was responsible for educating his children); the two areas are separated, however, by formal drawing rooms. The ASSEMBLY ROOM, which is over a thousand square feet in size, is the largest room in the palace. The WALNUT ROOM, with its painted ceiling and boiseries of Persian walnut wood, was Menshikov's favorite room; his BEDROOM (below) is covered with no fewer than 27,811 Delft tiles ● *64*. The restoring of the architectural decoration of the palace was completed in 2002, with the installation of the princely crowns and vases. The palace is now an annex of the Hermitage and contains an exhibition on "Russian Culture 1700–30".

MENSHIKOV'S OFFICE
On the walls are portraits of Menshikov's four daughters.

PAINTING, SCULPTURE, ARCHITECTURE
The Academy of the "three noble arts" was founded in 1757, at the instigation of Lomonosov.

ACADEMY OF ARTS (AKADEMIYA KHUDOSHESTV; Академия художеств). Further along the embankment, at no. 17, the building of the Academy of Arts may be found, which was constructed between 1764 and 1768 by the architects Alexander Kokorinov and Jean-Baptiste Vallin de la Mothe ● 86. The traditions of this academy are maintained today by the Repin Institute of Painting, Sculpture and Architecture. Also housed within the building is the Arts Academy of Research, and on the first floor a department exhibiting plaster casts of original artworks from all over the world. The department of architecture displays a variety of designs and projects, together with scale models of Smolny ● 84, St Isaac's Cathedral ● 88, the Engineers' Castle, and the Stock Exchange ● 87.

LIEUTENANT SCHMIDT EMBANKMENT

SPHINX QUAY ★
(SPUSK SO SPHINXAMI; Спуск со Сфинксами)
This quay was built (1832–4) to a plan by Konstantin Thon. The two sculpted sphinxes on either side of the steps leading down to the river were found at Thebes, the capital of ancient Egypt. Their features are those of the Pharaoh Amenophis III.

LIEUTENANT SCHMIDT BRIDGE. Both the bridge and the embankment are named for Nikolai Schmidt (center), who distinguished himself during the 1905 Revolution ● 44. The Lieutenant Schmidt Bridge (originally named the Nicholas Bridge) was the first permanent bridge across the Neva; it was built between 1847 and 1850 by the engineer S. Kerbedz and the decoration (sea shells and sea horses) is by Bryulov.
THE ACADEMICIANS' HOUSE (DOM AKADEMIKOV; дом Академиков). At no. 1 Lieutenant Schmidt Embankment (NAB. LEYTENANTA SCHMIDT; наб. Лейтенанта-Шмидта) stands the Academicians' House, which was constructed in the 1750's by Savva Chevakinsky. The building was completely reshaped in the early 19th century by the architects A. Bezhanov and Andrei Zakharov ● 87. The classical structure of the house is typical of the period; it has twenty-six plaques affixed to its walls, which commemorate the intellectuals who occupied it.

THE FRUNZE NAVAL STAFF COLLEGE (VYSSHEE VOENNO-MORSKOYE UCHILISHCHE IM. M. FRUNZE; Высшее военно-морское училище им. М. Фрунзе). This imposing building with its Ionic colonnade is the Russian Navy's principal educational institution. It was built between 1796 and 1798 by the architect F. Volkov, and succeeded the Navigation School, which had been founded in 1701 by an edict of Peter the Great. The Navigation School was converted into the Naval Cadet Corps School in 1752.

STATUE OF ADMIRAL KRUSENSTERN (PAMYATNIK ADMIRALU KRUSENSHTERNU; памятник адмиралу Крузенштерну). In front of the Naval Staff College stands the statue of Admiral Krusenstern (1770–1846), which was erected in 1873. Admiral Krusenstern is famous as the commander of the first flotilla of Russian ships to circumnavigate the globe in the early 19th century.

CHURCH OF THE DORMITION (USPENSKAYA TSERKOV; Успенская церковь). The pure lines of the monumental Church of the Dormition stand out clearly on the Neva's skyline. Built between 1893 and 1900 by B. Kosyakov, it stands on the former site of the Pskov Monastery's guest quarters, purchased in the 1880's by the Kiev Monastery ▲ 253.

MINING INSTITUTE (GORNY INSTITUT; Горный институт). Lieutenant Schmidt Embankment ends with the enormous Mining Institute, one of the oldest establishments of its kind in the world. When it was founded in 1773 it was known as the Mining School, later becoming the Mining Corps. The building, with its portico of twelve Doric columns, was built between 1806 and 1811 by Andrei Voronikhin. It houses a museum which contains one of the world's richest collections of minerals, stones and fossils. There are scale models of mines, and the museum also exhibits examples of the tools used in the mining industry.

THE "CHEKUCHI". Beyond the Mining Institute is the industrial and manufacturing quarter, which has always been known as the "Chekuchi" (The Crushers), on account of the mallets which were used to crush the lumps of damp flour piled in the warehouses here. Nowadays the area is a huge naval dockyard which, with its counterpart on the other bank of the Neva, frames the point where the river meets the Gulf of Finland.

PAVLOV (1849–1936)
Since 1949 there has been a museum at the Academicians' House dedicated to the work of the physiologist Pavlov, who lived at apartment no. 18 there from 1918 onward.

MIKHAIL FRUNZE (1885–1925)
This military commander distinguished himself during the Civil War (1918) and in 1924 was named Chief of Staff and Commandant of the Moscow Military Academy.

SMOLENSK CEMETERY ■ *26*
This is made up of three cemeteries: a Russian orthodox cemetery, a Lutheran cemetery and an Armenian cemetery.

ST CATHERINE'S CHURCH
The Bolshoy Prospekt begins with St Catherine's Church, built (1768–71) by Yury Velten ● *86* for the Evangelical Lutheran community of Vasilyevksy Island.

PASSENGER PORT
On Naval Glory Square, fronting the Gulf of Finland, the main building is the Passenger Port (1977–82), whose giant 240-foot spire is topped by a caravel, similar to the one at the Admiralty ▲ *190*.

BOLSHOY PROSPEKT

The buildings along the BOLSHOY PROSPEKT (Большой проспект) are less interesting for their architecture than for the memories that cling to them – above all, for the everyday life of the quarter.

ST ANDREW'S MARKET (ANDREEVSKY RYNOK; Андреевский рынок). The area between "lines" five and six is occupied by St Andrew's Market. The old part of the building dates from 1780–90, and its modern section from 1959.

ST ANDREW'S CHURCH (ANDREEVSKY SOBOR; Андреевский собор). The principal Orthodox church on the island, this building is a monument of mid-18th century Baroque architecture (1764–80, architect A. Vist). The carved iconostasis is a masterpiece in the genre.

PEL AND SON'S PHARMACY (APTEKA A. PELYA SYNOVEY; аптека А. Пеля и сыновей). On the first floor of a four-story house, situated at 16/18 Liniïa 7 – now transformed into a pedestrianised area, along with Liniïa 6 – was the original pharmacy of A. Pel (1900s). Pel, a doctor in chemistry, philosophy and pharmacology, was the first in Russia to make preparations based on organic constituents; he invented a number of medical compounds that are still in use today. Since 1983, a museum of Russian pharmacology has occupied Pel's old premises, with objects from the period.

From the Hermitage
to the Summer Palace

🕙 One day
◆ A-E

THE HERMITAGE

THE FIRST WINTER PALACES. The Winter Palace, now known as the Hermitage Museum, is the fourth building to have been constructed on this site. After the first "small Dutch-style house" built by Peter I it was probably the Italian architect Domenico Trezzini who built the nuptial palace which we consider to have been the first Winter Palace (1711–12). This building was destroyed in 1726. Meantime, the architect Mattarnovy had built a "winter house" next door (1716–19) for Peter I. In 1732 the Empress Anna Ivanovna from the Rastrellis another palace. It was razed in 1754 to make way for the current palace, built for Elizabeth Petrovna.

PALACE OF ELIZABETH. Built from 1754 to 1762 by Bartolomeo Rastrelli, this palace is renowned for its profusion of Baroque decoration: two stories of columns cover the facades.

✪ **THE HERMITAGE AND PALACE SQUARE**
The Hermitage, the city's symbol, is one of the largest museums in the world, with collections comprising about three million items. Now extending to the former General Staff Headquarters on Palace Square ▲ *180*, it constitutes a major cultural center. There are two exhibitions: "Under the Aegis of the Eagle", displaying artefacts of the Empire, and "History of the Guardsman", showing uniforms, flags and armor.

CATHERINE II'S WINTER PALACE. The interiors were still uncompleted when Rastrelli was dismissed by Catherine in August 1762. The director of the Buildings Chancellery, I. Betsky, called in several foreign architects to replace him: Jean-Baptiste Vallin de la Mothe, Antonio Rinaldi and the German Yury Velten. De la Mothe decorated Catherine II's private apartments (later destroyed in the 1837 fire), the Throne Room, the church, the apartments of the ladies of honor on the third floor, and the apartments of Count Grigory Orlov on the mezzanine floor. Felten reorganized the Portrait and the Mirror galleries, and Rinaldi changed the Throne Room into an oval salon. Catherine II had ten grandchildren, and the imperial apartments (including the theater) were altered to meet their needs by Giacomo Quarenghi and Ivan Starov. But the really major changes were to come with new construction work.

Built by Bartolomeo Rastrelli (1754–62), Elizabeth I's Winter Palace is laid out around an immense closed courtyard with four projecting pavilions at the corners. The main portions of the building facing the Neva and Palace Square are linked by closed lateral galleries with apartments, service areas and staircases giving on to them. The center of the façade giving onto the Neva is barely evident by comparison with the projecting pavilions on either side of it. Although the Palace Square was built much later, the entrance to the courtyard was always by way of the triple arch on the city side.

The entrance to the New Hermitage was from Khalturin (Millionaires') Street, through a monumental gateway. It was built by the German architect Leo von Klenze between 1839 and 1851 and is supported by ten sculpted figures of Atlas.

DURING THE REVOLUTION Guards occupying the Winter Palace, October 24, 1917.

THE THEATER (E)
Built in the antique
style, it has a semi-
circular auditorium
and décor inspired by
the Olympic Theater
at Vicenza (Italy).

**THE WINTER
PALACE (A)**
Major alterations
were made to the
Winter Palace's
corner pavilions in
the 19th century.
The Ambassadors'
Staircase (or Jourdain
Staircase) was built in
the northeast corner;
the sovereign used
this staircase on
January 6 (Epiphany)
each year on his way
to bless the waters of
the Neva in memory
of Christ's Baptism.

**THE SMALL
HERMITAGE (B)**
Beginning in 1736,
Vallin de la Mothe
built a hanging
garden here, with a
pavilion at each end.
The north pavilion,
which was called
the Hermitage, was
finished in 1770.
But Catherine II's
growing art collection
eventually required
another building, the
Large Hermitage, to
be built.

**THE LARGE
HERMITAGE (C)**
Built in two stages,
the Large Hermitage
was the work of Yury
Velten (1771–87).
It occupies a site
between the palace
and the Winter Canal
dug by Peter the
Great between the
Neva and the Moika.
Its name was changed
in the 19th century to
the Old Hermitage.

**THE NEW
HERMITAGE (D)**
The imperial
collections were
saved from the fire
which devastated the
Winter Palace in
December 1837.
To house and display
them to the public,
it was decided in
1839 that a New
Hermitage should be
built. The museum
was opened by
Nicholas I in 1852.

"COMPOSITION VI"
The work of
Vasily Kandinsky is
displayed on the third
floor of the south
wing of the Winter
Palace, after the
Fauvist section.
This painting,
Composition VI, is an
example of a work
from the artist's
Abstract period.

The War of 1812 Gallery (**2**) still bears the stamp of Rossi, its decorator. Here are displayed the portraits of the Russian generals who took part in the war against Napoleon. The Alexander Hall (**1**) contains a medallion with the profile of Alexander I, and m███s of warlike themes symbolizing the Czar's victory in the war of 1812–14. Bryulov ███ed this with ███ls of Gothic columns, two-headed eagles and classical medallions. The Hall of St George (**3**) ███ decorated with Carrara marble columns with gilded bronze capitals. The Throne, now installed in the Hall of Peter I, formerly stood below the bas-relief of Saint George and the Dragon. In the Pavilion Hall (**4**) copie█ mosaics from Roman spas are set in the floor. The █ also contain reproductions of the Fountain of Tears from the Bakhtchisarai Palace in the Crimea. On the orders of Catherine II Quarenghi painted a reproduction of Raphael's loggia (**5**) at the winter Canal side of this room (1783–92).

The history of the Hermitage as a museum began with Peter the Great, who himself bought a number of works of art – among them *David and Goliath* by Rembrandt and the *Tauride Venus*. In the reign of Catherine II the imperial collections occupied rooms in the Hermitage of the Winter Palace, which gave its name to the museum. The museum is considered to have been officially born in 1764, when the Berlin dealer Gotzkowski sent the Empress of Russia 225 paintings intended for Frederick II of Prussia, in payment of a debt. Later, on the advice of Diderot and many of the best art connoisseurs of the time, Catherine bought many more works of art (and above all complete collections) in Paris, Dresden and London. Toward the close of her reign the Hermitage collection numbered 3,000 paintings, almost 7,000 drawings as well as some 70,000 engravings, 10,000 carved stones and 38,000 books.

VENETIAN PAINTERS

The museum contains an outstanding collection of Italian paintings from the 13th to the 18th centuries. The Venetian collection at the Old Hermitage is particularly rich and includes works such as *Judith* (left) and *Madonna and Child* by Giorgione (1477–1510). One room is entirely devoted to paintings by Titian (c. 1490–1576), among which are several masterpieces, including *Danaë, Mary Magdalen, Portrait of a Woman, Christ Carrying the Cross* and *Saint Sebastian.*

17TH–18TH CENTURY SPANISH PAINTINGS

The Spanish collection includes impressive works by El Greco (*Saint Peter and Saint Paul*), José de Ribera (*The Vision of St Jerome*), Velasquez (*The Meal,* also known as *The Drinkers*), Zurbaran (*Saint Laurence*), Murillo (*Child with Dog*) and Goya's *Portrait of Antonia Zárate* (right).

THE GOLDEN COMB OF SOLOKHA
(above)
The collections of antique, oriental and Scythian jewelry, as well as gold and silverwork from Western Europe, are displayed in a special area. This golden comb is from the collection of Scythian jewelry, of which the Hermitage has some outstanding examples.

ITALIAN ART, 13TH–18TH CENTURIES

Among the many masterpieces in the section, don't miss the following: *The Virgin of the Annunciation* (Simone Martini); *The Vision of Saint Augustine* (a fresco by Filippo Lippi); *Virgin and Child with Saint Thomas and Saint Dominic* (Fra Angelico); *Saint Dominic and Saint Jerome* (Botticelli). The Italian majolica room has two paintings by Raphael: *Madonna Conestabile* (above) and *The Holy Family*. In the first glazed gallery are Veronese's *Conversion of Saint Paul* and Tintoretto's *Birth of John the Baptist*. In the large glazed gallery are 17th- and 18th-century paintings, including works by Tiepolo and Canaletto.

THE "BENOIS MADONNA"
The great gallery of the Old Hermitage exhibits two famous piantings by Leonardo da Vinci : *Benois Madonna*(1478, above) and the *Litta Madonna* (early 1490-1). This painting, previously known as the *Madonna of the Flower*, is named after one of its former owners.

Crouching Youth (right), the only work by Michelangelo in Russia, was created for the Medici Tombs in Florence.

DUTCH PAINTING IN THE 15TH AND 17TH CENTURIES

The most remarkable works in this collection are Campin's diptych, *The Trinity* and the *Virgin at the Hearth*, *Saint Luke Painting the Virgin* by Van der Weyden, *The Healing of the Blind Man at Jericho* by Van Leyden, and *The Adoration of the Magi* by Van der Goes. All 17th-century genres and great masters are represented, except for Vermeer. There are two portraits by Hals, landscapes by Van Goyen and Van Ruisdael, and pictures by Van Ostade, Steen, De Hooch and Ter Borch. In the Rembrandt Room are twenty-five pictures spanning the painter's entire career, from *The Sacrifice of Abraham* (1635) (right) and *The Descent from the Cross* (1634) to *David and Uriah* and *The Return of the Prodigal Son* (mid-1660's).

17TH–19TH CENTURY ENGLISH PAINTING

This section of the museum comes after the room devoted to works by Fragonard and Greuze. Note in particular *Love Untying Venus's Girdle* and *The Infant Hercules Killing the Serpents* (below, by Reynolds); and *The Duchess of Beaufort* (by Gainsborough). Also here is the work of landscape painters contemporary with Constable, including *Boats near the Shore* by Richard Parkes Bonington (1801–28)

Detail of Rembrandt's *The Return of the Prodigal Son* (left)

"SASKIA AS FLORA"

This painting by Rembrandt dates from the first years of his marriage to Saskia van Uylenborch, shown here as a goddess of Roman mythology.

15TH–19TH CENTURY GERMAN PAINTING

In this section religious painting is displayed alongside Renaissance portraits and 17th-century still lifes. The great masterpieces here include Cranach the Elder's *Venus and Cupid* (below), *Virgin and Child Under an Apple Tree* and *Portrait of a Woman*; as well as *Portrait of a Young Man* by Ambrosius Holbein and *Erasmus of Rotterdam* by Hans Holbein the Younger 1497–1543). There are also some fine still lifes by Christoph Paudiss (1618–66) and Hendrik van der Borcht the Elder 1583–1660).

Nineteenth-century German paintings are shown on the third floor, in a series of rooms parallel to those housing the Matisse collection. The group of paintings by the Romantic artist Caspar David Friedrich (1774–1840) are not to be missed.

17TH-CENTURY FLEMISH PAINTINGS

Many of the paintings exhibited in this section are works by the major Flemish portraitists of the period. The section includes twenty-six pictures by Van Dyck, including his fine *Portrait of Charles I, Self-Portrait* and *St Peter the Apostle*. Of the forty works by Rubens the most notable are *Christ with Crown of Thorns* (above), *The Alliance of Earth and Water, Perseus and Andromeda, Landscape with Rainbow* and *Portrait of Isabella of Spain's Lady-in-Waiting*. The fame of the collection of Flemish paintings in the Hermitage rests on the museum's holdings of works by these two masters.

"LA MUSIQUE"

"LA MUSIQUE"
The collection of paintings by Matisse (1869–1954) in the Hermitage is one of the largest and most representative in Europe. The thirty-seven paintings exhibited include *La Danse* and *La Musique*.

15TH–18TH CENTURY FRENCH PAINTING
This collection of French painting rivals that of the Louvre itself. The major works here are Le Nain's *The Milkmaid's Family*, Poussin's *Tancredi and Hermine* and *Landscape with Polyphenus*, Watteau's *The Little Savoyard* and *The Awkward Proposal*, and Fragonard's elegantly suggestive *Stolen Kiss* (left).

19TH CENTURY FRENCH ART
This collection is the pride of the Hermitage, particularly because it includes some paintings of international importance. Among the works dating from the first half of the 19th century are *Bonaparte at the Bridge of Arcole* (Gros); *Morpheus and Iris* (Guérin, left); *Portrait of Count Guriev* (Ingres); *Lion Hunt in Morocco* and *Arabs Saddling a Horse* (Delacroix).

FRENCH PAINTING, LATE 19TH TO EARLY 20TH CENTURY

Mainly assembled by the Muscovite collectors Morozov and Shchukin at the beginning of this century, this collection is one of the finest in the world. It includes six paintings by Renoir (among them *Portrait of Jeanne Savary* and *Young Woman with a Fan*), five pastels by Degas, including *Young Woman at her Toilet* (below, left); eight landscapes by Monet, eleven Cézannes, four van Goghs (including *The Bush*, above left), fifteen Gauguins from the artist's Tahiti period (left), eight paintings and thirteen panels by Denis, eight canvases and triptychs by Bonnard, two Vuillards and six Vallotons. The Fauvists are represented by nine Marquets, five Vlamincks, fourteen Derains and five Van Dongens. To cap it off, there are thirty-one paintings by Picasso and thirty-seven by Matisse. Below, *Absinthe Drinker*, 1901, by Picasso.

PALACE SQUARE

BLOODY SUNDAY
Gathered on Palace Square on January 22, 1905, the demonstrators asked to be allowed to present a petition to the Czar Nicholas II (who was not in the palace).

AN IMPERIAL ESPLANADE. Even though the entrance to the courtyard of the Winter Palace ▲ *168* was originally planned not for the Neva side but for the city side of the building, Palace Square (DVORTSOVAYA PLOSHCHAD; Дворцовая площадь) was laid out at a relatively late date. The architect Bartolomeo Rastrelli ● *84* had proposed a semicircular colonnade to transform the area into a gigantic courtyard and provide a counterpoint to the Baroque façade of the Winter Palace. But Empress Elizabeth died

The police fired on the crowd; the resultant carnage created an unbridgeable gulf between the Czar and his people and provided the impetus for revolution.

before the completion of the project and Catherine II dismissed Rastrelli when she ascended the throne. All this time the square was no more than a huge field; but in 1772 the architect Starov resurrected the idea of a colonnade, which Catherine had rejected, although the semicircular plan appealed to her. Finally, in 1779 the Arts Academy launched a competition, which was won by Yury Velten ▲ *162*. Opposite the palace he built a half-circle of houses with identical façades. Still, the ensemble lacked real grandeur, and Carlo Rossi ● *86* was commissioned in 1819 to lay out a more regular square.

PALACE SQUARE
The Winter Palace, Admiralty Gardens, former headquarters of the General Staff, and the Guards' former headquarters bound this huge area.

THE GENERAL STAFF HEADQUARTERS. The main function of the buildings fronting the square was to provide a general headquarters for the Army's main staff. In 1819 it was decided that Russia's administrative center should also be moved here, concentrating the Ministry of Finance and the Foreign Ministry in the same place. Carlo Rossi went back to the old semicircular layout as defined by the existing buildings, and put all of them behind a single façade, the center of which was pierced by a huge triumphal arch, the ARCH OF THE GENERAL STAFF. The skill with which this was accomplished is famous in the annals of architecture. The arch, sited directly on the axis of the main palace entrance, had to link the square with the curved street coming from the

Nevksy Prospekt. Rossi therefore devised a "turning" arch – that is, one doubled with a part forming an arc of a circle which made it possible to pass from the fixed plane to the curve of the street while preserving the illusion of depth. The Arch is decorated Roman-style with military trophies and laurel-crowned worthies. On its top is a team of six bronze horses harnessed to the chariot of Glory. In 1840 the square was rounded off on its east side by the Headquarters of the Guard, designed by Alexander Bryulov.

THE ALEXANDER COLUMN (ALEKSANDROVSKAYA KOLONNA; Александровская колонна). This gigantic column was raised in the middle of the square (1830–4) in honor of Alexander I ● *36*, who prevailed against the

CARLO ROSSI (1775–1849)
Rossi was born in St Petersburg, the son of an Italian ballerina. Beginning his career as the assistant of Brenna, he studied in Italy before returning to Russia to complete his architectural masterpieces, among them the Palace Square.

THE ALEXANDER COLUMN
The 600-ton column, brought from Finland in 1832, was raised onto its base using a system of winches similar to that later used for St Isaac's Church ▲ *195*. Myth has it that the column is perfectly balanced and whoever can lift it will find gold and treasure hidden underneath.

armies of Napoleon. The idea came from Rossi, but the design was completed by Auguste Ricard de Montferrand. The 90-foot monolith of pink Finnish granite is crowned by an angel: the total height of the monument is nearly 150 feet. The pedestal is decorated with allegorical bas-reliefs of the rivers Nieman and Vistula (crossed by the Army in pursuit of Napoleon) on one side, and Wisdom and Abundance, Peace and Justice, Victory and Peace on the other.

PUSHKIN'S HOUSE
The poet's study and
his 4,000-book library
(above) have been
carefully preserved as
they were when the
Pushkin family lived
here. Pushkin died in
this house on January
29, 1837 ● 117.

Arms of the
Volkonsky Family.

"The Neva, with its
bridges and piers, is
the true glory of
St Petersburg. The
prospect of it is so
immense that
everything else is tiny
by comparison. The
Neva is a basin filled
to the brim; its banks
merge with the water,
which seems about
to overflow on every
side. Venice and
Amsterdam seem to
me much better
defended against
the sea than is
St Petersburg."
Astolphe de Custine,
La Russie en 1839

THE MOIKA EMBANKMENT

CAPELLA ● **72.** The original Capella
(no. 20), known as the Glinka Singing
Academy in this century, was founded
by Peter the Great; the present school
was built in 1880 by the architect
Leonty Benois at the end of a courtyard.
The auditorium is separated from the
street by high cast-iron railings which
link two identical buildings. The
Capella ensemble is a fine example
of eclectic late 19th-century décor.

DLT STORE (Dom Leningradskoi Torgovli). This store backs
on to the Moika Embankment (NAB. REKI MOIKI; наб. реки
Мойки), although its main entrance is at no. 21 Bolshaya
Konnushenaya. Built by the architect E.V. Virrich (1908–10),
it is important in the history of St Petersburg architecture as
one of the first metal-and-glass structures in the city. The
huge salerooms were patterned on the Parisian *grands
magasins* built at the turn of the century.

PUSHKIN MUSEUM (MUZEY-KVARTIRA PUSHKINA; музей-
квартира Пушкина). An earlier house on this site (no. 12,
built in the 1730's) belonged to the Volkonsky family. This
mansion was replaced in 1770 by another in the classical
Russian style, and subsequently altered extensively. Six fluted
Corinthian pilasters distinguish the projecting central section,
of the height of two floors, with a curved façade reflecting the
bend in the river. On the courtyard side are broad arches
(now glassed in) which still incorporate elements of the
original building. The Pushkin family rented the second floor
here in 1836.

IMPERIAL STABLES. The first imperial stables were
built in 1720 for Peter the Great, by the architect
N.F. Gerbel. The buildings were laid out around a
polygonal courtyard. Although entirely
reconstructed on the same site by Vasily Stasov
between 1816 and 1823, they have retained their
original form, specifically the curve imposed by the
Moika. The CHURCH is contained in the square central
portion of the façade giving on to the square. This
somewhat complex ensemble included not only the stables
and the riding ring, but also several warehouses, the
administrative offices (the master of the stables was an

important figure in the imperial service), the lodgings of the staff and the church.

PALACE EMBANKMENT

THE WINTER CANAL BRIDGE. The Winter Canal meets the Neva by the Old Hermitage. The bridge that spans it is characteristic of those built by Yury Velten in the 1770's as part of the works carried out on the banks of the Neva, its tributaries and the various canals.

THE FORMER / NEW MIKHAIL PALACE. Built by Shtakenshneider (1857–61) for Mikhail Nicolayevich, son of Nicholas I ● *36*, this palace (no. 18) occupies a site bordered on one side by the Palace Embankment (DVORTSOVAYA NAB.; Дворцовая наб.) and on the other by Millionaires' Street. It follows the alignment of the other houses, blending well with the other private mansions of the quarter, although its lower level is notable for its French Renaissance-style panels and pilasters. The rear façade, however, is much more modest, and was reserved for the Grand Duke's domestic servants and staff. The dimensions of the palace are impressive, and it is said that one of the Grand Duke's sons would borrow a bicycle to visit his sister-in-law, whose quarters were located in another part of the palace.

Left to right: The galleried bridge across the Winter Canal, built by Yury Velten to link the Winter Palace with the theater ▲ *168*; the façade of the Hermitage ▲ *168* on the Neva side; and a detail of the façade of the Academicians' House. This former palace at no. 26 Palace Embankment, built by Alexander Rezanov (1867–71), includes many Italian Renaissance and Baroque elements. The red sandstone façade is itself strongly reminiscent of Florentine palaces.

BESIDE THE NEVA
The Palace Embankment owes its name to the residence of the Czars, today's Hermitage Museum ▲ *168*. The consolidation of the river banks with granite was undertaken over fifteen years, beginning in 1763, with the architect Yury Velten playing an important role.

THE MARBLE PALACE

FLOOR PLAN OF THE MARBLE PALACE
This follows the traditional U-design of urban palaces, with a courtyard fronting the main entrance.

A GIFT OF THE EMPRESS. For nearly twelve years Catherine II was the mistress of Count Grigory Orlov (1734–83). During this time she presented him with the Marble Palace (MRAMORNY DVORETS; Мраморный дворец). Orlov, with his brothers Alexei and Fyodor, led the conspiracy against Peter III that placed Catherine II on the Russian throne. The palace was built (1768–85) by the architect Antonio Rinaldi on a site between the Palace Embankment and Millionaires' Street. The main façade has four Corinthian columns at its center. The original entrance was via the Red Canal, which ran along the west side of Marsovo Pole. This canal was filled in during the 19th century, when a service wing was added and a new main entrance was built in the courtyard at the side of the palace.

GRANITE AND MARBLE. The contrast between the rough granite of the first floor and the refined marble of the upper levels, from which its name derives, gives

the Marble Palace an original if somewhat severe aspect. Its roof was formerly covered in copper sheeting, while the window frames of the *piano nobile* were of gilded bronze, with polished glass panes. Marble was as much in evidence inside the building as outside. The main FORMAL STAIRCASE and the MARBLE ROOM (left) are still in their original state. From 1937 to 1991 the Marble Palace housed the Lenin Museum. Serving since 1992 as an annex of the Russian Museum ▲ *225*, it now contains an exhibition of works by foreign artists living in Russia, and the Lüdwig Donation.

THE FIELD OF MARS

A RECENT ARRIVAL
In the courtyard of the Marble Palace stands an equestrian statue of Alexander III, which replaced Lenin's armored car in November 1994. The statue, originally erected on Insurrection Square (Pl. Vostaniya) ▲ *244*, was brought from the Russian Museum, its home since 1937.

MARSOVO POLE (MARSOVO POLE; Марсово поле). With the Summer Garden to eastward, the Moika to the south, the Red Canal to the west and the Neva to the north, this broad area was not given its final form until 1817–19, when the architect Vasily Stasov (1769–1848) built the Pavlovsky barracks at the same time as Carlo Rossi was completing the Mikhail Palace. Their joint efforts led to a definitive project for the quarter, and the layout of the various green spaces was dictated by the architecture they designed.

BARRACKS OF THE PAVLOVSKY GUARDS REGIMENT (KAZARMY PAVLOVSKOVO POLKA; казармы Павловского полка). The west side of the square is entirely occupied by this gigantic building. At the center of its long yellow façade are twelve Doric columns, crowned by a monumental pediment decorated with the usual trophies, weapons and winged victories. There are pavilions on either side in front of the building topped by a triangular pediment, which is echoed by a similar arrangement fronting Millionaires' Street. In the middle of Marsovo Pole, now laid out as a park, stands the Liberty Monument (right), formerly known as the Monument to Revolutionary Fighters. On the Neva side the quadrilateral ends at Suvorov Square; and in the center is a statue of Field Marshal Suvorov ▲ 252.

ADAMINI HOUSE. On the southwest side of Marsovo Pole, the corner house (no. 7) with a semicircular colonnade was built by the architect D. Adamini (1823–7) in the later classical style ● 86. The basement of this building was a meeting-place during World War One and the Revolution for Russian artists like Vsevolod Meyerhold, Alexander Blok, Anna Akhmatova,

MARSOVO POLE
Like its Paris equivalent, Marsovo Pole (Field of Mars) was used for military events, which played an important part in the daily lives of the Czars, notably that of Paul I.

Mikhail Kuzmin, Vladimir Mayakovsky and Anatoly Lunacharsky.

SALTYKOV AND BETSKY HOUSES. On the north side, fronting the waters of the Neva, Giacomo Quarenghi built the Saltykov House (1784–8); in 1820 it became the Austrian Embassy. It was celebrated for the salon over which presided the ambassador's wife, the grand-daughter of Marshal Kutuzov.

"MONTAGNES RUSSES"
In the old days Marsovo Pole was a favorite venue for the thoroughly Russian sport of sliding down an artificial slope on a small sledge or vehicle. In the rest of Europe this was known as *montagnes russes*; it was practiced as much by the Czars in their palaces as by peasants in the countryside. *Montagnes russes* could be extremely sophisticated, as at Oranienbaum ▲ 262.

The *Tauride Venus*.

SUMMER GARDEN (LETNY SAD; Летний сад)

A GARDEN IN THE FRENCH STYLE. In 1704 Peter the Great made a rough sketch of a Western-style garden, with rare plant species brought from Siberia, the Urals, Holland and Kiev. The French model won the Czar's favor after his visit to Versailles in 1717, and as a result the gardens, which extend between the Neva to the north, the Fontanka to the east and the Moika to the south, are regular and symmetrical. The gardens were divided into quadrilaterals which were planted with trees and (in the old days) shrubs and flowers. There were also cunningly devised fountains and sculptures.

GATES OF THE SUMMER GARDEN
After consolidating the Neva's banks, Velten worked on the Embankment fronting the gardens and on the Summer Palace. The wrought-iron garden gates that he competed in 1784 were considered to be one of the finest examples of metalwork of the period.

STATUES FROM ITALY. Most of the statuary in the Summer Garden was bought in Italy, according to the vogue of the early 18th century. Subjects from Greek mythology include

✪ **SUMMER GARDEN**
Praised by poets, the Summer Garden is particularly attractive in summer. From November to April its famous statues, masterpieces of European sculpture, are clothed in wooden cases to protect them from frost.

> "The Summer Garden is the Jardins du Luxembourg of the St Petersburgers; they are designed to form a square, with the Fontanka on one side and a ditch on the other. Everything, both inside and outside, is precisely measured."
>
> Alexandre Dumas

Cupid and Psyche, and the *Tauride Venus*, excavated at Rome; while real-life history is represented by the busts of Agrippina, Christina of Sweden and Jean Sobiesky. The *Venus*, transported with the utmost care from Italy, was Peter the Great's favorite piece. He placed it in the gallery at the entrance to the garden, but moved it later to the grotto, where he had it guarded by a sentinel for fear that it would be damaged. Today the *Venus* is in the Hermitage Museum ▲ *168*.

PLEASURE GARDENS. Pavilions, a grotto, an aviary, a menagerie and an orangery were installed in the Summer Garden, as Peter directed. Thirty-six granite monoliths, with alternating urns and vases as amortizements, frame the elements of the wrought-iron railing with its gilded points. In 1777 serious flooding destroyed the machinery, the channels and all the fountains, which were never repaired. Finally, Carlo Rossi built a COFFEE HOUSE (1826) and Louis Charlemagne a TEA HOUSE (1827) in the park. In 1855 a monument by Piotr Klodt was raised to Ivan Krylov, the "Russian Aesop".

"As I was smiling at this extraordinary collection, I saw the Czarina, preceded by Count Gregorius Orloff, and followed by two ladies, approaching . . .
I stood by the hedge to let her pass, but as soon as she came up to me she asked, smilingly, if I had been interested in the statues. I replied . . . that I presumed they had been placed there to impose on fools, or excite the laughter of those acquainted with history."

Jacques Casanova

SUMMER PALACE

PETER I'S PROPERTY. In 1711 Peter the Great built his Summer Palace ● *83* (LETNY DVORETS; Летний дворец) at the juncture of the Fontanka and the Neva beside his Summer Garden. The construction was based on the "model house" commissioned from the architect Domenico Trezzini ● *83*. In 1713 the German Andreas Schlüter doubled the size of the Summer Palace and completed the building's decoration, making bay windows in the pale yellow brick-and-staff walls. Between the windows he placed terracotta bas-reliefs; these were inspired by various mythological themes which could be seen to reflect Russia's military victories.

THE ROOMS. The interior of the Summer Palace is arranged in the Dutch style, with tall faience stoves and furniture which is simple in style. The walls of the vestibule are lined with beautifully carved panels, and also feature a relief depicting Minerva, who was the goddess of wisdom and of war.

SUMMER PALACE
To reach Peter the Great's Palace on the northeast side of the Summer Garden, turn off the Main Avenue in the direction of the Fontanka.

A WALK IN THE SUMMER GARDEN
In the 19th century the trees in the gardens were allowed to grow unpruned, in the English manner, and its shady avenues became famous. Pushkin, who lived nearby, often came here to read in the mornings, wearing his dressing gown.

187

BRIDGES ACROSS THE FONTANKA
The Prachechny Bridge (Laundry Bridge) was so named because of the laundries on the left bank of the Neva. Built at the junction of the Fontanka and the Neva (1766–9), it was one of the elements in the project to consolidate the banks of the Neva and was the city's first three-arched stone bridge. Between the Prachechny Bridge and the Panteleimon Bridge (right) runs the "green wall" of the Summer Garden.

MUSEUM OF DECORATIVE AND APPLIED ARTS
A huge dome spans the main exhibition room, covering a surface of nearly 4,000 square feet. The buildings belong to an art school, which contains sections on styling, decorative arts, haute couture and the restoration of works of art.

FONTANKA EMBANKMENT

LAW SCHOOL. The houses which ran along the Fontanka Embankment (NAB. REKI FONTANKI; наб. реки Фонтанки) in the 18th century were mostly rebuilt in 1835 by Melnikov, who adapted them for a new purpose. The Law School (no. 6) has two floors above a tall stylobate. A colonnade occupies the center and domes stand at the corners; the interior was completed by Vasily Stasov.

THE CHURCH OF ST PANTELEIMON (TSERKOV SV. PANTELEIMONA; церковь св. Пантелеймона). This church is the last remaining vestige of the old merchant shipyards, which occupied this quarter after 1739, and to which the salt warehouses were added at the end of the 18th century. It was dedicated to Saint Panteleimon, to commemorate the Russian fleet's victory over the Swedes in 1714 in Hangö Bay on St Panteleimon's Day. The church, which has a dome on an octagonal drum, is completed by a Baroque bell tower.

MUSEUM OF DECORATIVE AND APPLIED ARTS (MUZEY DEKORATIVNO- PRIKLADNOVO ISKUSSTVA; музей декоративно-прикладого Искусства). The glass cupola visible from the Fontanka Embankment is that of an art school (no. 12, Solyanoi Street) founded by Baron Stieglietz and built (1879–81) at his expense by the architects Krakau and Hedich. Within the complex is the museum, built (1885–96) by the architect Mesmacher for the students.

From the Admiralty to the Haymarket

1. ADMIRALTY
2. ADMIRALTY EMBANKMENT
3. DECEMBRISTS SQUARE
4. MONUMENT TO PETER I
5. RIDING SCHOOL
6. SENATE AND SYNOD
7. ALEXANDER GARDEN
8. ST ISAAC'S CATHEDRAL

🕐 **One day**
◆ **A-D**

In the early years of St Petersburg the smartest residential quarters extended over what is now the Petrograd Side ▲ *148* and Vasilyevsky Island ▲ *156*. By contrast, those of the Admiralty were purely utilitarian, occupied by craftsmen and soldiers in their barracks. With the closure of the Admiralty's naval dockyards an altogether grander kind of house began appearing on the far side of the Neva.

THE ADMIRALTY

THE NAVAL DOCKYARDS. The Admiralty (ADMIRALTEISTVO; Адмиралтейство) is a focal point of the city: three major thoroughfares converge on it, and its spire is one of the great landmarks of St Petersburg. The first Admiralty building marked the edge of the dockyards and gave onto the Neva. It was protected by a line of fortifications, with moats and bastions. After it was rebuilt in brick in 1738 the Admiralty was made up of two major constructions separated by an

CENTRAL TOWER
As the nerve center of the Russian Navy the 1,200-foot-long Admiralty building is sited around a gate tower. On this tower is an allegorical account of the history of the Russian Navy, sculpted by Terebenev. There are also an Ionic colonnade and various statues.

inner canal, which facilitated the transportation of goods. The government occupied the first building, while the second contained the carpentry shops, the forges, the cordwainers' shops, the general workshops and the reserve supplies needed for each body of craftsmen.

HEADQUARTERS OF THE GENERAL STAFF. In 1718 the Admiralty became the Headquarters of Peter I's General Staff. For a while after this the porches of the pavilions at its ends were fronted by a canal on its way to the Neva, which was not filled in until the mid-19th century. In the old days red flags would be hoisted on the roofs of these pavilions to warn the people of impending floods. Later a complex of buildings was erected on the site of the old dockyards between the Neva and the two wings, effectively concealing the Admiralty from passers-by on the embankment. It is now a military zone, closed to the public with the exception of the central tower.

▲ NAVAL CONSTRUCTIONS

Confronted by the naval power of Sweden Peter the Great, the "Father of the Russian Navy", decided to build a fleet worthy of the name. Originally the port of St Petersburg was set on Birch Island, where the city center evolved later in the 18th century. In 1733 it was transferred to the point of Vasilyevsky Island, and a stock exchange, a customs house, a merchant's court and other port installations were built. The Admiralty served both as the Navy Ministry and as a naval dockyard until 1844. At the close of the 19th century its precinct was densely built up and became known as the Admiralty Embankment.

KRONSTADT
From the 18th century onward Kronstadt was Russia's principal naval base; but after the appearance of steamships in the 1850's merchant cargoes began to be unloaded there, for transportation to St Petersburg on lighters. According to a popular saying of the period, "The voyage from London to Kronstadt is much shorter than the voyage from Kronstadt to the point of Vasilyevsky Island." In 1885 the port was moved to Gutuyevsky Island.

THE "GRANDFATHER OF THE RUSSIAN FLEET"
This was the name given to Peter the Great's first ship ▲ *149*, in which he learned to navigate.

THE ADMIRALTY

Toward 1738 the Admiralty was rebuilt. Its initial floor plan remained the same, but stone now replaced the original wood and clay materials. The Tower was raised to a height of over 200 feet. In 1823, after reconstruction works undertaken by the architect Andrei Zakharov, the building assumed its present appearance. Even before the completion of the works in 1829 the Navy Ministry was transferred here from Moscow, and a bureau was set up for the use of Czar Alexander I.

THE GALLEYS

In Russia the word "galley" was applied to any warship with oars. The crews of these vessels were made up of soldiers and sailors in the pay of the Army. The construction and repair of the galleys was carried out at the dockyards of Galley Island, west of the Admiralty.

THE FIRST DOCKYARDS

The construction of the first factory in St Petersburg, the Admiralty's naval dockyard, began on November 5, 1704. Peter I noted in his diary: "This day we laid the foundations of the Admiralty amid great joy and celebration. The building is to be 200 sagens in length and 100 sagens broad [1 sagen = 6½ feet]."

THE EMBLEM OF THE CITY

A spire was added to the Admiralty Tower in 1719, with a golden apple and a weathercock in the form of a caravel.

PETER THE GREAT

Peter I surveys the city he founded from horseback, in the pose imagined for him by the French sculptor Etienne Falconet, who won a competition arranged by Catherine II in 1765. The sculpture was not completed until 1778; it represents the Czar ascending a rock and trampling a serpent (symbolizing the Swedes) underfoot. This statue was the inspiration for one of Pushkin's most celebrated poems, "The Bronze Horseman" ● 118. In 2003, another monument dedicated to Peter I was restored to its original position, on the Admiralty's quay. It is a copy of the statue of the "Tsar Carpenter", inaugurated in 1900, then lost during the Revolution. It recalls the stay of the sovereign in Holland.

✪ A VISTA OF BRIDGES

On summer evenings, when the bridges ● 90 spanning the Great Neva are bathed in the mysterious light created by diffused sun beams ● 28 (known in Russia as "white nights"), enthusiasts for the nightly opening of the bridges gather around the statue of the Bronze Horseman. As orchestras assemble on the English Embankment and Admiralty Embankment, bankside cafés and restaurants begin to fill with customers. It is worth being there when the bridges are opened: Palace Bridge opens at 1.35am and Lieutenant-Schmidt Bridge at 1.40am.

DECEMBRISTS SQUARE

DECEMBRISTS SQUARE (PL. DEKABRISTOV; пл. Декабристов) owes its name to the protagonists of one of the more painful episodes in the history of St Petersburg and Russia ● 42.

EQUESTRIAN STATUE OF PETER I. Contrary to the fashion of the day, the Czar is represented neither as a Roman emperor nor as a prince of his own time. Instead he wears a long robe, a mantle, soft leather boots and a simple sword at his side – the garb of an ordinary Russian prince. Only the crown of laurels on his head, sculpted by a pupil of Falconet's, Anne-Marie Collot, reminds us of his rank. On either side of the plinth are four words, which translate as: "To Peter I, Catherine II".

THE RIDING SCHOOL (THE MANÈGE). Designed by Quarenghi (1804–7), with sculpted décor by Paolo Triscorni, the Riding School is a low quadrangular building not unlike a Greek temple, with a double colonnade and pediment.

VICTORY COLUMNS. Following the disappearance of the Admiralty dockyards, the canal connecting the site with the New Holland district was covered by a brick arch that became the Horseguards Boulevard. On a granite pedestal here are winged Victory figures in bronze, modeled by Christian Rauch (1845–6) and presented to the Czar by the King of Prussia in commemoration of their joint victory over Napoleon.

SENATE AND SYNOD. By creating new institutions for Russia Peter the Great managed to disarm those of his opponents who were obstructing his reforms. He suppressed the Patriarchate which had hitherto wielded absolute power over the Church, and replaced it by a Synod, with authority to settle all religious questions. Likewise in 1711 he outmaneuvered the Duma of the Boyars by setting up a nine-member Senate to manage affairs of state in his absence. The architects Rossi and Stasov designed twin buildings for these institutions

MONUMENT TO PRZEVALSKY
This statue in the Alexander Garden, sculpted by Schroeder in 1882, celebrates the explorer Przevalsky (1839–88), who went out to discover Asia on behalf of the Imperial Geographical Society. In his account of his travels Przevalsky described the wild camel whose image now graces his statue's plinth, along with the rare Siberian horse species which was named after him ▲ 151.

(1829–34), which were connected by an arch spanning Galernaya Street. The columns are set forward, with a heavy entablature decorated with statues of angels. A frieze in bas-relief emphasizes the attic, in the center of which is a sculpted group featuring allegories of Probity and Justice. In the direction of the Neva, the Senate building is distinguished by a colonnade which curves round to meet the embankment. Today the Senate and Synod buildings contain historical archives; they also incorporate the Palace of Count Laval, whose daughter followed her husband, the Decembrist Trubetskoy, into exile in Siberia.

ALEXANDER GARDEN. The Alexander Garden (ALEKSANDROVSKY SAD; Александровский сад) was planted for the two-hundredth anniversary of the birth of Peter the Great, and covers the fortifications and moats which formerly defended the Admiralty. The statues here are mostly copies of antique originals made in the 18th century, along with busts of famous Russians like Gogol, Lermontov, Glinka and Zhukovsky.

ST ISAAC'S CATHEDRAL

St Isaac's Cathedral had difficult beginnings. Between the first church, built of wood on the present site of the Senate, and the project of Rinaldi, inherited by Renna and rejected by Montferrand, nearly a dozen architects seem to have tried to build this cathedral on its sodden, unstable site.

THE FIRST ST ISAAC'S CHURCH
Wishing to honor the saint on whose feast day he was born, Peter I dedicated what was later to become St Petersburg's largest place of worship to an obscure Dalmatian monk.

Montferrand left an album of watercolors showing the different stages of the cathedral's construction, from the transportation of the columns to their erection.

A TECHNICAL EXPLOIT. The architect Auguste Ricard de Montferrand, who designed the cathedral as we know it (1818–58), gave it a Byzantine floor plan, somewhat lengthened. He solved the problem of unstable foundations by setting the 300,000-ton building on 11,000 pilings, reconciled the dictates of the disposition of the square and the orientation of the Christian sanctuaries, and added deep porches with double rows of columns to the north and south façades. These monolithic columns, made of Vyborg granite brought by sea from Finland, are over 50 feet high and weigh 114 tons each. Before constructing the main dome Montferrand made a study of similar European buildings; his greatest innovation was his use of cast iron for the rafters.

REALISTIC DÉCOR. To give his monstrous brainchild at least a veneer of lightness, the architect used materials of contrasting colors: for example, the gray granite of the walls offsets the pink columns, while the bronze of the pediments, statues, monumental doors and capitals echoes the gold of the domes. The décor of the interior ● 88 is extremely lavish; the two columns supporting the central door of the iconostasis ● 56 are paneled with lapis lazuli, while all the inside columns are covered in malachite.

ST ISAAC'S CATHEDRAL
The upper parts of the building are classical in style, with a huge dome, four smaller bell towers, and abundant statuary on the roof.

ST ISAAC'S SQUARE ★

Conceived as a whole and remodeled by Montferrand as part of the work on the cathedral, St Isaac's Square (ISAAKIEVSKAYA PL.; Исаакиевская пл.) was no more than a huge building site at the time when Rossi was busy with the Senate and the Synod.

MONUMENT TO NICHOLAS I. This equestrian statue (1859), the work of the sculptor Piotr Klodt, represents the Czar in the uniform of the Horse Guards. The pedestal is decorated with four bronze bas-reliefs of the principal episodes of his reign.

The pedestal is decorated with four bronze bas-reliefs of the principal episodes of his reign. Between the motifs are allegorical statues of Justice, Strength, Faith and Wisdom, which have the features of the Empress and the daughters of the Czar, who together commissioned the monument.

MARIINSKY PALACE (MARIINSKY DVORETS; Мариинский дворец). This palace, built (1839–44) by Shtakenshneider, is the final element of the square. Intended for the Grand Duchess Maria, daughter of Nicholas I, it replaced an older construction of Vallin de la Mothe. It was purchased by the State in 1884 and was used thereafter by the Council of the Czar's Ministers. After the Revolution it became the seat of the Provisional Government of the Russian Republic; today it is the headquarters of the St Petersburg Legislative Assembly.

BOLSHAYA MORSKAYA

This main thoroughfare (once Herzen Street) begins at the Arch of the General Staff ▲ *180* and intersects Nevsky Prospekt ▲ *214* and St Isaac's Square.

ASTORIA HOTEL. The Astoria (neoclassical and Art Nouveau) was designed by the architect Lidwal in 1911. The first and second floors are faced with granite decorated with medallions, garlands and mascarons, while the façades are punctuated with pilasters. In 1917 the Astoria was a focus of resistance to the Revolution, which was invested on November 7 by Red Guards

and sailors. In the first years of the Soviet regime it was the headquarters of the Petrosoviet. In 1990 it was merged with the neighboring Angleterre Hotel (where poet Sergei Esenin committed suicide in 1925) and was entirely renovated.

THE BLUE BRIDGE
Despite its diminutive span the Blue Bridge (SINY MOST; Синий мост) across the Moika is the broadest in St Petersburg (nearly 300 feet). It was once made of wood and painted blue – hence the name – while its neighbors were red and green.

LOBONOV-ROSTOVSKY MANSION
This majestic private mansion on the corner of Decembrists Square and the Voznesensky Prospekt occupies a three-cornered site. It was built by the architect of St Isaac's Cathedral, Auguste Ricard de Montferrand (1817–20).

DEMIDOV MANSION. This building (no. 43) bears the name of an industrialist whose family made a fortune from mines in the Urals. Constructed between 1836 and 1840, the Demidov Mansion was inspired by Italian Renaissance architecture and is laid out around an inner courtyard. Formerly it had a hall that was entirely covered in malachite taken from its owner's mines, and this served as the model for the one in the Winter Palace ▲ *172*.

NABOKOV'S HOUSE. Vladimir Nabokov (below, with his mother) was born in St Petersburg in 1899 and grew up in no. 47. The scion of a liberal aristocratic family, Nabokov was a privileged child and idolized by his mother; he recalls his happy youth in his memoir *Other Shores*. Following the October Revolution the Nabokovs left Russia for Europe; the writer then emigrated to the United States in 1940, adopting U.S. citizenship. The house contains the Nabokov Museum.

POLOVTSEV MANSION. This lavish townhouse (no. 52), also called the Architects' House, was built (1835–6) by Pel. The Senator A. Polovtsev, who acquired it in 1860, was also the president of the Russian Historical Society. The interior is notable for its neo-Gothic library, a gilded hall and a salon decorated with malachite and bronze. The restaurant at Polovtsev Mansion, which was once used exclusively by architects, is now open to all.

CENTRAL POST OFFICE

The first post office, or Postamt, founded by Peter I in 1714, was on Suvorov Square ▲ *186*. It was later transferred to larger premises on the present Millionaires' Street; and in 1782 Catherine II moved it to the present site. This was the departure point for the post coaches which criss-crossed the Russian Empire; all the milestones in the nation indicated their exact distance

DEMIDOV MANSION
The gateway here is flanked by Atlas figures and caryatids supporting a richly sculpted balcony. At the turn of the 20th century Demidov Mansion was the Italian Embassy; today it is a machine-tool training institute.

GAGARIN HOUSE
The pavilion at no. 45, next door to Demidov Mansion, was built in the 1840's. It is now the Composers' House.

from the Postamt. In 1859, when the Post Office was in need of more space, it expanded to the other side of Postamt Street and a covered gallery in the form of an archway was built to connect the two buildings. Clocks were hung here, showing the time in the major foreign capitals. Today the Postamt still fulfills its original function.

NOVAYA GOLLANDIYA (NEW HOLLAND DISTRICT)

THE FORMER TIMBER STORES. The Novaya Gollandiya district covers an area that was once a Navy storage depot constructed on an artificial island skirted by the Admiralty, Kryukov and Moika canals. Before the depot was built, timber used for shipbuilding was kept at the Admiralty ▲ *190*, in close proximity to the yards, where it was seasoned in the Dutch fashion; for this reason the wood store was known as "New Holland". The immense building with its rounded corners is characteristic of the work of the architect Vallin de la Mothe, who was commissioned to construct the market galleries. The bare brick edifice that ultimately resulted is virtually blind on its exterior, with nothing but small-paned bay windows on the corners.

THE ARCH ● *88*. A large pool stands at the center of the store area, which can be reached by boat through an archway high enough to admit fairly substantial superstructures. This arch is classical in design, framed by two columns bearing a Doric frieze. The arch itself rests on smaller columns. The austerity of the architectural design is relieved to some extent by the colors of the brick walls and the metopes, which contrast with the gray granite columns and triglyphs. The district of Novaya Gollandiya has been associated with the Russian Navy for as long as it has been in existence; today it remains a military zone, and is not open to the public. In the 19th century it was used as a prison. In more recent times it has been suggested that the Novaya Gollandiya district should be converted into a cultural center, or a tourist area which would incorporate hotels and boutiques. A third project has been proposed that would move the Naval Museum into the precinct, as this institution is at the moment somewhat cramped in its present building at the Stock Exchange ▲ *157*.

"My mother's boudoir had an overhanging window, which was convenient for looking outside, since it had a view across Morskaya Street toward Mariya Square . . . from this window, a few years later, at the start of the Revolution, I observed more than one skirmish, and for the first time in my life I saw a dead man."
Vladimir Nabokov

APARTMENT OF ALEXANDER BLOK The apartment in which the writer spent a few months (no. 57, Decembrists Square) is now a museum displaying mementos of his life, amid the sober surroundings he favored.

From the 18th century onward the Mariinsky was the imperial ballet theater. Among the five theaters maintained by the court (two in Moscow and three in St Petersburg) it was especially favored from the time of Nicholas I. Nothing was too lavish for the ballets of the Imperial Theater, which was endowed with sumptuous décors created by court artists such as Roller and (later) Golovin and Benois. Known as the Kirov under the Soviet regime, the Mariinsky reverted to its original name in 1992.

MARIUS PETIPA (1818–1910)
A world-renowned choreographic genius, Petipa was ballet master at the Mariinsky from 1869 to 1903. He put on more than sixty performances and was one of the architects of academic ballet.

THE KIROV BALLET
From 1935 the Mariinsky Ballet was known as the Kirov Ballet, in honor of Sergei Kirov ● *49*. The repertoire of the Soviet period included Tchaikovsky's *Queen of Spades*, among other productions.

PAVLOVA (1881–1931)
No choreographer before Petipa had celebrated the ballerina with so much brio. His ballets brought a whole constellation of dancers to the fore, including Mathilda Kshesinskaya, O. Presbrazhenskaya and Anna Pavlova.

THE CORPS DE BALLET
The genius of Petipa reached its climax in his collaboration with the composers Tchaikovsky and Glazunov. With *The Sleeping Beauty* (1890), *Swan Lake* (1895) and *Raymonda* (1898) Petipa created a style in which the *corps de ballet* became an essential component of the choreographic language.

Yusupov Palace

Built by Vallin de la Mothe in the 1760's, the Yusupov Palace (YUSUPOVSKY DVORETS; Юсуповский дворец) was converted at the end of the 19th century for Princess Zinaida Yusupov. Seriously damaged during World War Two, it has since been heavily restored and its magnificent art collection moved to the Hermitage. The interior decoration of the palace testifies to its former brilliance; the formal salon, the MOORISH SALON, and the Buffet Room (where the acoustics are extraordinary) in particular. So as not to overload the slender vaulting of the BALLROOM, which was not strong enough to support crystal or gilded bronze, the chandeliers were fashioned of gilt papier-mâché so that they resembled metal. An Italianate THEATER (above) is situated in the North Wing of the building.

THE POISONING OF RASPUTIN
In the basement of the Yusupov Palace there is a waxwork which recreates the décor and atmosphere of Rasputin's gruesome murder.

THE DEATH OF RASPUTIN. On the first floor of the Moika side of the building a concealed entrance leads to a salon in which exclusive parties were given; it was in this salon that Rasputin ● 37, the hypnotic monk who oscillated between spirituality and debauchery, met his horrible end. In the uneasy atmosphere of the period, Rasputin's mesmeric gift had given him enormous power over the Empress and her entourage. To rid the court of this inconvenient character Prince Felix Yusupov plotted his murder, in which the Grand Duke Dmitry also had a hand. Felix Yusupov died in Paris in 1967.

Theater Square ✪

✪ **NEW LIFE FOR THEATER SQUARE**
The area around Theater Square is the focal point of the city's artistic life. Once the place where wealthy princes bought residences for their favorite ballerinas, the area later became an official showcase for Soviet culture. Today it has a new lease of life, thanks to the Mariinsky Theater. This musical theater, which is renowed for its festival "Stars of the Night", has broadened its repertoire by staging innovative productions of such classic works as Tchaikovsky's *The Nutcracker* and Mussorgsky's *Boris Godunov*, with a cast featuring eminent performers from other countries.

Theater Square (TEATRALNAYA PL.; Театральная пл.) contains, in close proximity, two of the main institutions of the musical life of St Petersburg.

THE MARIINSKY THEATER. Between 1847 and 1848, A. Kavos, St Petersburg's chief theatrical architect, built a theater that also doubled as a circus. Circus acts with performing horses, acrobatic shows and trapeze acts took place in its central arena. Badly damaged by fire in 1859, the building was replaced the following year by a conventional theater. Named the Mariinsky Theater in honor of the Empress Maria Alexandrovna, consort of the Emperor Alexander II, the theater began its first season with *A Life for the Czar*, a work by Glinka that signaled the birth of classical Russian opera. It was nationalized in 1917, and from 1935 to 1993 was known as the Kirov Ballet. It has now reverted to its original name. During the Soviet era the theater continued to mount operas and ballets by native Russian composers such as Prokofiev and Shostakovich. The theater's current director is Valery Gergiev, whose primary objective is to revive the great masterpieces of Russian opera. The ballet company, which still enjoys international renown, continues to tour the major capitals of the world.

THE CONSERVATOIRE. The site on which the Conservatoire now stands was originally occupied by the Great Theater. Built in the late 1770's, during the reign of Catherine the Great, it was at the time the only permanent theater in St Petersburg. Between 1891 and 1896 it was completely rebuilt: the new building, designed by the architect V. Nicol, was to house the Conservatoire that the pianist Anton Rubinstein had founded in 1862. It was the first advanced music school in Russia, teaching seven disciplines; these were musical theory and composition; choir and orchestra conducting; singing; orchestral instruments; piano and organ; ballet and opera direction; and traditional instruments. The Conservatoire has two auditoriums: in the larger of the two, pupils give public performances; the smaller one, which has magnificent acoustics, a painted ceiling and a gallery of portraits of musicians, is used for Russian and international festivals and competitions.

Statue of Nikolai Rimsky-Korsakov ▲ *239* in front of the Conservatoire.

SYNAGOGUE
The Jewish community of St Petersburg was heavily repressed prior to the reforms of Alexander II ● *36*. In 1893 the construction of a synagogue and cultural center confirmed these reforms; the synagogue, at no. 2 Lermontov Street, is built in the Moorish style.

In an area once overwhelmingly inhabited by sailors, this cathedral was understandably dedicated to their patron, Saint Nicholas. With its blue, white and gold exterior, St Nicholas' Cathedral is similar in many ways to Smolny, which was built by Rastrelli; indeed Chevakinsky, the architect of St Nicholas, was a pupil of the Italian. A remarkable illustration of religious Baroque, this church remained open throughout the Soviet era.

BESIDE THE KRYUKOV CANAL
The cathedral is built to the classic Greek cross plan, with a central cupola and four turrets at each corner, topped by onion domes ● 57. On the exterior the composition is punctuated by columns backed against the walls. The lower church (there is no crypt, because of likely flooding) supports a richly embellished upper one. Services are held on the upper level, where the décor is especially lavish because of the largesse of Catherine II, who presented ten gold-covered icons to commemorate ten naval victories. The equally gold-laden iconostasis ● 57, of carved wood, was executed between 1755 and 1760. The bell tower is separate from the church proper ● 85, standing at the entrance to the cathedral precinct, where it is reflected in the Kryukov Canal ▲ 210.

1. Main entrance
2. Secondary entrance
3. Lower church
4. Stairs leading to upper church
5. Iconostasis
6. Portal
7. Altars
8. Central cupola
9. Onion-domed corner turret

SENNAYA PLOSHCHAD
In Dostoevsky's time the crowded and filthy Haymarket was known for its low dives, taverns, cabarets, brothels and prostitutes' hotels. The district exercised a deep fascination on Raskolnikov, the hero of *Crime and Punishment*: at the close of the novel, visiting the Haymarket for the last time, "... he let himself fall to the ground ... on his knees in the center of the square, he bent and kissed the muddy stones with ecstasy and delight ... then he straightened, and prostrated himself a second time."

HAYMARKET SQUARE

From St Nicholas' Cathedral, Sadovaya Street (SADOVAYA UL.; Садовая ул), typical of 19th-century St Petersburg, leads through to Haymarket Square (SENNAYA PL.; Сенная пл.).
At the end of the 18th century there was a huge market here where hay, oats and straw were sold, hence the name.
The Haymarket area was once one of the worst slums of St Petersburg, but today the old buildings have been replaced by buildings constructed after World War Two. The only original edifice still standing is the Police Station, with its four-columned classical portico.
THE CHURCH OF THE ASSUMPTION IN HAYMARKET SQUARE, now demolished, was built in the mid-18th century to a project by A. Kvasov, in which Rastrelli had a hand. It was the architectural focus of the square. Closed in 1938, the church was knocked down in 1961 to make way for the Sennaya metro station.

DOSTOEVSKY DISTRICT ★

HERMETIC SPACE. Dostoevsky never had a house of his own in St Petersburg; instead he was constantly on the move,

> "Few places exercise on the human spirit so somber,
> violent, and strange an influence ..."
>
> Fyodor Dostoevsky

changing his domicile a score of times in the eight years he lived in the city center. As a rule he chose buildings that faced churches. Whether large and spacious or narrow and closed off, a room for Dostoevsky had a profound underlying meaning. Time and again the image of the oppressive, constricting bedroom appears in his books. This hermetic space, bounded by a corner, a wall, a palisade or an alleyway, is a frequent characteristic of his work; it has the value of a symbol, expressing the inner life of the hero and his state of mind.

CUT OFF FROM THE WORLD. Dreamers, "men of the underworld" with ravaged consciences, the heroes of Dostoevsky always live in "corners"; they flee the reality that surrounds them. The writer himself nearly always lived on street-corner houses, which made him feel even more isolated from the rest of the world than he actually was. He had a clear preference for Vladimir Square ▲ 238 and the Haymarket. It was here that he set his characters, who walked the same streets as he did and saw the same buildings and scenes from their windows as he saw. The lives of both Dostoevsky and his heroes are seamlessly blended with the life of St Petersburg itself. Indeed, this may be one reason why Dostoevsky moved with such regularity: once he had completed a novel, he became impatient to leave the places which his art and his imagination had transformed into fiction.

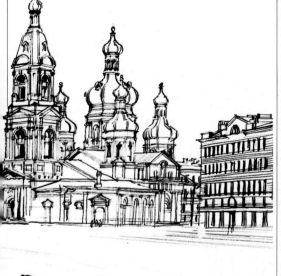

A CITY REINVENTED
Dostoevsky's St Petersburg has two dimensions, one real, the other imaginary. On the one hand, there is the city which really existed, with real people and locations; and on the other, there is the imagined metropolis, peopled by invented characters, which is such a strong characteristic of his work. Dostoevsky loved his city, where he had grown up and made his literary career. St Petersburg is present in about twenty of his thirty novels, sometimes as a background but more often as a character in its own right.

GRIBOEDOV CANAL

Every episode in the novel *Crime and Punishment* is centered around the Griboedov Canal ▲ *217* (КАН. ГRIBOEDOVA; кан. Грибоедова), formerly called the Catherine Canal. Soniechka lives at no. 63 and patrols the canal bank looking for clients. On the far side of the canal stands the building occupied by the moneylender Alena Ivanovna, the old woman whom Raskolnikov robs and kills with an axe. No. 65 was the old Police Station to which Raskolnikov is summoned, and which Dostoevsky himself visited.

PRZEVALSKY STREET

RASKOLNIKOV'S HOUSE. The corner house here, no. 5, is thought to be the model for Raskolnikov's. In the mid-19th century this three-story building belonged to a man called Joachim. If you turn right after entering the porch you will see in the corner the door which gives onto the staircase described in the novel. Dostoevsky gives an exact account of Raskolnikov's comings and goings, and his hero's fate is decided by a series of coincidences. Thus Raskolnikov, who has carefully thought out everything he needs to do before he commits his crime, finally forgets to bring an axe with which he intends to do the deed.

ASCENSION BRIDGE
❝Raskolnikov went straight to X Bridge, stopped in the middle of it, leaned his elbows on the parapet, and looked down . . . with his head craned over the water, he began mechanically to contemplate the last pink rays of the setting sun … Eventually red circles emerged before his eyes, and the houses, passers-by, quays, coaches and everything else began spinning and dancing around him.❞

Crime and Punishment

TREASURY STREET

Dostoevsky occupied three different houses in Treasury Street (KAZNACHEYSKAYA UL.; Казначеская ул.), close by the Haymarket, known as Petit Bourgeois Street until the turn of the century. The writer, who was already famous, lodged in one of the most wretched slums in St Petersburg; not

> "He hadn't the least desire to go into the street like that. And as for going home, that would be even worse. 'A beautiful opportunity, lost forever!' he muttered, standing with dangling arms under the porch just in front of the concierge's tiny lodge, which was also open. Suddenly he gave a start. Within the lodge two steps away, something was shining on the bench, just to the right."
>
> *Crime and Punishment*

because he liked the romantic, meandering Catherine Canal, or because he wanted to study the sordid existence of the tenants of the surrounding buildings, but because he simply did not have the means to live elsewhere. Considering that "the mind is narrowed by small lodgings", he preferred to have two spacious rooms, a luxury which was very expensive in the grander districts of the city.

OLONKIN HOUSE. This house (no. 7), on the corner of Treasury and Przevalsky streets (the latter used to be called Carpenters' Lane), was Dostoevsky's home from August 1864 to January 1867. It was here that he wrote *Crime and Punishment* and received his second wife, Anna Grigorievna Snitkina, for the first time. The two also worked together for the first time at this house, when Anna (whom he had engaged to help him finish a novel, *The Gambler*, in double-quick time) took down his dictated text in twenty-six days. The building contained a wine-shop and tavern kept by a tradesman, Efimov; and although the district was noisy at all hours Dostoevsky mostly worked at night.

THE "TIMES". Dostoevsky's elder brother also lived on Petit Bourgeois Street; together they edited and published the *Times* and *Epoch* reviews.

ASCENSION PROSPEKT

Ascension Prospekt (VOZNESENSKY PR.; Вознесенский пр.) features in nearly every one of Dostoevsky's novels set in St Petersburg. He lived there himself between 1847 and 1849, and again in 1867. In the 1860's one of his friends, Apollo Grigoriev, also lived in the street, which appears often on the itineraries of Raskolnikov, of Arkady Dolgoruky in *Raw Youth*, and of the characters in *Insulted and Injured* and *The Eternal Husband*.

THE CHIL HOUSE. Dostoevsky lived here, at nos. 8–23, from spring 1847 to April 23, 1849 while he was writing *White Nights*, *The Landlady* and *Netoshka Nezvanova*. And it was here, also, that he was arrested, in the night of April 22–3, 1849.

> "With his heart failing him, trembling with nerves, he approached an enormous house, one side of which backed on to the canal, with the other overlooking X Street. This building was divided into a crowd of small apartments, whose tenants were artisans of every kind: tailors, locksmiths, cooks, Germans, prostitutes, petty functionaries, etcetera. People went in and out through the two carriage entrances."
>
> *Crime and Punishment*

THE KOLOMNA DISTRICT ✪
Between Kryukov Canal and the Great Neva to the west lies the Kolomna district. This quiet quarter of the city seems still to be slumbering in the 19th century, and this is how Pushkin described it in his poem "The Little House in Kolomna". Consisting of four islands and having nine embankments and twenty bridges, the appealing Kolomna district can be explored by boat, revealing yet another aspect of St Petersburg, "the Venice of the North".

TRINITY CHURCH
This five-domed building, constructed by Stasov between 1828 and 1830, supplanted an 18th-century wooden church.

"We, the Petrashevtsy, heard out our sentence of death standing on the scaffold without a trace of remorse. I cannot speak for all of us, but I do not think I am mistaken when I affirm that at that instant, in that minute, the majority among us were very close to dishonoring themselves by forsaking their convictions."
Journal of an Author

KRYUKOV CANAL

Beside the Kryukov Canal stands the clock tower of St Nicholas' Cathedral ▲ *204*, a fine three-story building of harmonious proportions. This is one of the most romantic corners of St Petersburg. Dostoevsky set what is perhaps his most poetic novel, *White Nights*, around the Kryukov and Catherine canals.

2ND ISMAILOV BATTALION STREET

From this street, where Dostoevsky lived in 1872 and 1873, the writer could see the Trinity Church, which was where he married Anna Grigorievna Snitkina in 1867. The central cupola was destroyed by fire in 2006.

PIONEERS' SQUARE

It was on Pioneers' Square (PIONERSKAYA PL.; Пионерская пл.), formerly known as Semenovsky Square, that the members of the Semenovsky circle were led to believe they

had been condemned to death (December 22, 1848). Those who had been present at the meetings of this literary and political group, at which Vissarion Bielinsky's letter was read out ▲ *237*, appeared before a military tribunal, who condemned them to death after eight months' imprisonment in the Peter and Paul Fortress ▲ *146*. At the last moment the sentence was commuted to deportation to a labor camp. Afterward Dostoevsky recorded in *The Idiot* Prince Myshkin's description of the minutes they spent in the full expectation of death.

Around
Nevsky Prospekt

The buildings along Nevsky Prospekt recount the history of this main thoroughfare, laid down through the forest in the decade following 1710. The road was originally laid with tree-trunks; gradually houses and palaces began to be built along its length, the most beautiful structures concentrated between Palace Square and the Fontanka (the original limit of the city). In the mid-18th century it was baptized Nevsky Prospekt, after the monastery to which it led. This avenue, over 2½ miles long, is "at once the most elegant street and the chief shopping area of St Petersburg . . . being an original blend of shops, palaces and churches; on the signs gleam the beautiful characters of the Russian alphabet." (Théophile Gautier)

✪ AT THE HEART OF THE CITY

In St Petersburg, every street leads to Nevksy Prospekt, which, according to Nikolai Gogol, was "the hub of all communication". Shops selling all sorts of goods attract a cosmopolitan crowd. At the corner of no. 56 Malaya Sadovaya Street, a pedestrianized thoroughfare lined with cafés, benches and old-fashioned street lights, is a fountain with a granite globe that is turned by the flow of water. Visitors will also admire the attractive interior courtyards that line the street.

CITY OF PETERSBURG (NO. 1)

SHADY SIDE (UNEVEN NUMBERS) Here the buildings were provided with galleries, loggias and colonnades to make the most of the shade.

CITY OF PETERSBURG (NO. 1)
This late 18th-century building was altered between 1910 and 1912 by Ziedler, on behalf of the Commercial Bank of Petersburg.

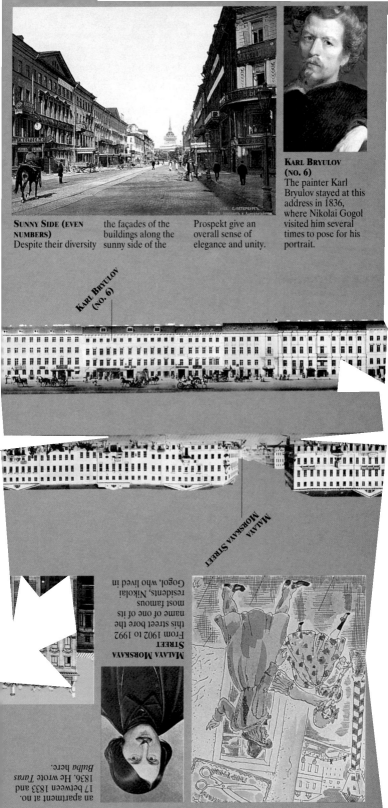

SUNNY SIDE (EVEN NUMBERS)
Despite their diversity the façades of the buildings along the sunny side of the Prospekt give an overall sense of elegance and unity.

KARL BRYULOV (NO. 6)
The painter Karl Bryulov stayed at this address in 1836, where Nikolai Gogol visited him several times to pose for his portrait.

KARL BRYULOV (NO. 6)

MALAYA MORSKAYA STREET

MALAYA MORSKAYA STREET
From 1902 to 1992 this street bore the name of one of its most famous residents, Nikolai Gogol, who lived in an apartment at no. 17 between 1833 and 1836. He wrote *Taras Bulba* here.

DURING THE SIEGE
No. 14 has a poignant reminder of the siege of Leningrad: a plaque reads, "Comrades! In the event of artillery fire, this side of the street is the most dangerous."

BOLSHAYA MORSKAYA STREET
Before reverting to its original name Bolshaya Morskaya Street was rebaptized Herzen Street, after the writer (right) who lived at no. 14. Bolshaya Morskaya Street cuts directly across Nevsky Prospekt. The even street numbers end at the Arch of the General Staff. At nos. 3–5 the former Azovsko-Donskoy bank (1908–9) provides another example of the luxurious tastes of the old financiers. This building has now been converted into a telephone exchange.

"WOLFF AND BÉRANGER" (NO. 18)
Pushkin met his second, Danzas, at this pastry-shop on January 27, 1837, before his final duel ● *116.* The literary café here opened in 1985.

No. 14

BOLSHAYA MORSKAYA STREET

CHICHERIN PALACE (NO. 15)

POLICE BRIDGE
The rearrangement of the banks of the Moika took place earlier than that of the other canals. Nevertheless it was only in the years 1798–1810 that these were completely reconstructed in granite. The Police Bridge, which spans the Moika, owes its name to its proximity to the Chicherin Palace (no. 15) and the central police building.

DUTCH CHURCH (NO. 20)

The central part of this long building (1830–3, designed by Paul Jacot) had a massive portico behind which the church was situated; the wings contained the residences of the pastor and the members of the Dutch mission. In the 19th century the offices of the Society for the Encouragement of Painters occupied the first floor.

"WOLFF AND BÉRANGER" (NO. 18)

DUTCH CHURCH (NO. 20)

POLICE BRIDGE

STROGANOV PALACE (NO. 17)

CHICHERIN PALACE (NO. 15)

Built in the 1760's for the Chief of Police, this palace was a gift of Catherine II to her servant. Today it is the Barrikada Cinema.

STROGANOV PALACE (NO. 17)

This palace was built between 1752 and 1754 by Rastrelli for his friend Baron Sergei Stroganov. The latter's son Alexander, an art lover and patron, commissioned Andrei Voronikhin to redecorate the interior. The Palace, an annex of the Russian Museum ▲ 225, houses several exhibition rooms.

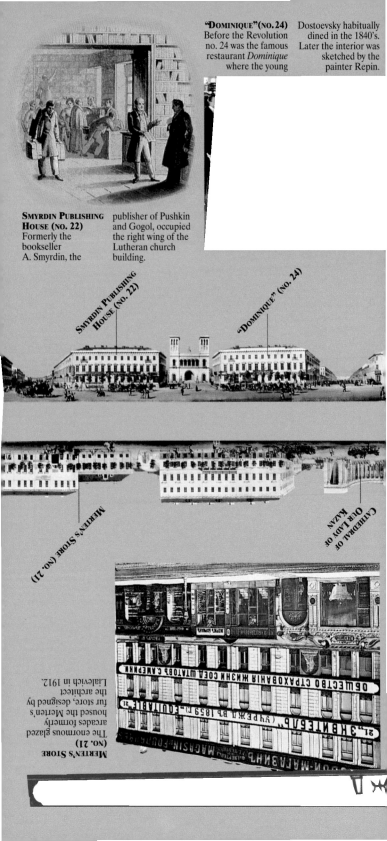

"DOMINIQUE"(NO. 24)
Before the Revolution no. 24 was the famous restaurant *Dominique* where the young Dostoevsky habitually dined in the 1840's. Later the interior was sketched by the painter Repin.

SMYRDIN PUBLISHING HOUSE (NO. 22)
Formerly the bookseller A. Smyrdin, the publisher of Pushkin and Gogol, occupied the right wing of the Lutheran church building.

SMYRDIN PUBLISHING HOUSE (NO. 22)

"DOMINIQUE" (NO. 24)

MERTEN'S STORE (NO. 21)

CATHEDRAL OF OUR LADY OF KAZAN

MERTEN'S STORE (NO. 21)
The enormous glazed arcades formerly housed the Merten's fur store, designed by the architect Lialevich in 1912.

21, "ЗНАМЕНЬ" (учрежд. въ 1859 г.) "EQUITABLE"

ОБЩЕСТВО СТРАХОВАНІЯ ЖИЗНИ "ЗНАМЕНЬ" (учрежд. въ 1859 г.) "EQUITABLE"

GRIBOEDOV CANAL

This waterway was cut between 1764 and 1790 to avoid flooding. Hilarion Kutuzov, the father of Marshal Kutuzov, originally proposed this idea to Elizabeth I.

SINGER BUILDING (NO. 28)

The Singer Sewing Machine Company decided to build a ten-story building on this site and, despite the opposition of the municipality, constructed it in 1907 with a glass globe on its dome.

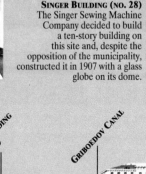

SINGER BUILDING (NO. 28)

GRIBOEDOV CANAL

CHURCH OF OUR LADY OF KAZAN

Designed by Voronikhin and built between 1801 and 1811, this church reflects both Russian and Western styles. While it respects the Orthodox canon of an altar facing east, its lateral colonnade (like that of St Peter's in Rome) is very striking. It was reinstated as a functioning church in 1999.

KAZAN SQUARE
The church of Kazan, with its semicircular colonnade of ninety-six columns, forms one of St Petersburg's most majestic squares.

The tomb of Marshal Kutuzov (1745–1813) is preserved in the cathedral.

ул. "ЭНВITEБУР" (уч

TOWER OF THE DUMA (NOS. 31–3) It was decided that the Municipal Duma (town hall) would occupy a part of Quarenghi's building. The tower, built between 1799 and 1804 by the architect Giacomo Ferrari, is the tallest construction on the Prospekt. It served as a semaphore for the optical telegraph and as a beacon for fires (the signals informed the fire brigade of the location of conflagrations).

THE "PORTIK"

DUMA TOWER (NOS. 31–3)

ARTS SQUARE

"GRAND HOTEL EUROPE" (NO. 36)

ST CATHERINE'S CHURCH (NOS. 32–4)

ST CATHERINE'S CHURCH (NOS. 32–4) The refined Baroque elegance of St Catherine's (1763–83, Vallin de la Mothe) contrasts strongly with the massive buildings around it.

GRAND HOTEL EUROPE (NO. 36)

Beyond the Grand Hotel Europe, now restored by European investors to its pre-Revolutionary glory, cross Mikhailovskaya Street, to reach the Arts Square.

ARMENIAN CHURCH

This wonderful little church was built by Yury Velten in 1780 and restored between 1835 and 1837 by the architect A. Melnikov.

САНКТ-ПЕТЕРБУРГ
ST. PETERSBURG

НЕВСКИЙ ПРОСПЕКТ
NEVSKY PROSPEKT

30 ← → 36

MEETING PLACE OF THE DECEMBRISTS (NO. 42)

The Decembrist Gavril Batenkov (1793–1863) lived at no. 42, where he entertained other conspirators such as Kondraty, Ryleyev, Trubetskoy and Bestuzhev (left).

ARMENIAN CHURCH

No. 42

GOSTINY DVOR (NO. 35)

GOSTINY DVOR (NO. 35)

After a series of fires and lootings, the tradespeople of Nevsky Prospekt decided to finance the construction of a stone galleried market by Vallin de la Mothe. Behind these façades, which have a total length of more than half a mile, is the largest store in the city. Maintenance work on the gallery in 1965 brought to light over 300 lbs of gold hidden by merchants.

THE "PORTIK"

This neoclassical portico, the work of the architect Rusca (1802–6), was restored in 1972. Today it is a sales office for theater and exhibition tickets.

219

THE "PASSAGE" (NO. 48)

This 180-yard gallery, built in 1846, was commissioned by Count Essen-Stenbock from the architect R. Zheliazevich as a site for shops, a concert hall and a *salon de thé*. The façade, which the tradesmen thought too modest, was altered in 1902 by the engineer Kozlov.

THE "PASSAGE" (NO. 48)

SADOVAYA STREET

SCHROEDER PIANO WORKS (NO. 52)

SALTYKOV-SHCHEDRIN LIBRARY (NO. 37)

A MAJOR RESERVE In addition to a large stock of French books (among them the 7,000 books of Voltaire's library) are a number of other treasures, notably rare 11th- and 12th-century manuscripts such as the *Ostromir Gospels* (1056), documents and autographs of Peter the Great and Mozart ▲ 231.

К.М. ШРЕДЕР

SCHROEDER PIANOS (NO. 52)
No. 52 belonged to Karl Schroeder, the piano manufacturer. Today it is a bookshop.

MALAYA SADOVAYA STREET
The "Street of the Gardens" (left) leads through to the Michael Garden, the Summer Garden and the Engineers' Castle.

ELISEEV STORE (NO. 56)
This foodshop was built in 1907 by G. Baranovsky for the Eliseev brothers. Don't miss its magnificent Art Nouveau interior.

MALAYA SADOVAYA STREET

ELISEEV STORE (NO. 56)

OSTROVSKY SQUARE

SALTYKOV-SHCHEDRIN LIBRARY (NO. 37)
The curving façade giving onto Nevsky Prospekt is the work of the architect Sokolov, built between 1796 and 1801; the rectilinear colonnade was added by Rossi thirty years later, when the Library (inaugurated 1814) needed to be enlarged. It is named for the Russian writer Saltykov-Shchedrin (1826–89).

Many well known figures, including Tolstoy, Gorky, Mendeleev, Pavlov, Plekhanov and Lenin all frequented the Saltykov-Shchedrin Library.

THE BOOK HOUSE
(NO. 62)
Or 'Dom Knigi',
the largest bookstore
in the city.

APARTMENT BLOCKS
(NOS. 64–6)
Nos. 64–6 are typical
of late 19th-century
St Petersburg
apartment buildings.

ANICHKOV BRIDGE
The four horses and
their tamers (all
different) on the
Anichkov Bridge
were sculpted by
Klodt in 1849 and
1850.

THE BOOK HOUSE
(NO. 62)

APARTMENT BLOCKS
(NOS. 64–6)

ANICHKOV PALACE
(NO. 39)
This palace,
completed by
Rastrelli in 1751 after
a project by Zemtsov,
was frequently altered
prior to the 19th
century. First of all it

was given by
Elizabeth I to her
morganatic husband
Alexei Razumovsky.
Later Catherine II
gave it to Prince
Potemkin, on two
occasions: the first
time in 1776, then a

second time after he
had sold it to pay his
debts. Potemkin gave
lavish balls here.

222

FONTANKA

The Fontanka, named for the fountains of the Summer Garden which it fed with water, was only a muddy watercourse when Elizabeth ordered it to be dredged and reinforced, first with wood and later with granite.

ANICHKOV BRIDGE

ANICHKOV PALACE (NO. 39)

> "A PERPETUAL STREAM OF CARRIAGES GOES BY AT FULL SPEED, AND CROSSING THE PROSPEKT IS NO LESS PERILOUS AN UNDERTAKING THAN CUTTING OVER THE BOULEVARD FROM RUE DROUOT AND RUE DE RICHELIEU IN PARIS."
>
> THÉOPHILE GAUTIER

THE HEIRS OF THE PIONEERS After 1817 the Anichkov Palace became the residence of the heirs to the Russian throne. Alexander III liked it so much that he remained there after his coronation, filling the house with his art collections, which were later to be exhibited at the Russian Museum ▲ 225. In 1935 the Anichkov buildings became the Palace of the Pioneers, where the red-scarfed pioneers came to spend their free time.

223

⌚ **Half a day**

◆ **A–E**

The former Mikhail Square thoroughly deserved its new name of Arts Square (Pl. Iskusstv; площадь Искусств) since institutions of music, literature, painting and sculpture are all concentrated here behind Carlo Rossi's façades, on a site which was no more than a swamp at the beginning of the 19th century. In the center of the square is a statue of the poet Pushkin ● *114*, whose imperious gesture seems to invite you to begin your visit on the left hand side of the square.

BRODSKY MUSEUM

STATUE OF PUSHKIN
Sculpted in 1957 by Mikhail Anikushin, the statue is the first thing you see when you arrive from the Mikhail Street side.

The painter Isaac Brodsky (1883–1939), after whom Mikhail Street was named during the Soviet era, lived between 1924 and 1939 at no. 3, which was a building constructed in the early 19th century according to plans by Rossi. Those who admire socialist realism will look for Brodsky's edifying canvases, such as *Lenin's Speech at the Putilov Factory Workers' Meeting* (1929) and *Lenin at Smolny* (1930) ▲ *248*. Others, however, may prefer his comprehensive collection of 19th- and 20th-century paintings, which includes works by Repin, Surikov and Serov.

LITTLE THEATER OF OPERA AND BALLET

THE FORMER MIKHAILOVSKY THEATER

● *68.* At no. 1 Arts Square is the old
Mikhailovsky Theater (now called the
Little Theater of Opera and Ballet,
Maly Theater or Mussorgsky Theater),
built by the architect Alexander Bryulov,
partly to plans by Rossi, between 1831
and 1833. "Certain productions have
their premieres in St Petersburg almost at
the same time as in Paris. We may be
forgiven a certain pride at seeing, some
six or seven hundred leagues from Paris,
at a latitude of sixty degrees, that our
language is sufficiently widely spoken
to maintain full houses in an exclusively
French theater." Thus Théophile Gautier

described the "French Theater of St Petersburg", as it was
sometimes known at that time; it is now a mecca for ballets
and musical productions.

RUSSIAN MUSEUM ★

MIKHAIL PALACE (RUSSKY MUZEY/MIKHAILOVSKY DVORETS;
Михайловский дворец). The central building of the Russian
Museum, with its Corinthian façade, was built between 1819
and 1825 for the Grand Duke Mikhail, brother of Alexander I,
by Carlo Rossi. This architect, who laid out Mikhail Square in
its entirety, also arranged the interior details of the palace.
All that survives of this today is the vestibule and main
staircase, along with the White Room (where visitors can see
sculptures by Mikhail Kozlovsky, bas-reliefs by Stepan
Pimenov and murals by Vighi).
FIRST RUSSIAN MUSEUM. In 1898 Nicholas II transformed
the Palace into the Russian Museum of Alexander III,
bringing in some of the paintings and art objects earlier
assembled by his father at the Anichkov Palace ▲ *223.*
Works from private collections, from the Hermitage ▲ *168*
and from the Fine Arts Academy ▲ *162* were added to
these, leading to the construction of a west wing in the
direction of the Griboedov Canal, by Leonty Benois,
between 1914 and 1916. The
nationalization of private
property in 1917 also
greatly enriched
the museum.

✪ ARTS SQUARE
With three museums,
two theaters and
the Shostakovich
Philharmonia
building, Arts Square
is an artistic hub.
A café on the square,
the Stray Dog
(Brodiarchaya
Sobaka), was popular
in the 1910's with
artists and writers
like Vladimir
Mayakovsky and Anna
Akhamatova. Nearby,
beside the
Mikhailovsky Garden,
is the art market, a
picturesque place
between four bridges.

Created by an *ukaze* of the Emperor Alexander III, the Russian Museum opened its doors on March 7, 1898 in Carlo Rossi's Mikhail Palace. Today it is one of the largest museums in the world, with reserves of over 380,000 paintings and *objets d'art*. The purpose of the museum is to exhibit Russian works of art that range in date from the 10th century to our own time; among them is an extraordinary collection of some six thousand icons.

"THE SWAN PRINCESS" (1900)
Superb and disquieting, *The Swan Princess* by Mikhail Vrubel (1856–1911) illustrates Pushkin's story *The Czar Saltan*.

"EVGRAV DAVYDOV" (1809)
Since the creation of the Academy of Arts of St Petersburg the teaching reflected mainly French art. The Russia of the early 19th century did not escape the vogue for Romanticism, fueled by the patriotic war of 1812, as this portrait of Evgrav Davydov by Orest Kiprensky (1782–1836) shows.

"THE DINNER" (1902)
The collections of the museum reflect the artistic and cultural blossoming of Russia on the eve of the Revolution. One of the movements of the period, the World of Art, adopted an esthetic that was simultaneously predominant in Berlin, Vienna and Paris. Leon Bakst (1868–1924) went to the French capital; a lover of 18th-century painting and the poetry of the French Symbolists, he knew how to pay homage to them without compromising any of the essentially Russian character of his art.

"THE ZAPOROZHIAN COSSACKS WRITE A LETTER TO THE TURKISH SULTAN", ILYA REPIN (1891)
National traditions, historical episodes, legends and tales supplied many favorite themes of the 19th century.

"THE PROMENADE" (1917)
Marc Chagall, who was initially influenced by the World of Art movement, later looked for a means of escape into the world of fantasy.

"ANNA YOANNOVNA" (1741)
Artists whose destinies were closely linked to that of Russia were also represented: left, the Empress Anna Yoannovna and her servant, by Rastrelli.

▲ AROUND ARTS SQUARE

Details of the façade
of the Church of the
Resurrection,
representing the arms
of all the regions of
Russia.

THE ASSASSINATION OF ALEXANDER II

On March 1, 1881 the carriage of Czar Alexander II was bowling along the Griboedov when a bomb, hurled by the Narodnaya Volia ("People's Will"), missed its target; but a second bomb mortally wounded the Czar. The members of the commando were tried and executed on April 3.

CHURCH OF THE SPILT BLOOD

Alexander III built the Church of the Resurrection on the very spot where his father Alexander II was assassinated. This explains why the church projects so far out into the street, and why it is also called the Church of the Spilt Blood.

ETHNOGRAPHIC MUSEUM

The Mikhail Palace is flanked, on its left, by a wing built (1900–11) by Vasily Svinin to house the ethnographic section of the Ethnographic Museum (MUZEY ETNOGRAFII; Государственный музей Этнографии). Founded in 1901, it was not opened to the public until 1923; it became a separate museum in its own right in 1934. The richness of its collection makes it far and away Russia's most important ethnographic museum. All the peoples of the former Soviet Union are represented: for example, Moldavians and Bielorussians, Azeris and Turkmens, Evenks and Nenets.

MARBLE HALL. The great entry hall of the museum is sumptuous: Svinin had its walls covered with delicate pink Carelian marble, while the sculptor Kharlamov executed a 300-foot frieze representing all the peoples of the former Russian Empire.

SHOSTAKOVICH PHILHARMONIA

The building constructed by Paul Jacot in 1839 for the Assembly of the Nobility was the scene of major concerts organized by the St Petersburg Philharmonic Society; here, in the Great Hall, Tchaikovsky, Berlioz and Wagner came to conduct their own works, and Isadora Duncan danced. After the Revolution the Great Hall and auditorium became the property of the Philharmonic Society (founded in 1921); a year after the death of Shostakovich (left) in 1976 it was renamed after him. The Philharmonia building projects into the ITALIANSKAYA with two further theaters, the MUSICAL COMEDY THEATER (no. 13) and the KOMISSARZHEVSKAYA THEATER (no. 19). The latter opened in October 1942, hence its nickname the "Blockade Theater".

THE "LENINGRADSKAYA". On the evening of August 9, 1942, the date that had been fixed by Hitler for the fall of Leningrad, the Philharmonia gave the city's first performance of Shostakovich's *Leningrad Symphony*, or *7th Symphony*, which was broadcast from the Great Hall by all the nation's radio stations. Some of the members of the orchestra were still in uniform, having been recalled from the front for the occasion. Others wore the traditional white tie and tails.

CHURCH OF THE RESURRECTION ★

THE NEO-RUSSIAN STYLE ● 89. The twisted onion domes, proliferating mosaics and asymmetry of the Church of the Resurrection (KHRAM VOSKRESENIYA KHRISTOVA; храм Воскресения Христова) come as a surprise in this city known for its Baroque curves and classical rigor. The mosaics have just been restored and are magnificent.

Alfred Parland, who built the church (1883–1907), won the competition set up by Alexander III, which stipulated that it had to be in the "purely Russian style of the 17th century".

ENGINEERS' CASTLE ★

A walk through the MIKHAILOVSKY GARDEN will take you past the rear façade of the Mikhail Palace to the Engineers' Castle (INZHENERNY ZAMOK; Инженерный замок), which since 1991 has served as an annex of the Russian Museum ▲ *225*.

STATUE OF PETER THE GREAT. Bartolomeo Carlo Rastrelli, the father of the architect, began this equestrian statue of Peter I while the Czar was still alive, and ultimately used his death-mask as a model. In 1800 Paul I placed the statue in front of the Castle's main entrance, with the inscription: "To the great-grandfather, the great-grandson."

MIKHAILOVSKY CASTLE. Paul I decided to build a secure fortress on the site of Empress Elizabeth's Summer Palace. The castle was inaugurated on November 8, 1800, St Mikhail's Day in the Orthodox calendar. The name Mikhailovsky, contrary to that of Arts Square or the Russian Museum, has nothing to do with the Grand Duke Mikhail; instead it refers to the Archangel Mikhail, who, according to Paul I, appeared and commanded him to build a chapel bearing his name on this site. This inspiration, which obliged the architect Brennan to design each of his four façades completely differently, did not mitigate the castle's frowning, military aspect.

SCHOOL OF ENGINEERING. Alexander I abandoned the castle, with its sinister associations. It later became the barracks of a squadron of the Imperial Guard, the headquarters of an institute for the blind, and the Chancellery of the Ministry of Instruction and Religious Affairs. In 1822 the Military Engineering School moved here, and it assumed the name of Engineers' Castle. Fyodor Dostoevsky ▲ *207* was a student at the school in 1838, occupying a corner room on the third floor overlooking the Fontanka, where he liked to read and work.

MIKHAILOVSKY CASTLE
Designed by Bazhenov, this massive building was built by Brenna to a medieval plan. The castle was surrounded by water (the Fontanka, the Moika and two other canals, now running underground), and was linked to the city by drawbridges, which were raised every evening.

ASSASSINATION OF PAUL I
In the night of March 11, 1801, supporters of Alexander murdered Paul I in Mikhailovsky Castle, where he had resided for only forty days. The secret rooms and passages Paul I (justifiably paranoid) had devised stopped many of the plotters from reaching the murder scene.

🕐 **Three hours**

◆ A-E

"If God did not exist, it would be necessary to invent him." One of the famous Voltaire manuscripts in the Public Library.

OSTROVSKY SQUARE (PL. OSTROVSKOVO; площадь Островского) is bordered on one side by Rossi's Saltykov-Shchedrin Library ▲ *221*, and on the other by the pavilions of the Anichkov Palace ▲ *223* and its gardens. This square, even more than Arts Square, is an example of the architectural ensemble of balanced proportions and restrained ornamentation for which Carlo Rossi was famous ▲ *181*. It formerly bore the name of the wife of Nicholas I, Alexandra; in 1923 this was changed in honor of the celebrated Russian dramatist Alexander Ostrovsky, whose most famous works were *Poverty No Vice* (1854), *The Storm* (1860) and *Snegurochka* (1873), which had been performed at the Alexandrinsky Theater.

CATHERINE II SQUARE

STATUE OF THE EMPRESS. This massive monument (over 40 feet tall standing in the center of the square was sculpted in 1873 by Matvei Chizhov and Alexander Opekuchin, after a project by Mikhail Mikechin. Catherine the Great is shown in her state robes, while around the plinth cluster sundry personalities of the period: the officers Suvorov ▲ *252*, Rumantsev, Orlov ▲ *184* and Chichagov, the statesmen Potemkin ▲ *251*, Bezborodko and Betskoy, the poet Derzhavin and Princess Dashkova, President of the Academy of Sciences.

ALEXANDRINSKY THEATER ★

Known as the Pushkin Theater during the Soviet era, the Alexandrinsky Theater (ALEXANDRINSKY THEATR; Александринский

театр) was built in 1832, to a project by Ca~~rlo Rossi~~ in
the Russian classical style ● 86. It was named in honor
of the Empress Alexandra Fyodorovna. The troupe at
this theater, one of the oldest in Russia, was founded
in 1756 during the reign of Elizabeth I ● 36. In 1836 it
staged the first production of Nikolai Gogol's
The Government Inspector.

RUSSIAN DRAMA. The history and development of theatrical
genres in Russia (classicism, Romanticism, Realism) are
linked to the evolution of this theater, which became the
de facto national dramatic academy. The repertoire during
the second half of the 18th century included the works of
Russian authors such as Alexander Sumarokov, Iakov

Kniazhnin, Vasily Kapnist and Ivan Krylov, as
well as Western European masters, such as
the French playwrights Corneille, Racine,
Molière and Beaumarchais. At the dawn of
the 20th century the Imperial Alexandrinsky
Theater turned to the new drama of Anton
Chekhov, whose *Seagull* flopped badly
in 1896. After the 1917 Revolution
the theater actively promoted new
Soviet-style plays, and today it remains
one of the most popular with the
St Petersburg public. Its repertoire
is a blend of Russian and Western
classics, along with contemporary
plays. The leading actors of the
decades between 1950 and 1980 used
the title of "Artists of the People of
the USSR".

**ORIENTAL
MANUSCRIPTS**
The Saltykov-
Shchedrin
Library has,
among its
oriental treasures,
this manuscript of
the Hindu poem, the
Bhagavad-Gita.

THEATER MUSEUM ★

This museum, founded in 1918, was established on
the premises of the former Management of the Imperial
Theaters of Russia. Its collections were assembled from
the imperial archives and from the private collections of

people connected with the
theater; today the Theater
Museum includes many items, all
of which are on display, which
document 250 years of Russian
music and theater.

Another special jewel of the Theater Museum is its collection of ballet shoes, which gives an idea of the technical evolution of the ballerina's art.

AGRIPPINA VAGANOVA (1879–1951)

From 1921 until her death Agrippina Vaganova reigned supreme over the dance school which was named after her in 1957. A former pupil of O. Preobrazhenskaya, E. Vazem and P. Gerdt, she became the star dancer of the Mariinsky Theater ▲ 200. Nicknamed the "Czarina of Variations", she described her teaching system in her book *The Foundations of Classical Dance* (1934). According to Vaganova all the expressive power of dance derives from the assimilation of technique combined with a rigorous mastery of the body and of the positioning of the feet and hands.

COLLECTIONS. The museum also displays the personal archives of Marius Petipa, Maria Savina and Fyodor Shalyapin (including the jeweled robe that he wore as Boris Godunov), along with the autographed musical scores of Nikolai Rimsky-Korsakov, letters of Piotr Tchaikovsky and projects for costumes and décors of many different periods throughout the history of Russian theatrical production. The museum's collection of costumes is one of the world's largest, and includes, among others, those of SLEEPING BEAUTY (1890).

FOR MUSIC LOVERS. In the evenings people crowd into the museum's small concert hall. The piano on which Tchaikovsky once played bursts into sound; recordings of former stars are played; contemporary artists perform, and videos of the greatest ballets and operas are screened.

ROSSI STREET

VAGANOVA CHOREOGRAPHIC SCHOOL. In 1737 the dance teacher of St Petersburg's Polish aristocracy, the Frenchman Jean-Baptiste Landet, who had danced professionally in Paris and Dresden and had been master of ballet in Stockholm, suggested to the Empress Anna Yoannovnathat a dance school should be founded to train the leading dancers of the imperial court's ballet troupe. In 1738 Her Majesty's Dance School was inaugurated, exclusively for children of Russian families of modest means. The first class was made up of twelve girls and twelve boys. The best pupils of this first generation (1742) soon demonstrated a mastery of their art that astonished everyone. In the 19th century the director Charles Didelot ● *71* was replaced by Marius Petipa ▲ *200*, who formed a strong pedagogical team. Since that time the school has regularly sent its pupils on to glittering careers on the Russian stage. The School of St Petersburg has exercised a very powerful influence on the development of European and American ballet; indeed ballet of the 20th century would have been considerably the poorer had it not been for such figures as George Balanchine, Rudolph Nureyev, Natalia Makarova, Anna Pavlova, Tamara Karsavina and Mikhail Baryshnikov, brilliant choreographers and dancers who were all trained at the Vaganova Choreographic School.

ROSSI STREET
The height of the buildings and the width of Rossi Street are exactly equal (66 feet), while its length is exactly ten times this (660 feet). The street was laid out by Carlo Rossi between 1828 and 1834, and was originally known as Theater Street.

LOMONOSOV SQUARE

Rossi Street leads on to another of that architect's projects, Lomonosov Square (PL. LOMONOSOV; Ломоносова). The austerity of the buildings here accorded well with the use that was made of them, prior to the Revolution, by the Ministry of Public Instruction and the Interior Ministry. At that time the square was named after Peter the Great's companion-in-arms,

Chernyshev. In the middle of the square stands a bust of Mikhail Lomonosov ● *53* by Sabello (1892).

LOMONOSOV BRIDGE ● *90*. The turrets of this bridge formerly concealed the chains used to raise and lower its ramp. Today the turrets are purely ornamental. The Lomonosov Bridge was identical to another bridge further along the Fontanka, opposite the Anichkov Palace, before the latter was reconstructed and provided with its celebrated horses ▲ *222*.

FONTANKA EMBANKMENT

To the right, on the way down the Fontanka Embankment (NAB. REKI FONTANKI; наб. реки фонтанки), is the Press Building, the offices of several newspapers and at one time the *Leningrad Pravda*'s nerve center. Beside it stands the Tovstonogov Theater ● *69*.

TOVSTONOGOV THEATER
The Tovstonogov was one of the first post-Revolutionary theaters in the city. Its inaugural play, performed in 1919, was Schiller's *Don Carlos*; later repertoires included contemporary pieces such as Mayakovsky's *The Bedbug* and *The Bath-House* (both 1929). The theater originally bore the name of one of its founders, Maxim Gorky, before adopting that of Tovstonogov, the director who ran it from 1956 onward.

Details of the various bridges spanning
St Petersburg's canals.

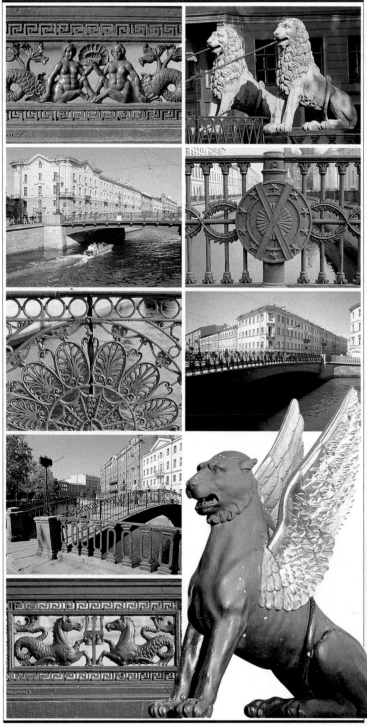

From the Fontanka
to Insurrection Square

1. INSURRECTION SQUARE
2. MOSCOW STATION
3. LIGOVSKY PROSPE

🕐 **Half a day**
◆ E

"Over that noble
   abode
I have no rights nor
   pretensions,
But it happens that I
   have spent
Almost all my life
   beneath the roof
Of the Palace of
   Fountains:
I was poor when I
   entered it,
And I leave it poor"
   Anna Akhmatova

FOUNTAINS HOUSE ★

On the Fontanka Embankment the regularity of the
19th-century façades is broken by a green park, at the
end of which is Fountains House (no. 34) (FONTANNY
DOM; Фонтанный дом).

SHEREMETEV PALACE. In 1712 Marshal Sheremetev was
allotted a large building site beside the river, where he
erected a wooden country house. This was replaced in the
1730's by a stone house. In 1750–5 the architect Argunov,
who came from a family of serfs famous for their artistic
talents, added a floor to the palace and transformed its
façades, giving it its present aspect. The central façade of the
main building was heightened by the addition of a mezzanine
and a semicircular pediment.

MUSIC AND CULTURE. Many famous writers, artists and
intellectuals have lived and worked in Fountains House,
beginning with the actress Prascovia Kovaleva
(Zhemchugova), who married Nikolai Sheremetev in 1801.
From the mid-18th century to the 1870's the house was the
venue for the concerts
of the Sheremetevs'
Capella, which was one
of the best private
choirs in Russia and
greatly admired by such
figures as Glinka, Liszt
and Berlioz. After the
Revolution the house
was used by a series of
different organizations
and its interior was
much altered. A few
years ago it was
reallocated to the
State Museum of
Theater and Music,
which is currently
restoring the prestige
of this former center
of musical and cultural
life. The building's
reception rooms and
the Museum of Music
that has been laid out
there are now open to
the public.

AKHMATOVA MUSEUM. (MUZEY ANNY AKHMATOVOI; музей Анны Ахматовой). The poet Anna Akhmatova lived from 1924 to 1952 in the apartment on the third floor of the south wing, overlooking the courtyard. During the 1920's this place was frequented by poets, painters and writers, among them Mayakovsky, Tatlin, Lebeder and Tyrssa. Akhmatova's rooms were made into a museum in 1989; one of them has been redecorated to look as it would have appeared between 1938 and 1941. Here Akhmatova's husband and later her son were arrested. In the other room a display of her poetry explains how she won so important a place in the history of Russian society, culture and literature between 1910 and 1960. There is also a portrait of the poet by Modigliani, executed during a visit to Paris in 1911.

HOUSE OF LETTERS

The house that was situated at the intersection of Nevsky Prospekt and the Fontanka Embankment (nos. 40–60) was entirely destroyed during the siege of World War Two ● 50 but subsequently rebuilt. The critic Vissarion Bielinsky lived here from 1842, in what was known during the 19th century as the "House of Letters". Bielinsky was an influential journalist, and had a powerful effect on the younger generation of writers. He gathered around him a circle of Russia's intellectual avant-garde which included the writers Nekrasov, Turgenev, Grigorovich and Dostoevsky. Today the house is used by the regional tax office.

VISSARION BIELINSKY (1811–48)
Bielinsky's ideas about the condition of the people and the role of Russian writers are expressed in his letter to Gogol, which was clandestinely circulated among the intelligentsia. Dostoevsky spent four years in a labor camp and six years in exile in Siberia, partly because he had read this letter.

237

BELOSELSKY-BELOZERSKY PALACE

The house of Prince Shakhovskoy was bought in the mid-18th century by Myatlev, the head of the Assignat bank. It was subsequently altered by the classical architect Thomas de Thomon and became the palace of Prince Beloselsky-Belozersky. The new owners were wealthy and famous, members of a family that dated back to Vladimir Monomachus, the Kievan Grand Duke. Their double-barreled name originated in 1798, when Paul I gave Beloselsky the right to use the name of Belozersky, in recognition of his ancestors' services to Russia. The palace was rebuilt between 1846 and 1848 by the architect Shtakenshneider. From 1898 to 1917 it belonged to the imperial family; one of its last owners was the son of Alexander II, Prince Sergei Alexandrovich.

MUNICIPAL CULTURE CENTER AND MUSEUM After the Revolution the Beloselsky Palace was occupied by the Communist Party's regional committee. Today it is the Municipal Culture Center. The Hall of Mirrors and the Oak Room are used for plays and concerts, while other rooms provide exhibition areas. The palace also houses the Museum of the Development of Russian Democracy, which is named after Anatoli Sobtchak, the first mayor of the city following the Soviet period.

VLADIMIR SQUARE Vladimir Prospekt leads to the square of the same name, whose buildings form a circle around the Vladimir Church (dedicated to the Virgin and Saint John of Damascus).

VLADIMIR PROSPEKT

LITTLE (MALY) DRAMATIC THEATER ● 69. At no. 18, on the corner of Rubinstein and Count streets, is the Little Dramatic Theater (MALY DRAMATICHESKY TEATR; Малый драматичесий театр). Since its creation in 1944, it has gained worldwide fame under the direction of Lev Dodin.
LENSOVIET THEATER (LENSOVETA TEATR; Леисовета театр). This single-story building (no. 12) has a striking façade with an eight-column portico, Ionic pilasters and masks. It was built in the 1820s by the architect Mikhailov as a wealthy mansion for the Korsakov family. After the Revolution it was occupied by a number of different theatrical institutions. Today it is once again known by its original name, the Lensoviet Theater, and is under the direction of Vladimir Paze.

VLADIMIR SQUARE (VLADIMIRSKAYA PL.; Владимирская пл.). The first church in the center of this square was built in 1747 and replaced in 1761 by a stone building. Its anonymous architect may have been Trezzini, who worked under Rastrelli. In 1783 a two-story bell tower was erected alongside the chirch by Quarenghi; in 1848 the architect Ruska added two further stories. Closed since 1932, the Vladimir Church has been reopened by the Russian Orthodox authorities.

RIMSKY-KORSAKOV MUSEUM

The famous composer Rimsky-Korsakov lived for the last fifteen years of his life at no. 28 Zagorodny Prospekt. In 1971 his apartment was transformed into a museum (MUZEY-KVARTIRA RIMSKOVO-KORSAKOVA; музей-квартира Римского-Корсакова). The vestibule, study, salon and dining room here recreate the atmosphere of what was one of the centers of St Petersburg culture, where Rimsky-Korsakov held his musical evenings, the "Korsakov Wednesdays". Glazunov, Lyadov, Rachmaninov, Taneyev and Shalyapin all attended these events. Today an entire room is devoted to musical life in St Petersburg in the late 19th and early 20th centuries, and every Wednesday meetings of singers and musicians are once more held in the concert room. In this apartment Rimsky-Korsakov wrote over forty romances, as well as his *Principles of Orchestration*, *Chronicle of My Musical Life* and the operas *Sadko*, *Czar Saltan*, *The Czar's Bethrothed* and *Kashchey the Immortal*.

"LOUSE EXCHANGE"
The intersection of Nevsky Prospekt, Vladimir Prospekt and Liteiny Prospekt used to be known as the "Louse Exchange"; porters and craftsmen looking for work used to gather here, along with itinerant barbers who sat their clients on stools to cut their hair.

RIMSKY-KORSAKOV (1844–1908) ● *72*
The composer's name is closely linked with the Conservatoire, where he taught the composition class.

DOSTOEVSKY MUSEUM ★

This museum (MUZEY-KVARTIRA F.M. DOSTOYEVSKOVO; музей-квартира Ф. М. Достоевского) was opened in 1971, ninety years after the death of Dostoevsky ▲ 206. The apartment had to be reconstituted, but its atmosphere remains faithful to the personality of the master and to the spirit of his time.

A WRITER'S PRIVACY. Dostoevsky lived in this apartment on two occasions (for a few months in 1846, and during the last years of his life) with his wife Anna Grigorievna and their two children, Lyuba and Fedya. Here he wrote his celebrated *Discourse on Pushkin*, as well as *The Brothers Karamazov*. Dostoevsky liked his study (above) because it was spacious and isolated from the rest of the apartment. The place was austere and ascetic. Above the sofa on which he slept is a reproduction of Raphael's *Virgin of Saint Sixtus*, a painting he especially loved. Beyond the windows are the domes of the Vladimir Church, of which he was a parishioner. The streets and the passers-by in this district still compose the same ". . . inexhaustible, magnificent almanac, which one can leaf through in one's spare moments, when one is bored, after a meal . . .".

MARATA STREET

RADISHCHEV (1749–1802)
This celebrated writer, the first thoroughgoing Russian dissident, lived at no. 14 Marata Street from 1775 to 1790. He was arrested, imprisoned at the Peter and Paul Fortress, and sent to Siberia on the orders of Catherine II for his revolutionary *Journey from Petersburg to Moscow*. Freed in 1796 by Paul I, he was amnestied in 1801 by Alexander I, but killed himself in 1802.

MUSEUM OF THE ARCTIC AND ANTARCTIC (MUZEY ARKTIKI I ANTARKTIKI; музей Арктики и Антарктики). The former St Nicholas Church is the only building of the United Schismatics (a branch of the Old Believers ● 56) which remains intact at St Petersburg; it was closed in 1932 to make way, in 1937, for the Museum of the Arctic and Antarctic, which houses, among other exhibits, stuffed polar wildlife and items from expeditions. Today there is a project to return the church to the Old Believers and move the museum elsewhere.

NEVSKY PROSPEKT

On the section of Nevsky Prospekt between Liteiny and Vladimir prospekts and Marata Street is a series of apartment blocks dating from the second half of the 19th century and early 20th century. At no. 60 lived the satirical writer Mikhail Saltykov-Shchedrin ▲ 221; in 1815 Vladimir Zhukovsky, the translator of English, French and German poetry, lived at no. 82.

Actors' House. This building (no. 86), with its white-columned portico, is known in St Petersburg as the Actors' House. It unites several theatrical associations, such as the Union of Theater Workers, the Russian Theater Society and the Stanislavsky Palace of the Arts. Built in the 18th century as a private mansion, then reconstructed between 1820 and 1830 by the architects Ovsianikov and Fossati, it belonged in the 19th century to the Yusupov family, who organized concerts and exhibitions there. Today the Actors' House still mounts soirées, seminars, conferences, and exhibitions of theater décor as well as international festivals and competitions.

"Nevsky Palace". No. 57, opposite the Actors' House, was built in 1861 by the architect Langé and belonged to the craft school of Czarevich Nicholas ● *36*. It was formerly the Renommée Hotel, which rented furnished rooms, before it became the Hermès and finally the Baltic Hotel at the end of World War Two. It was restored in 1993, and is today a luxury establishment.

Samoilov Museum. In the same block as the Nevsky Palace, on the Groom Street side, is the Samoilov family museum which was opened 1994. From 1869 onward a number of famous actors, composers, painters and writers frequented this house.

Pushkin Street

On a square halfway down Pushkin Street (Pushkinskaya Ul.; Пушкинская ул.) is a statue of the writer, which was the first to be erected to him in St Petersburg. It is the work of the sculptor Opekushin, who was also responsible for the Moscow statue of Pushkin (1880), this monument was unveiled in 1884.

No. 10 Pushkin Street. Today a number of artists inhabit this derelict house. As representatives of alternative culture in St Petersburg they organize exhibitions, entertainments and concerts in the courtyards of the building and in the street outside. The creative drive behind this unusual center is currently a popular phenomenon in St Petersburg.

▲ St Petersburg in the Movies

The first Russian production company was founded in 1907. St Petersburg at that time appears (with the help of Czarist censors) as a 19th-century city, a sumptuous décor perfect for adaptations such as *The Queen of Spades* (1916) by Iakov Protazanov, the greatest director of the early Russian cinema.

Max Linder, immensely popular in Russia, came to St Petersburg in 1913. The public flocked to see his movie, which ended with a ballooning scene. Then the theater lights came on, and Linder himself appeared on the end of a rope, as if he had come in through the roof.

St Petersburg's first movie theater was established on the Nevsky Prospekt, on the initiative of the Lumière brother. Although Moscow was the cinematic capital for Russia under the Czars, St Petersburg was an inspiration to a number of directors and developed a distinct cinema tradition of its own. Today directors no longer seem threatened by censors, but the new economic situation of the Russian cinema is making movie production extraordinarily difficult.

КВАРІУМЪ

4-го Мая 1896 года

Вниманіе! Откр

Съ 4 Мая и ежд. первый разъ въ Россіи
Живая фотографія Синематографъ-Лю
мієрѣ послѣднія чудеса науки.
Завтра, въ Воскресенье, 5 Мая, выходъ і ж
ВАЯ ФОТОГРАФІЯ послѣднія чудеса науки
Лица.

Certain Soviet directors rapidly established their "Leningrad" credentials, notably Kozintsev and Trauberg. Ermler (with Johanson) was mainly concerned to film a city transformed by socialism (*Ruins of Empire*, 1929).

This was held on May 4, 1896 at the Aquarium Theater, and was organized by the Lumière brothers.

242

In 1927 Greta Garbo played Anna Karenina in Goulding's movie. Seven years later Marlene Dietrich marched through Sternberg's unreal Peterhof (*The Scarlet Empress*). More recently American stars have ventured into revolutionary Petrograd (Warren Beatty in *Reds*).

With the Russian vogue of the 1930's pasteboard Petersburgs sprang up like mushrooms. Harry Borg played a disquieting Rasputin in the French movie *La Tragédie Impériale* (1938).

John GILBERT

Greta Garbo in **LOVE**

An Edmund Goulding PRODUCTION

from the novel AnnaKarenina by Lyof N. Tolstoi. Adaptation by Lorna Moon, Continuity by Frances Marion, Directed by Edmund Goulding

A Metro-Goldwyn-Mayer PICTURE

The recasting of the Leningrad studios under the name of Lenfilm in 1936 (the name has survived to this day) sounded the death-knell of their creative insolence. Experimentation was definitely out of favor when Heifitz and Zarkhy filmed *The Baltic Deputy* (1936).

For its epics the Soviet cinema often used the streets of Leningrad. Crowds of extras, directed by Eisenstein, flooded past in his theoretical and disturbing *October* (1927).

INSURRECTION SQUARE

In 1909 a statue of Alexander III by Trubetskoy was erected in the center of the square; at the time this monumental sculpture ▲ *184* was nicknamed "The Scarecrow".

BREAD MUSEUM
At no. 73 Ligovsky Prospekt is an industrial bakery; on the fourth floor is the Bread Museum. The exhibition here traces the history of breadmaking from the foundation of St Petersburg, and describes the various uses to which bread has been put over the centuries.

LIGOVSKY PROSPEKT

Nevsky Prospekt intersects Ligovsky Prospekt (LIGOVSKI PR.; Лиговский пр.), laid out in the late 19th century on a part of the canal of that name, now filled in, which fed the fountains in the Summer Garden ▲ *186*. In the 18th and 19th centuries this street was famous for its queues of carriages, its supply of drinks, its tearooms, taverns and cheap hotels.

OCTOBER CONCERT HALL. At the head of the Prospekt there used to be a remarkable Greek Orthodox church. This was built between 1861 and 1866 in a Byzantine style that was highly unusual for St Petersburg. It was demolished in 1961 and replaced by the October Concert Hall (1967).

"WRITERS' WALKWAYS". In the Volkovskoe Cemetery at the end of Ligovsky Prospekt is a mausoleum where some great Russian intellectuals, including the writer Turgenev and the chemist Mendeleev, are buried.

INSURRECTION SQUARE

INSURRECTION SQUARE (PL. VOSTANIYA; пл. Восстания) was the original terminal point of Nevsky Prospekt before it was extended to the Alexander Nevsky Monastery ▲ *253*. It was the scene of some of the most violent encounters between police and demonstrators during the February Revolution.

FROM THE CHURCH TO THE METRO. Until 1918 this square was called Our Lady of the Sign, after the church built here by Elizabeth I in 1767. At the end of the 18th century plans were made for the original wooden church to be replaced by a stone one. Work began in 1794 and continued for ten years. The result was a five-domed church dominating the square. It remained in use until 1938 but was demolished in 1940. The Ploshchad Vostaniya metro station now stands on the site.

MOSCOW STATION (MOSKOVSKY VOKZAL; Московский вокзал). The inauguration on November 1, 1851 of the railway linking St Petersburg with Moscow was a momentous event in the life of the capital. The original Nicholas Station was designed by Thon. The central part of its grand green and white façade was decorated on two levels, with Corinthian columns, and now this is all that remains of the old building, as it has now been completely modernized inside. In 1967 a bust of Lenin was placed in the main hall on a monumental pedestal, and on its walls were inscribed the decree of the second Party Congress of 1924 which changed Petrograd to Leningrad ● *33*. Now that the city has reassumed its original name the bust of Lenin has been replaced by that of Peter the Great. For St Petersburg's statues "musical chairs" has always been the norm.

From Smolny
to the Alexander Nevsky
Monastery

SMOLNY

Suvorov Avenue leads to the remarkable Smolny architectural complex. Behind the Dictatorship of the Proletariat Gardens rises the austere yellow and white façade of the Smolny Institute, while to the left, behind the trees, rise the Baroque domes of the Cathedral and Monastery. The origin of the name Smolny goes back to the time of Peter the Great. Until 1723 this site was occupied by the Smolny Dvor (tar depot), where tar was prepared and stored for caulking ships' timbers.

DICTATORSHIP OF THE PROLETARIAT SQUARE

(PL. PROLETARSKOY; пл. Пролетарской Диктатуры Diktatury). The access to the Smolny Institute, which played so prominent a role in the Revolution, had to be on a par with its symbolic importance; this, at any rate, is what the architects Vladimir Shchuko and Vladimir Guelfreikh must have thought when they erected their massive neoclassical propylaea (1923–4) on either side of the main thoroughfare, and complemented them ten years later with a rectilinear garden. In the garden the architects installed busts of Karl Marx and Friedrich Engels, sculpted by Sergei Yevseyev.

SMOLNY MONASTERY AND CATHEDRAL
Visitors can attend concerts and view an exhibition on the site's history. From the top of the bell tower (accessible on request) are fine panoramic views.

🕐 **One day**

◆ E

SMOLNY MONASTERY AND CATHEDRAL (SBOR SMOLNOVO-MONASTYRIA; собор Смольного-Монастыря) ★.

A convent at Smolny was first founded by the Empress Elizabeth I ● *37*, who decided to take the veil toward the end of her life. The project (a maquette of it is on display at the Academy of Arts ▲ *162*), which was designed by Rastrelli and begun in 1748, originally allowed for a 420-foot bell tower. Catherine II, once she was on the throne, sacked the Italian architect in 1764 and founded a school for young ladies in the convent.

A LAVISH CATHEDRAL ● *85*
The cathedral as completed by Vasily Stasov in 1835 preserves the style of Rastrelli, in which the ornamental exuberance of Baroque includes purely Russian elements such as the five onion domes.

247

▲ LENIN AND THE REVOLUTION

For taking part in an illegal political meeting the seventeen-year-old student Vladimir Ilyich Ulyanov was arrested, banned from the University and exiled to a distant village in Kazan. Thus began Lenin's life as a dedicated revolutionary. By 1916 he was living in Zurich and had despaired of any revolution in his lifetime; the spontaneous rising of the Russian masses in October 1917 came as a total surprise to him.

A CLANDESTINE EXISTENCE
Lenin lived clandestinely in St Petersburg during the 1905–7 Revolution ● *44* and in the same city (by then named Petrograd) under the Kerensky regime from July 5 to October 25, 1917. Left, Lenin disguised as a worker, under the name of K. Ivanov.

APRIL 1917
Lenin outlined his program at the Tauride Palace in April 1917. He declared the "Tasks of the Proletariat" to be of the utmost urgency; and to the astonishment of his listeners he proposed an immediate end to the war, the overthrow of the government, and the handing over of all political power to the soviets.

LENIN AT THE SMOLNY INSTITUTE
Lenin arrived at the headquarters of the Petrograd Soviet, the Smolny Institute, on the evening of October 24, 1917 to direct the coup d'état. He stayed there until the government left for Moscow on March 11, 1918. He ran the Council of People's Commissars within the Palace, wrote, and received delegations and journalists; among the latter was J. Reed, author of a celebrated account of the October Revolution, *Ten Days that Shook the World*.

POWER TO THE BOLSHEVIKS

On October 25, 1917, at 10.40pm, even as the attack on the Winter Palace ● *44* was under way, the Second Pan-Russian Congress of Soviets opened at Smolny. The Mensheviks and right-wing Socialist Revolutionaries disapproved of Lenin's coup d'état. They proposed to open talks with the Provisional Government, with a view to setting up a democracy. After a short, violent debate they walked out in a body, abandoning the field to the Bolsheviks.

BACK IN PETROGRAD

In July 1920 Lenin took part in the Second Congress of the Komintern at the Tauride Palace. The same month he sent a message to Stalin, then fighting at Kharkov: "The situation in the Komintern is excellent. Zinoviev, Bukharin and I believe that we should immediately encourage the Revolution in Italy. In my view, we should first Sovietize Hungary and perhaps the Czech state and Romania. This requires mature consideration. Let us know your conclusion."

LENIN'S TRAGEDY

On May 25, 1922 Lenin fell ill, with a paralyzed right arm and leg and acute aphasia. He returned to work in October, but by December was once more confined to his bed. His health declined progressively thereafter, and he was cut off from the levers of power within the Kremlin.

THE DEIFICATION OF LENIN

Krupskaya, Lenin's wife, entreated the Politburo in vain not to embalm his body but to bury it as he had wished.

NIKOLAI KARAMZIN (1766–1826)
The great historian and writer Nikolai Karamzin spent the final years of his life at the Tauride Palace.

THE FIRST KUNSTKAMMER
After Kikin's death his palace was used for the Kunstkammer, Peter the Great's assemblage of curiosities. Here was displayed a collection bought from the Dutch anatomist Frederik Ruysch (1717), a specialist in embalming. In 1727 the Kunstkammer was transferred to Vasilyevsky Island ▲ 160.

SMOLNY INSTITUTE (SMOLNY INSTITUT; Смольный институт) ★. This long neoclassical building, built by Quarenghi in 1806–8, was a school for young ladies until August 1917, at which time the Soviet of Workers' and Soldiers' Deputies of Petrograd ● 46 was installed there. On October 24, 1917, in the evening, Lenin arrived to seize control of the insurrection. The long corridors of the Institute swarmed with Red Guards, soldiers, sailors and factory delegates seeking weapons, tracts or newspapers. On October 25, while the fighting was still going on, the Second Pan-Russian Congress of Soviets opened, at 10.40pm in the Lecture Hall. At 3.10am the delegates greeted the news of the fall of the Winter Palace with wild cheering. That evening they ratified the decrees proposed by Lenin on peace and land ownership, as well as on the formation of the Council of People's Commissars. The Council, headed by Lenin, operated from Smolny until it was moved to Moscow in March 1918. Since 1991 the Institute has housed the offices of the Mayor of St Petersburg, but the historic Lecture Hall, Lenin's study and the bedroom he occupied with his wife, Nadezhda Krupskaya, now form part of the SMOLNY MEMORIAL MUSEUM. There is also a permanent exhibition about the Institute as it was at the time of Catherine II.

KIKIN PALACE

At the Stavropol intersection stands one of the oldest buildings in St Petersburg, the palace of the Boyar Alexander Kikin. Kikin was an opponent of Peter the Great's policies who supported the Czarevich Alexei in his doomed attempt to overthrow the Emperor ● 39. After fleeing to Austria on the advice of Kikin the Czarevich returned to Russia in January 1718 and was condemned to death a few months later. Most of the people he denounced as his accomplices, among them Kikin, were executed. Nowadays the Kikin Palace building houses a music school.

"Stand up straight and speak French!" was the admonishment given to the six- to eighteen-year-old pupils at the Smolny Institute. Here the young ladies were taught such subjects as religion, languages, arithmetic, drawing, dancing, sewing and good manners.

TAURIDE PALACE

Nearby, on the left-hand side of Shpalernaya Street, runs the 760-foot yellow façade of the Tauride Palace (TAVRICHESKY DVORETS; Таврический дворец), which has a stark Doric pediment crowned by a green dome. Constructed between 1783 and 1789, this was one of the first classical buildings in Russia ● *86*.

POTEMKIN'S REWARD. Catherine II was much given to showering palaces on her favorite, Prince Potemkin. After presenting him with the Anichkov Palace ▲ *222* she had the Tauride Palace built for him, modeled on the Pantheon in Rome. Scarcely was it finished than she offered to buy it back for 460,000 roubles; Potemkin, a notorious spendthrift, was always heavily in debt and needed the money. In February 1791, on his return from Iasi, the former capital of Moldavia, where he had negotiated an advantageous peace with the Turks, Catherine gave the palace to Potemkin a second time. He used it to throw parties of legendary extravagance.

OTHER OCCUPANTS. After Prince Potemkin's death the Tauride in 1792 was decreed an imperial palace. When the Empress died Paul I revenged himself on his mother and her favorite by stripping the place bare and converting it into a

barracks. The Column Room was converted into a stable, and its furnishings and works of art were moved to the Mikhail Castle ▲ *229*. Alexander I had the palace restored by Luigi Rusca (1802–4).

FROM THE DUMA TO THE SOVIETS. After the February Revolution ● *46* the left wing of the palace was occupied by the Soviet of the Workers and Soldiers of Petrograd, while the right wing was used by the Committee of the Duma, which formed the Provisional Government. The Tauride Palace was later used as the Leningrad Higher Party School before becoming the seat of the Assembly of the CIS.

TAURIDE GARDENS. (TAURICHESKI SAD; Таврический сад). Although probably not as luxuriant today as in Potemkin's time these gardens are still a pleasant place to walk. In winter its avenues are used by cross-country skiers.

POTEMKIN, PRINCE OF THE TAURIDE
The Greeks called the Crimea the Tauride; they believed that its barbarian inhabitants were in the habit of burning foreigners on sight (Euripides states this categorically in his *Iphigenia*). When the Crimea was annexed to Russia in 1783 it reverted to its original name; and Potemkin, who led the campaign against the Ottomans, was named Prince of the Tauride by Catherine II. His palace, built at this time, was given the same name.

A MAJESTIC FAÇADE
The stylistic restraint shown by the architect Starov in his design for the palace provoked the enthusiasm of poet Gavril Derzhavin: "Its exterior is distinguished neither for its sculptures, nor its gilding . . . old-fashioned, elegant good taste is the true source of its dignity and majesty."

WATER MUSEUM
Situated opposite the Tauride Palace is an old water tower, dating from the 19th century. Since 2003, it has housed a water museum.

ALEXANDER SUVOROV (1729–1800)
Alexander Suvorov was born in Moscow. His father was a general who had fought with Peter the Great. During the Russo-Turkish War (1787–91) Catherine II conferred on him the rank of Field Marshal after he crushed the Polish uprising (1794).

Suvorov Museum

The popularity of Field Marshal Alexander Suvorov made possible a nationwide subscription toward the Suvorov Military History Museum (Voenna-Istorichesky Muzey Suvorova/военно-исторический музей А. В. Суворова). In 1904 the architects Guerman Grimm and Alexander Gogen completed this building, with its enormous panels of mosaic illustrating the principal events in Suvorov's life. Inside, a selection of the general's possessions is on display, together with maps, weapons and various other items that have survived from his campaigns.

Toward the Monastery

Suvorov Avenue (Suvorovsky Prospekt; Суворовский проспект). This broad thoroughfare, which leads to the Smolny District, used to be known as Elephant Avenue. In the early 18th century the Persian shahs were in the habit of sending elephants as gifts to the Russian emperors (indeed, in 1741 Nadir Shah gave a total of fourteen elephants). One of the special stables constructed for these somewhat cumbersome offerings stood by the side of today's Suvorov Avenue; it was by this route that the elephants would travel on their way to drink from the waters of the river Neva.

ALEXANDER NEVSKY
Prince Alexander Novgorod was given this sobriquet after he won the 1240 battle by the Neva.

Nevsky Prospekt. The section of the Nevsky Prospekt ▲ *212* which leads to the Alexander Nevsky Monastery was built shortly after the foundation of the monastery; the idea behind its construction was to give the monks access to the road to Novgorod, where the metropolitan resided. Close by what has now become Insurrection Square ▲ *244* the monks' route joined with the road linking the dockyards of the Admiralty to this same Novgorod road. It was during the reign of Anna Ivanovna – in fact on April 20, 1738 – that it was finally decreed that "the great thoroughfare from the Admiralty to the Nevsky Monastery should be called the Nevsky Prospekt".

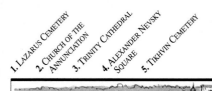

ALEXANDER NEVSKY MONASTERY

BY PETER'S WILL. In 1710 Peter the Great built the Alexander Nevsky Monastery (ALEKSANDRO-NEVSKY LAVRA; Александро-Невская Лавра) in honor of Prince Alexander Novgorod, on the site of his victory over the Swedes in 1240. The construction work began in 1712, and by the following year a wooden church had been consecrated and monks had moved in. After the death of Peter the Great the works continued, but the building was not completed until the last years of the 18th century, during the reign of Catherine II. In 1797 the Alexander Nevsky Monastery took the title of *lavra*, reserved for the most important monasteries. In addition to the St Petersburg *lavra*, there are others at Pechersky (Kiev, Ukraine), Trinity-St-Sergei (Sergiyev Posad) and Pochaevsky-Uspensk (Volhynia, Ukraine).

TOURING THE MONASTERY. In the recess of the curving monastery wall rises the dome of the main entrance, built between 1783 and 1785 by the architect Ivan Starov. Once through the gateway arch you will see beyond the walls surrounding them the Lazarus cemetery (on the left) and the Tikhvin cemetery (on the right). Some of the tombstones here are the work of famous sculptors, such as Ivan Martos, Mikhail Kozlovsky, Auguste Montferrand and Vasily Demut-Malinovsky.

LAZARUS CEMETERY (LAZAREVSKAYE KLADBISHCHE; Лазаревское кладбище). The Lazarus Cemetery, also known as the 18th-century Necropolis, is the oldest cemetery in St Petersburg. It was inaugurated in 1716 with the burial of Natalia Alexeyevna, who was the much-loved sister of Peter the Great. Later it was mainly used for the deceased of the great aristocratic families, but it also harbors the remains of such luminaries as the encyclopedist Mikhail Lomonosov (1711–65) ● *53*, the architects Adrian Zakharov (1761–1811), Carlo Rossi ▲ *181*, Giacomo Quarenghi (1744–1817), Andrei Voronikhin (1759–1814), as well as Thomas de Thomon ● *87*, who had been appointed court architect in 1802.

🕐 **Two hours**

◆ **E**

✪ **RUSSIA'S NATIONAL MAUSOLEUM**
The Alexander Nevsky Monastery is one of the rare architectural complexes to have survived intact from the early 18th century. The Museum of Sculpture keeps more than 2,000 funerary monuments of great historical or artistic value here. Don't miss the Artists' Necropolis (in the Tikhvin cemetery), where are laid to rest the great figures of Russian culture, such as Dostoevsky and Tchaikovsky.

RELICS OF ALEXANDER NEVSKY
In 1742 Peter the Great decided to move the relics of Alexander Nevsky (then in the town of Vladimir) to St Petersburg. To begin with they were displayed at the Church of the Annunciation, and then transferred to Trinity Cathedral in 1790, where they were placed in a silver sarcophagus (now at the Hermitage).

CHURCH OF THE ANNUNCIATION
(BLAGOVESHCHENSKAYA TSERKOV; Благовещенская церковь). The avenue between the two cemeteries crosses a small canal (which joins the Obvodny "lateral" canal, built between 1805 and 1834, to the southward) and leads on to the Monastery entrance.

The Church of the Annunciation, which lies immediately to the left, is the oldest in the Monastery. Built between 1717 and 1725 by Domenico Trezzini, it was from the start used as a burial place for major figures such as Vasily Dolgoruky, who traveled to Europe with Peter the Great; Alexei Razumovsky, the morganatic husband of the Empress Elizabeth; Ivan Shuvalov (who was another celebrated favorite of the Czarina's); and the great strategist Field Marshal Alexander Suvorov ▲ 252. At Suvorov's funeral on December 6, 1800, his coffin appeared to be too wide to be able to pass through the door, but one of the soldiers carrying the bier gave the order: "Forward! Nothing ever stopped Suvorov!" and somehow they managed to force it through. Today the church contains a part of the collection belonging to the Sculpture Museum. Among the items on display are maquettes of a variety of different monuments and statues of St Petersburg (including the Alexander Column ▲ 181 and the Monument to Peter I ▲ 194).

LAVISH DECORATION
The interior décor of Trinity Cathedral contains an altar of marble and agate, and walls covered in copies of works by Guercino, Van Dyck, Rubens and such Russian painters and other masters as Grigory Ugriumov, Marcin Bielsky and Nikolai Utkin.

TRINITY CATHEDRAL (TROITSKY SOBOV; Троицкий собор). A church built by Schwertfeger originally stood on this site, but its walls were so fissured that in 1753 the Empress Elizabeth I ● 37 ordered its demolition. The stones were reused to pave Nevsky Prospekt; and the subsequent cathedral was built by Ivan Starov between 1778 and 1790, with a restrained pediment, colonnade and single dome, in the classical style that was then in fashion. It is the only place of worship in the Monastery precinct that is still open for services. Behind it stretches the St Nicholas Cemetery (NIKOLSKOYE), where many prominent personalities from the Soviet era are buried.

FEDOROVSKAYA CHURCH (FEDOROVSKAYA TSERKOV; Федоровская церковь).
This church (right), built between 1742 and 1750 by Trezzini, to the south of Trinity Cathedral, was also used as a mausoleum for the last kings and princes of Georgia.

Palaces on the outskirts of St Petersburg

GULF OF FINLAND

Hermitage

Toward Marly • Eve Fountain

Toward landing-stage

Catherine Wing • Monplaisir

Little Divan Fountain • Sun Fountain

Adam Fountain

LOWER PARK

Oak Fountain

Aviary

Umbrella Fountain

Great Cascade

Pine Fountains

Favorite Fountain • Great Glasshouse

Roman Fountain

Triton Fountain

GREAT PALACE

Chessboard Cascade

Toward the Cottage

UPPER PARK

Neptune Fountain

0   110   220 yds

Toward Oranienbaum

🕐 **Half a day**

STRELNA
On the way to Peterhof note (on the right) Strelna Palace (dating from the first half of the 18th century), along with the grand-ducal

residences of Mikhailovka and Znamenka, which were built for the sons of Nicholas I. Restored in 2003, following designs by architect Nicolas Mechetti, Strelna Palace is now the maritime residence of the president of the Russian Federation.

Peterhof (Петергоф) is one of the oldest summer palaces in the region of St Petersburg, and it is perhaps the most exotic of all because of its unusual seaside situation. In the 19th century Peterhof was one of the world's most extraordinary palace and garden complexes, covering a total area of nearly 2,500 acres. Like the city 20 miles away it is named after the first Emperor of Russia (Peterhof means "Peter's Court"). Peter the Great built a preliminary residence here in 1710, on the edge of a plateau of land commanding fine views of the Gulf of Finland. Then, in place of this small wooden building, in which he would habitually stay on his way to Kronstadt ▲ *192*, he proceeded to construct a far bigger palace (1714), broadly sketched out by himself as a basic plan from which his architect Johann Braunstein worked.

UPPER PARK

The Upper Park (VERKHNY SAD; Верхний сад) ". . . is no less beautiful than that of the King of France" according to the archives. This area served as an ostentatious front courtyard to the Great Palace, the main residence of Peterhof. It was to the Great Palace that Peter the Great summoned the entire corps of foreign diplomats to celebrate the official inauguration of the building that became known as the "Russian Versailles".

Lili

GREAT PALACE ★

As we see it now the Great Palace (BOLSHOY DVORETS; Большой дворец) still has the exterior planned by the Empress Elizabeth I ● 37. After 1745 she had the initial building altered by the architect Bartolomeo Rastrelli ● 84, who, after enlarging Peter I's original palace, added to it a couple of single-floor galleries, each ending with a pavilion (a church on the east side and an armorial pavilion of the west side). He also surrounded the Upper Park with a long railing punctuated by broad pillars, later designing a formal enfilade in the purest Baroque style.

BAROQUE STAIRCASE
The grand staircase was entirely restored in 1985.

FORMAL STAIRCASE. The stairway to the second floor is typical of the Russian Baroque period. Its décor, designed by Rastrelli in about 1750, combines richly carved and gilded elements in wood (mostly limewood) with numerous trompe-l'oeil features.

CHESME HALL. Contiguous with the ballroom is a large space dedicated to the naval victory of Chesme (1770); this was altered by Yury Velten ● 86 to house major commemorative paintings by Hackert (1737–1807).

THRONE ROOM. In the Throne Room, alongside portraits of Russian sovereigns, is a canvas by the Danish painter Vigilius Erichsen of Catherine II on her horse Brilliant. There are also four pictures of the Battle of Chesme by Joseph Wright of Derby. The Audience Chamber, with its décor by Rastrelli, offers an interesting collection of Russian marquetry gaming tables which date from the latter part of the 18th century.

WHITE DINING ROOM ★. The table set in the White Dining Room, whose neoclassical décor was redesigned by Velten toward 1775, displays a complete set of Wedgwood china delivered from England in 1768.

CHINESE ROOMS. On either side of the Portrait Hall are extravagant Chinese Rooms decorated by Vallin de la Mothe with walls set with lacquer screens and exotic marquetry floors.

LAVISH STUCCO
The walls of the White Dining Room are decorated with white stucco bas-reliefs.

FOUNTAINS AT PETERHOF

The wide variety of fountains at Peterhof is the principal feature of the park. Elsewhere (notably at Versailles) all the surviving fountains are classical in design; not so at Peterhof, where their extravagance and sheer playfulness give us a vivid idea of the atmosphere that must have reigned in a park of this kind during the early 18th century. The Great Cascade, with its Samson Fountain, is the most impressive of all.

FESTIVALS AT PETERHOF ✪

The Baroque masterpiece of Peterhof is now a site for several festivals, the most popular of which are those marking the opening and closing of the fountains (in May and October respectively). Cultural events held between these two festivals include the music festival (June) and the festival of the city of Peterhof (July).

GREAT CASCADE
On the slope between the upper and lower terraces, the Great Cascade is a major feature of Peterhof. The statue of *Samson and the Lion* symbolizes the Russian victory over the Swedes at Poltava (1709).

MARLY CASCADE
▲ *260*. Also called the "Golden Mountain", the Marly Cascade is made of white marble and plaques of gilded copper, which cover its successive levels.

CHECKERBOARD CASCADE
The water spouts from the jaws of fierce dragons above giant sloping checkerboards.

THE SUN
The perpetually spinning sun and its silvery rays.

ROMAN FOUNTAINS
Erected in 1739 at the foot of the Checkerboard Cascade, these statues are reminiscent of those by the fountains of St Peter's in Rome. They were reconstituted in 1792; gilded bronze masks spout water from their plinths.

OAK STUDY
This room, with its carved oak boiseries after drawings by Nicolas Pineau (1684–1754), contains assorted personal possessions of Peter I.

A SEA VIEW
Monplaisir, on the seafront, was a favorite with Peter the Great, who liked to spend several months a year there. William Coxe, visiting the palace in 1784, wrote: "We can form an idea of the austere simplicity in which this sovereign was accustomed to live . . .".

PORTRAIT HALL. In 1764 the Portrait Hall in the central part of the Palace was decorated by the architect Vallin de la Mothe ● 86 with a rare ensemble of 368 portraits of women painted by Count Pietro Rotari.

PARTRIDGE ROOM. The adjoining Partridge Room takes its name from its partridge-design hangings. These hangings were woven in Lyons, France, after cartoons by Philippe de la Salle.

DIVAN ROOM. This room has walls covered with Chinese silk, and contains an enormous sofa framed by a balustrade in the Turkish manner.

CROWN ROOM. The Crown Room is also covered in 17th-century Chinese silk. During the 18th century the imperial crown was kept in this room when the Court was residing at Peterhof.

LOWER PARK

LOWER PARK (NIZHNY PARK; Нижний парк) was originally planted with lime trees, oaks, elms and maples from Holland, Germany, Estonia and the regions of Moscow and Novgorod. The geometrical parterres are crowded with the sculptures and fountains that were at that time deemed to be the essential features of any princely park. At the ends of the domain's various prospects there are pavilions designed for the pleasures of the Russian sovereigns and their courtiers.

HERMITAGE PAVILION (PAVILION ERMITAZH; павильон Эрмитаж). In the main room of the Hermitage Pavilion, used for dining, there is a mechanism that lifts the central section of the table, loaded with the dishes ordered by guests, from the first floor straight to the second floor.

MARLY PALACE (DVORETS MARLY; дворец Марли). Marly Palace, a favorite of Peter the Great, is furnished according to his own simple taste.

MONPLAISIR ★ (MONPLEZIR; Монплезир). In 1714, work began on the construction of a small palace the far end of the Lower Park. It was named Monplaisir after the French palace on which it was based. Monplaisir's paintings gallery, which has a ceiling decorated to a design by Philippe Pillement (1684–1730), contains a collection of Dutch and Flemish pictures of battle scenes. In 2001, some of the

BENOIS MUSEUM
East of the Palace are former court buildings
which now contain a museum dedicated to
the Benois family ● *104*.

MONPLAISIR
In 1723 the Marquis
de Campredon gave
this report to Louis
XV: "One enters the
house by way of a
remarkably well-kept
garden. It is square in
shape, with double
banks of greenery on
either side,
contiguous to the
rooms, in which one
can walk unseen . . .
lulled by the sound of
the great fountain in
the garden."

palace's attractive buildings, including the imperial baths and
the Chinese garden around them, were opened to the public.
CATHERINE WING (EKATERININSKY KORPUS; Екатерининский
корпус). In the Catherine Wing, added to Monplaisir in the
1740's, a remarkable china service , made at the imperial
St Petersburg works between 1809 and 1817, is on display. It is
known as the Guriev Service, after the director of the factory.
The gilded chandeliers in the Yellow
Salon, of pasteboard and carved wood,
are remarkable for their quality.

ALEXANDRIA PARK

IMPERIAL STABLES (TSARSKIE
KONIUSHNI; Царские конюшни). Beyond
the Benois Museum stand the extensive
imperial stables (which are now a rest
home and closed to the public). They are
the work of the architect Nikolai Benois
(1856–1928) and their extraordinary
neo-Gothic style bears witness to the
Czar Nicholas I's pronounced taste for this style.

Nicholas I's study.

GOTHIC CHAPEL (KAPELLA; капелла). By continuing toward
the east through the gates of the Alexandria Park you will
reach the imperial family's private oratory, a Gothic chapel
built (1831–3) to a design by the Berlin architect Karl
Schinkel (1781–1841).
COTTAGE (KOTTEDZH; Коттедж)★. You can reach this small
pavilion (right) either by walking through Alexandria Park or
by car. The cottage was constructed by the architect Adam
Menelaws between 1826 and 1829, and it has now been
carefully restored to display collections of objects and
furniture, along with Russian porcelain and crystal in the
dining room. The original stairway leads to the study of
Nicholas I, from which he communicated with his fleet by
semaphore. The Czarina's study has a stained-glass screen
and a remarkable frieze around the bay window. Another
interesting feature is the intricate star-burst ceiling of the
Grand Drawing Room next door to the Czarina's study.
NEO-GOTHIC STATION. To the north of Alexandria Park stands
the picturesque neo-Gothic railway station, which was built by
Nikolai Benois.

"[The Cottage] is a
small house built in
the new Gothic style
currently fashionable
in England."
Astolphe de Custine

▲ PALACES ON THE OUTSKIRTS
ORANIENBAUM

COURTYARD/GARDEN
Like Peterhof, the
Great Palace is
fronted by a huge
courtyard/garden
surrounded by open
land. Two levels of
terraces and steps
link it to a lower
garden area.

CHINESE STUDY
The fine marquetry
floors and boiseries of
the Chinese Study
illustrate large exotic
scenes. All are by
Russian master
cabinet-makers.

About 25 miles from St Petersburg, not far from
Peterhof ▲ 256, is the Oranienbaum estate, which
occupies a comparable sloping site and dates from exactly
the same period. It was originally given in 1710 by Peter
the Great to his companion-in-arms and political advisor
Prince Alexander Menshikov ▲ 161 as a summer residence,
but it soon reverted to the Crown and was regularly
embellished in the 18th century. Until the 1990s, foreign
tourists were excluded from Oranienbaum, which stands
directly opposite the Kronstadt Naval Base ▲ 192.
Nevertheless, it is one of the very few residences around St
Petersburg that did not suffer heavily during World War Two,
and has more or less remained in its original state.

GREAT PALACE

Giovanni Maria Fontana began the
building works in 1710. The Great Palace
(BOLSHOY DVORETS; Большой дворец)
takes full advantage of its elevated
position, with a central section and two
single-story galleries curving round on
either side to domed pavilions (a chapel
to the west and a Japanese pavilion to
the east). Long occupied by government
bodies, the Great Palace, also known as
the Menchikov Palace, is nowonce again
open to visitors.

CHINESE PALACE ★

Detail of the Glass
Study in the Chinese
Palace.

The stucco walls and
ceilings of the
Chinese Palace
(KITAISKY DVORETS;
Китайский дворец),
built by Rinaldi ● 86
in 1762, provide the
background for
frescos and oil
paintings by Italian artists. The interior style is is Rococo,
while outside it is a less flamboyant Baroque.
GLASS STUDY. On the floor, once of glass, are two
extraordinary "smalt" marquetry tables.
CHINESE KITCHEN. In the Chinese Kitchen and the Cavalry
House, both nearby, are objects from the Far East and 17th-
and 18th-century paintings.

PETER III'S PALACE

Near the Great Palace is the Palace of Peter III (DVORETS PETRA III; дворец Петра III), to which Oranienbaum devolved in 1743. Peter III, nephew of Empress Elizabeth I ● *36* and a monarch of rabid military bent, built a fortress here called Peterstadt, where he had Russian troops parade about in German uniforms. Nothing remains of it but this small, two-story palace, constructed by Antonio Rinaldi ● *86* and decorated in Chinese style with silk hangings, lacquer paintings and dress cabinets. The Picture Hall houses Italian and Flemish paintings.

"SLIDING HILL" ★

Heading toward the sea, you come to "Sliding Hill" (PAVILION KATALNOY GORKY; павильон Катальной горки; currently closed for repairs), also designed by Rinaldi (1762–74). Built on a helical plan, until the early 19th century it had an extension in the form of a 1,500-foot wooden colonnade, in the middle of which was a *montagne russe* ▲ *185* for the diversion of the court (a model of this is displayed on the first floor). From the second-floor windows you can see the island of Kronstadt, and notably the dome of its huge Byzantine-style cathedral (1902–13).

ROUND ROOM. The central salon, or Round Room, still has its original *scagliola* floor, made of powdered marble mixed to imitate colored marble marquetry.

PEARL GLASS
The Glass Study in the Chinese Palace, a masterpiece of extravagance, has eleven panels and two door lintels in pearl glass made in the workshops of the great Russian scientist and writer Mikhail Lomonosov, after whom Oranienbaum was renamed in 1948.

MEISSEN PORCELAIN
In the Porcelain Room is a rare series of Meissen figurines, which symbolize the prestige of the Russian Empire.

263

▲ PALACES ON THE OUTSKIRTS
TSARSKOE SELO

🕐 **Half a day**

Although history tends to associate its name with Catherine the Great the palace of Tsarskoe Selo (TSARSKOÏE SELO; Царское Село) was built at the beginning of the 18th century. In 1710 Peter the Great gave his second wife, Catherine, a small property 15 miles south of St Petersburg. When Elizabeth, Catherine's daughter, came to the throne in 1741 she found the house too small; and in 1743 she commissioned Mikhail Zemtsov to enlarge it. This he did by adding two wings, linked to the main building by single-story galleries leading to pavilions. The finished

ensemble, however, lacked unity, and in 1752 Bartolomeo Rastrelli ● *84* was asked to entirely redesign it. The building we see today is the result of his work, is a surprising 900 feet in breadth.

CATHERINE PALACE ★

FAÇADE. The columns, with composite capitals, are themselves supported by massive Atlas figures; they punctuate most of the bays in the façade of the Catherine Palace (BOLSHOY EKATERININSKY DVORETS; Большой Екатерининский дворец), which incorporates no fewer than five projecting and pedimented buildings. The series of diverse rooms within, restored in the 1960's, gives an idea of the development of the Russian interior through three very different epochs.

STATE STAIRCASE. This was installed between 1860 and 1864 by Hippolyte Monighetti (1819–78) in the center of the palace. On the upper landing are folding chairs with the monogram of Elizabeth I, made in the workshops of Tula ● *60*.

Catherine Palace.

GREAT HALL. Decorated in a generous Baroque style, with a painted ceiling representing "The Triumph of Russia", this immense room is the focal point of the palace as it was redesigned by Rastrelli in the late 18th century.

State Staircase.

KNIGHTS' BANQUETING HALL. In this hall the table is set with china that was made to order

Great Hall (detail below).

for Catherine II by the Gardner works in Moscow. The banqueting hall was formerly heated by a pair of enormous Dutch faience stoves.

PICTURE GALLERY. There are 117 works altogether, by painters such as Luca Giordano, David Teniers and Jean-Marc Nattier, which hang here side by side in the decorative spirit of the 18th century.

AMBER ROOM. This famous rococo room – presented to Peter the Great by the King of Prussia in 1716 and then lost at the end of World War Two – has been reopened to visitors since 2003. Twenty-four years of work have been necessary to restore its exquisite panels, decorated in mosaics and amber.

FIRST APARTMENT. The rooms of the first apartment, converted by the Scottish architect Charles Cameron ● *86* for the heir to the throne Czarevich Paul Petrovich ● *37*, are decorated in the neoclassical style, Catherine II's favorite. In the GREEN DINING ROOM ★ (details on the left and right of these pages) the accent is deliberately innovative; on the ceiling, which is bare of ornamentation, are ample white stucco figures in relief, alternating with tall matching antique tripods. The BEDROOM is even more surprising, with its multiple colonnettes delineating the alcove and punctuating the walls.

OLD GARDEN

All too often the visit to Tsarskoe Selo is confined to the Catherine Palace, but the park and its many pavilions hold much of interest. Below the eastern façade of the Palace extends the Old Garden (STARY SAD; Старый сад); here are the Upper and Lower Baths, built by the architect Ilya Neelov in the late 1770's.

HERMITAGE

Down from the Old Garden stands the Hermitage (ERMITAZH; павильон Эрмитаж), built by Rastrelli, where receptions were held in the summer; nearby is the Hermitage Kitchen, in a remarkably composite style.

AGATE PAVILION ★

In the vicinity of the Palace the Old Garden is delineated by two of the most interesting buildings of Tsarskoe Selo: the Agate Pavilion (AGATOVY PAVILION; Агатовый павильон) and the Cameron Gallery, both built after 1780.
COLD BATHS. The first floor of the Agate Pavilion was occupied by the Tsarina's cold baths. On the second floor the AGATE BEDROOMS open on to a hanging garden, which in turn gives access to the elegant CAMERON GALLERY. There are also a large salon and two studies with walls richly covered in semi-precious agate from the Urals, after which the pavilion is named. (These rooms are currently closed to visitors.)

CATHERINE PARK

The lower reaches of Catherine Park (EKATERININSKY PARK; Екатерининский парк) are taken up by a lake; nearby is a series of follies.

GROTTO, OR MORNING SALON. Originally decorated with thousands of seashells, the grotto was built in the reign of Elizabeth I by Rastrelli. Catherine II liked to come here from time to time, early in the morning, after her marathon work sessions.

AROUND THE LAKE. The Turkish-inspired "Admiralty" and the Chesme Column (CHESMENSKAYA KOLONA; Чесменская колонна) in the middle of the lake are succeeded by the Turkish baths built by Monighetti toward 1850. The Pyramid, where Catherine II's dogs are buried, is close to the Palladian bridge. Other monumental features include the Orlov Gate and the impressive ruined tower designed by Yury Velten ● 86.

UPPER GARDEN. North of Catherine Park are the Evening Hall, the Concert Hall and the Creaking Pavilion. The Great Caprice, an elaborate arch standing at the end of the avenue that separates Catherine Park from Alexander Park, has a pagoda-like roof supported on Ruskeala marble columns.

ALEXANDER PARK

ALEXANDER PARK (ALEKANDROVSKY PARK; Александровский парк) is named for the Grand Duke Alexander Pavlovich, the future Alexander I and favorite grandson of Catherine II.

CHINESE VILLAGE. This echoes the pavilions described, with its painted roofs, its theater and its various quaint bridges, such as the cross-shaped one with four ramps.

ALEXANDER PALACE (ALEKSANDROVSKY DVORETS; Александровский дворец). This classical building, built by Quarenghi in 1792 for the future Emperor, was also the favorite residence of the last members of the imperial family.

KAGUL OBELISK
This monument stands opposite the side wing of Catherine Palace.

THE ARCH
On the way to Catherine Palace you pass beneath an arch; this communicates with the Lyceum, a building converted into a school in the 19th century. The poet Pushkin was educated here.

АЛЕКСАНДРУ СЕРГЕЕВИЧУ
ПУШКИНУ.

▲ PALACES ON THE OUTSKIRTS PAVLOVSK

Pavlovsk is the most elegant of the summer palaces around St Petersburg, in its decoration and the quality and quantity of the objects it contains. Although PAVLOVSK (Павловск) is no more than four miles from Tsarskoe Selo, visitors from abroad seldom take the trouble to go there. None the less, there is a striking contrast between the majestic aspect of the latter and the more homely character of the former. The histories of the two palaces would have been very similar had it not been for an adventure unique in the annals of the 18th century. In order to get away from the court, and above all to visit the capitals of Western Europe and acquire works of art for their residence, Paul Petrovich and the Grand Duchess Maria Fyodorovna set out on a tour lasting over a year. They left St Petersburg on September 19, 1781 and embarked on a 428-day journey that would take them the length and breadth of Europe, with the objective of embellishing the palace of Pavlovsk.

GREAT PALACE ★

STATE APARTMENTS. The central block of the building is classical in structure. On the second floor are the apartments of Paul and Maria Fyodorovna, set around a central salon known as the Greek Hall. On the Grand Duke's side this leads on to a room called the Hall of War and on the Grand Duchess's side the Hall of Peace. The décor, begun by Charles Cameron ● 86, was mostly completed by Vincenzo Brenna (1740–1819), an Italian artist whom Paul and Maria Fyodorovna met in Poland on their travels.

GALLERIES. After Paul I's accession in 1796 Brenna was commissioned to enlarge the palace, now an imperial residence. He heightened the two single-story side galleries

Paul Petrovich and Maria Fyodorovna.

PAVLOVSK
The original wooden houses on the site, known as Krik and Krak, were succeeded by two small palaces, also in wood, called Marienthal ("Maria's Valley") and Paulslust ("Paul's Joy"). No doubt these were still considered inadequate, so the decision was made to build yet again. The result was what we know as Pavlovsk Palace (Pavlovsky Dvorets; Павловский дворец), much larger and in brick; it was designed by Charles Cameron ● 86, one of Catherine II's favorite architects.

A LAVISH GIFT
Originally a hunting estate, the
domain of Pavlovsk was given by
Catherine II to her son Paul,
when the Grand Duchess produced a male
heir for the dynasty, Alexander, on
December 12, 1777.

Rotunda
Alleya Krasnovo Molodtsa

Battery Tower

Amphitheater

Mausoleu

PAVLOVSK PARK

Great Cascade

Rose Pavilion

Iron Gates

Ulitsa Revolyutsii

Detskosselskaya Ulitsa

Humpbacked Bridge
Cold Bath
Centaur Bridge
Colonnade of Apollo

Temple of Friendship

Dairy

PALACE

4-ia Paradnaya Alleya

**Pavilion
of Three Graces**

Aviary

Marienthal
Pond

Obelisk

Ulitsa Marata

Ulitsa Revolyutsii

Ul. Karla Lebknehta

Ulitsa Michurina

0   220   440 yds

Slavianka

☑ **Half a day**

VESTIBULE
The Vestibule
(where the tour
begins) was decorated
by Voronikhin with
twelve allegorical
sculptures in the
Egyptian style, very
fashionable at the
time. On the upper
landing can still be
seen the elaborate
stucco décor designed
by Brenna.

built by Cameron. He then added two ample pavilions to
house the new Throne Room and chapel; and finally he
included two other service wings, on the same quarter-circle
plan.
HALL OF WAR. The carved and gilded wooden *torchères* of the
Hall of War (opposite page, top left) are additional tangible
proof of the special talent of Russian artisans for woodwork,
such as the chairs in the Greek Hall and the marquetry floors
of the Grand Duchess's apartment.
BOUDOIR. The Boudoir is decorated with porphyry columns
and painted pilasters brought from Italy by the royal couple
(left page, center).

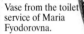

▲ PALACES ON THE OUTSKIRTS
PAVLOVSK

Vase from the toilet service of Maria Fyodorovna.

GRAND DUCHESS'S STATE APARTMENTS. In the apartments of Maria Fyodorovna (center) is a magnificent series of Gobelins and Savonnerie tapestries, along with a sixty-four piece toilet service in Sèvres porcelain kept in a glass cabinet opposite the bed, which was given to Paul I and the Grand Duchess by Louis XVI and Marie-Antoinette during their visit to France.

THE ROSE
Maria Fyodorovna dedicated a pavilion to her favorite flower, the rose, a motif which covers the chairs and everyday objects.

". . . 1,500,000 roubles are invested in perpetuity for the upkeep of Pavlovsk . . I give to my son the Grand Duke Mikhail the castle of Pavlovsk . . . the Grand Duke Mikhail will gain possession of Pavlovsk on condition that the castle, the gardens, parks, orangeries, hospital and invalids' home . . . that, in a word, all the dependencies of that beautiful place, are maintained . . . "
Maria Fyodorovna

PICTURE GALLERY. In the picture gallery Russian furniture and vases relate harmoniously with European paintings and French objects in gilded bronze purchased on the orders of Paul I, who originally wanted them for his St Petersburg residence, the Mikhailovsky Castle ▲ 229.

THRONE ROOM ★. In the Throne Room, or State Dining Room (above left), are magnificent displays of porcelain ● 64 from the various palace collections, both French (Sèvres) and Russian (St Petersburg). The dominant feature of this room is its enormous ceiling fresco by the set designer Pietro di Gottardo Gonzaga.

FAMILY ROOM. The Family Room on the first floor is especially touching, with personal mementos of the palace's founders, drawings of Maria Fyodorovna and a charming family portrait.

CORNER SALON. With its 1815 décor by the architect Carlo Rossi ● 86, the Corner Salon shows the evolution of taste during the reign of Alexander I.

BALLROOM. In the gay pink and blue ballroom are four major canvases by the French artist Hubert Robert, of which Paul I was particularly fond.

MUSEUM OF INTERIORS. On the third floor the Museum of Interiors exhibits a collection of Russian furniture and objects from the late 18th and 19th centuries.

> "A home, a colonnade, a temple at Pavlovsk give me
> greater joy than all the beauties of Italy."
>
> Maria Fyodorovna

PARK AT PAVLOVSK

AVIARY. Near the palace stands an aviary, designed by Cameron, in which the Grand Duchess bred her songbirds.
TEMPLE OF FRIENDSHIP. Further on is the Temple of Friendship, also built by Cameron, which symbolized the reconciliation between Paul Petrovich and Catherine II. The walls bear depictions of platonic and romantic love.

THE SLAVYANKA
On the banks of the Slavyanka, and overlooking it, are the foundation obelisk and the Marienthal staircase, formerly a landing stage.

PIL TOWER. Beyond the cast-iron bridge designed by Rossi and the amphitheater is the thatched Pil Tower.
NEW WOODS. In the New Woods overlooking the Slavyanka are the monument to Maria Fyodorovna's parents, the Duke and Duchess of Württemberg (their profiles appear on a marble pyramid inside) and the mausoleum of Paul I.
VANISHED PAVILIONS. Other favorite retreats of the owners of Pavlovsk (the Old Chalet, the Elizabeth Pavilion by the Slavyanka Valley, the New Chalet and the farm in the Great Star area) have disappeared since World War Two. The Great Star is formed by twelve paths which converge on a statue of Apollo at the center. A statue of a mythological figure stands at the entrance to each path.
ROSE PAVILION. This place, much loved by Maria Fyodorovna (especially after she became a widow), stands on an expanse of parkland known as the White Birch. It was here that the Dowager Empress met her son Alexander I ● *36* after his victory over Napoleon. In seventeen days the decorator Pietro Gonzaga managed to add a ballroom, dedicated to the liberator of Europe. The current restoration of this building, so dear to the creator of Pavlovsk, at a time when Russia is going through times of special difficulty, is a striking symbol of the nation's deep attachment to its history and culture.

PAVLOVSK PARK
(Pavlovsky Park; Павловский парк). The grounds of Pavlovsk, covering nearly 2,000 acres, were a major interest of Paul Petrovich and Maria Fyodorovna from the start. They beautified the estate with artificial lakes and follies. The meandering river Slavyanka served as the basis for Cameron's first landscape project.

▲ PALACES ON THE OUTSKIRTS
GATCHINA

APARTMENTS
The State Staircase leads directly to the Great Antechamber, which is followed by the Marble Dining Room and Paul I's Throne Room (the tapestries here were a gift from Louis XVI). In the White Room (below) the walls are covered in stucco by Rinaldi.

In 1766 Catherine II gave Gatchina (Гатчина) to Count Orlov. On this estate, 28 miles from St Petersburg, the architect Antonio Rinaldi ● *86* built a country residence. After 1783 Gatchina belonged to Paul Petrovich, who had it altered to some extent by the architect Vincenzo Brenna ▲ *268*. Following Paul I's assassination, the palace was left empty until Nicholas I ordered its restoration in 1844.

GATCHINA PALACE

State bedroom of Maria Fyodorovna (right).

ENGLISH GARDEN
An English garden was fashioned from the original hunting estate, described by Orlov in a letter to Rousseau: "Sixty versts from St Petersburg I have a property where the knolls surrounding the lakes are an inspiration ... to reverie." The park is filled with picturesque monuments, notably the Chesme Obelisk.

FAÇADE. Gatchina Palace (GATCHINSKY DVORETS; Гатчинский дворец), faced entirely in limestone, is made up of a central block with galleries on either side leading to service wings. The plan is quadrilateral, with an inner courtyard.
"SQUARE" WINGS OF THE ARSENAL AND KITCHENS. Under Nicholas I the main central building was converted into a memorial of filial devotion, and comfortable apartments were set up in the lateral wings.

INTERIOR DÉCOR. The décor of the central building nearly all dates from Rinaldi's time (elaborate marquetry floors and fine stuccos).

GATCHINA PARK

After the death of Orlov the park at Gatchina (GATCHINSKY PARK; Гатчинский парк) was embellished with several new buildings. By the White and Silver lakes are two pavilions: the Venus Pavilion, a copy of the Prince de Condé's original at Chantilly, in France, and the Birch Pavilion, whose rustic exterior belies an interior of great refinement.

Practical information

◆ GETTING THERE

USEFUL ADDRESSES

→ CONSULATES OF THE RUSSIAN FEDERATION

■ IN THE UK
5 Kensington Palace Gardens
London W8 4QP
Tel. 020 7499 1029
Visa Information:
Tel. 0906 550 8960
(£1/min.)
www.russialink.org.uk

■ IN THE USA
– 2641 Tunlaw Rd
NW, Washington, DC 20007
Tel. (202) 939 8907
– 9 East 91st St
New York, NY 10128
Tel. (212) 348 0926
– 2790 Green St
San Francisco,
CA 94123
Tel. (415) 928 6878
www.russianembassy.com

■ CANADA
3655 Avenue du
Musée, Montreal
Quebec H3G 2EI
Tel. (514) 843 5901

→ TOURIST OFFICES

■ IN THE UK
Russian National
Tourist Office
70 Piccadilly
London W1J 8HP
Tel. 020 7495 7555
Intourist Travel Ltd
7 Wellington Terrace
London W2 4LW
Tel. 020 7727 4100
www.intourist.com

■ IN THE USA
Russian National
Tourist Office
224 West 30th St,
Suite 701,
New York, NY 10001
Tel. (646) 473 2233
Tollfree (US):
Tel. 877 221 7120
www.russia-travel.com

FORMALITIES

→ TOURIST INVITATION
Contact your nearest consulate or consult one of the websites listed below where you can download a visa application form and get the "invitation" you need to enter the Russian Federation (and where all other formalities are clearly explained). The invitation must come from a business relation or a friend in Russia, or confirmation of your hotel booking in St Petersburg.
www.russianvisas.org
www.waytorussia.net
www.traveldocs.com/ru/

→ VISAS AND PASSPORTS
Russian visas come in six types, each corresponding to your purpose of visit: short 72-hour, tourist, student, business, personal or transit. Tariffs vary a lot. Tourist visas cost between US$50 and US$150 and take at least eight working days to be processed. The price for a business visa varies on the length of stay and the speed at which you need your visa. Business visas cost from US$80 to US$300, depending on the processing speed.

■ PASSPORT
Must be valid for six months beyond your intended stay.

→ TRAVEL INSURANCE
Your insurance policy must cover medical expenses as well as costs of repatriation and funeral expenses in the case of death. It must be issued by an insurance company that has a reinsurance agreement with a Russian equivalent company.

→ CUSTOMS
When entering the Russian Federation you must fill out one of the two copies of the customs declaration form provided, indicating the amount of foreign currency as well as any valuables you are bringing into the country. Be sure to keep this form safe, together with the receipts for all currency exchange transactions and purchases as you may be required to produce these documents upon leaving the country. You must fill out the second copy of the customs form at the end of your stay. The amount declared when you leave the country must not be superior to the amount declared when you arrived.

→ DRIVING LICENSE
An international driving license is strongly recommended.

MONEY

→ CURRENCY
The ruble.
Warning: rubles issued before 1998 are no longer valid.

■ COINS
1, 2, 5 rubles and kopecks (1 r = 100 k)

■ BILLS
10, 50, 100 and 500 rubles.

→ EXCHANGE
Rubles cannot be converted. Exchange can only take place in the Russian Federation.
US$1 = 26.796 rubles,
CA$1 = 23.97 rubles
UK £1 = 50 rubles,
(at the time of going to press). There's more information on money on p. 279.

TELEPHONE

Dial 00 (from the UK) or 011 (from the US) + 7 (Russia) + 812 (area code for St Petersburg), followed by the seven-digit number.

TIME DIFFERENCE

GMT + 3.
St Petersburg is eight hours ahead of Eastern Standard (New York) time and three hours ahead of London all year round.

CLIMATE

→ GEOGRAPHY
St Petersburg is the most northerly of the world's large metropolises. Its geographical location – at the mouth of the Gulf Stream, close to the Arctic Circle – is the reason for the extreme changes and capricious variations of its continental climate.

→ TEMPERATURES AND RAINFALL
Winters at this latitude are extremely hard, and the short springs and falls are often wet and rainy. Summers are usually mild. See the chart opposite.

WHEN TO GO

The best months to visit St Petersburg are May to July, September to Oct, December to January.

■ MARCH–APRIL
The city is quieter, with fewer visitors, and prices are not as high, especially for accommodation.

■ MID-MAY–MID-JULY
Days seem never-ending during the city's "white nights" that occur around the summer solstice (June 11 to early July). This is the perfect time for romantic night-time walks along the Neva. It is also the festival season (see Celebrations and Festivals p. 284).

■ SEP–OCT
In fall visitors can

enjoy in peace the lovely colors of St Petersburg's numerous parks and gardens, as well as cruise down the Neva before it becomes solid ice.

■ **DEC–JAN**
There are barely five hours of sunlight a day in December. With luck you may see the Neva frozen over and may be able to walk on the icy solid Gulf of Finland. The Russians hold four end-of-year celebrations: on Dec. 25 and 31 and on Jan. 6 and 13 (Roman Catholic and Orthodox Christmasses and New Year's Days, respectively). Various public events take place (see p. 284), and major hotels and restaurants also organize end-of-year parties.

■ **"WHITE DAYS"**
Since 2000, the city has had a winter celebration of its culture, named after the white covering that lies on the ground between November and March. There are programs of ballet, concerts and art exhibitions, and hotels offer attractive rates at this time (except Christmas and New Year). Browse www. whitedays.com for more information.

TRAVEL

→ **BY AIR**
From the UK, Aeroflot and British Airways operate

direct flights to St Petersburg. In the USA, Continental offer direct flights to St Petersburg from Los Angeles. Other major airlines offer connecting flights. International flights arrive in St Petersburg at Pulkovo 2, while domestic flights arrive at Pulkovo 1 (see also p. 276), both about 10 miles south of the city. Check with the following airlines for details of fares and conditions:

■ **FROM THE UK**
Aeroflot
Tel. 020 7355 2233
www.aeroflot.co.uk
Austrian airlines
Tel. 0845 601 0948
www.aua.com
British Airways
Tel. 0870 850 9 850
www.ba.com
Finnair
Tel. 0870 241 4411
www.finnair.com
Lufthansa
Tel. 0870 8377 747
www.lufthansa.co.uk

■ **FROM THE US**
Aeroflot
Tel. 1 888 340 6400
www.aeroflot.com
British Airways
Tel. 1 800 AIRWAYS
www.ba.com
Continental
Tel. 1 800 231 0856
www.continental.com
Delta
Tel. 1 800 241 4141
www.delta.com
Lufthansa
Tel. 1 800 399 5838
www.lufthansa.com/us

→ **BY TRAIN AND SEA FROM THE UK**
■ **BY TRAIN**
Eurostar from London Waterloo to Brussels,

then another train to Berlin. From Berlin the 'Moskva Express' travels direct to St Petersburg (journey time about 36 hours). Trains leave daily (except Sat.) June–Sep.; Tue., Thu. and Sun. only Oct.–May. A Belarus transit visa is required, as well as your Russian visa.
Information
Eurostar (London)
Tel. 0870 160 6600
www.eurostar.com
For train information throughout Europe:
www.seat61.com
■ **BY SEA**
There are sea links between London, Göteborg, Oslo and Helsinki, and numerous cruises in the Baltic Sea that include St Petersburg on their route. Contact the Russian National Tourist Office or Intourist Travel Ltd (see p. 274) or a specialized tour operator.

HEALTH

→ **FIRST-AID KIT**
Take your usual medicines with you, such as antibiotics and anti-diarrhea tablets, but make sure all packages are intact in order to avoid trouble at customs when entering the country. If you are undergoing a course of treatment, keep a prescription with you bearing the generic names of the drugs you need.

→ **VACCINATIONS**
None required from European or American visitors,

however DT polio, typhoid, and hepatitis A inoculations are recommended. Any visitor intending to stay in the Russian Federation for more than three months must produce a certificate confirming that they are not HIV-positive. This certificate must mention their passport number and be signed by a doctor. It remains valid for three months. More about health p. 279.

VOLTAGE

220 Volts. Plugs are similar to the straight pins of continental European plugs, but slightly thinner. Adapters and power converters are recommended for all American appliances.

PHOTOGRAPHY AND VIDEO

Film, tapes, batteries available from specialized stores, but make sure you take enough equipment with you. In most national museums you can take photographs without a flash for a nominal fee. Never take pictures in theaters or circuses.

RUSSIA ON THE NET

General information: cultural and travel information on St Petersburg:
www.travel.spb.ru
http://petersburgcity. com
Travelers' Yellow Pages online:
www.infoservices.com/ stpete
Travel information on the Russian Federation:
www.geographia.com/ russia
www.russian-tours. spb.ru

TEMPERATURE AND RAINFALL						
	JAN.	FEB.	MARCH	APRIL	MAY	JUNE
T. maxi °F	9	10	18	32	43	52
T. mini °F	19	23	32	46	59	68
R. (inches)	1½	1¼	1	1⅓	1½	2
	JULY	AUG.	SEP.	OCT.	NOV.	DEC.
T. maxi °F	55	55	48	39	28	18
T. mini °F	70	68	59	48	36	27
R. (inches)	2¾	3	2¼	2	1¾	1½

◆ STAYING IN ST PETERSBURG FROM A TO Z

Accommodation, arrivals and departures, bridges

When in St Petersburg you do not need to dial the city code 812 before the seven-digit phone number.

ACCOMMODATION

The number of foreign visitors to St Petersburg has been growing steadily in recent years, and unfortunately the Russian hotel infrastructure has not been able to keep up with the demand. It is still undergoing major transformation, and prices vary greatly according to the season (they actually double during the "white nights" period from mid-May to mid-July). Hotels with fewer than three stars are practically non-existent in the city center.

■ **HOTELS**
Average price for a double room, excluding breakfast:
★★★
US$55–140 (add $13 per day if half-board)
★★★★
US$150–470 (add $25 if half-board)
★★★★★ from US$380 (add up to $110 if half-board)

■ **YOUTH HOSTELS**
US$19–44 per night per person.
www.ryh.ru

■ **STAYING WITH A RUSSIAN FAMILY**
US$38–63 per room
www.homestay.ru
To reserve contact a tour operator (see under Useful addresses p. 283.)

■ **APARTMENTS**
US$38–190 per night for the apartment (may vary according to the size of the apartment and to the distance from the city center).

■ **RENTAL AGENCIES**
Becar
Bolshoy Sampsonievsky Prospekt 61, Business-Center Becar

Tel. 812 324 31 31
Open 9am–10pm, Sat.–Sun. 10am–8pm
http://en.becar.ru/
Itaka
Bolshoy Prospekt VO 36
Tel. 812 325 21 12 or 812 327 98 02
www.petersburg-estate.com
Open Mon.–Fri. 10am–7pm

ARRIVALS AND DEPARTURES

→ **BY AIR**
http://eng.pulkovo.ru

■ **PULKOVO 2 INTERNATIONAL AIRPORT**
Located 10 miles south of the city center, on Startovaya Ulitsa.
International flights
Tel. 812 704 34 44
Tourist Information Bureau
Arrival hall, or Nevsky Prospekt 41
Tel. 812 311 28 43

■ **PULKOVO 1 AIRPORT**
Located 10½ miles south of the city center, on Pulkovsky Road.
Domestic flights (C.E.I.)
Tel. 812 704 38 22

■ **AIRPORT LINKS FROM PULKOVO 1**
Express bus no. 39 to Moskovskaya Metro station (15–20 mins); tickets sold on the bus (under US$1). Change at Moskovskaya for Nevsky Prospekt station (or other destinations), duration: 15–20 minutes.

■ **AIRPORT LINKS FROM PULKOVO 2**
Express bus no. 13 or shared taxi (*marshrutnoye taksy*) to Moskovskaya station. Tickets from the bus driver (under US$1).
Taxis
Taxi rank outside the

terminal; fares go from US$20–50, according to the length of the journey. Many private cab drivers will offer you their services inside the airport arrival hall; agree on the fare before starting your journey. (See City Transportation, p. 282).

■ **AIRLINES**
Aeroflot
– Nevsky Prospekt 7/9
Tel. 812 314 69 59
– Pulkovo Airport
Tel. 812 104 34 44
British Airways
– Sweden House, Malaya Konyushennaya Ulitsa 1/3A, Office B23
Tel. 812 329 25 65
– Pulkovo Airport
Tel. 812 346 81 46
Finnair
– Kazanskaya Ulitsa 44
Tel. 812 326 18 70
– Pulkovo Airport
Tel. 812 324 32 49
Lufthansa
– Nevsky Prospekt 32 (2nd floor)
Tel. 812 320 10 00
– Pulkovo Airport
Tel. 812 324 32 44
Pulkovo Airlines
Pervaya Krasno armeyskaya Ulitsa 5
Tel. 812 303 92 68 or 812 303 92 67
Central Ticketing Office
Nevsky Prospekt 7/9
Tel. 812 571 80 93
Open 8am–8pm, Sat.–Sun. 8am–6pm.

→ **BY BOAT**
Passenger maritime port (*Morskoy Passajirsky Port*)
Morskoy Slavy Pl. 1
Tel. 812 355 13 10 or 812 322 60 52
Also known as Gavan (harbor), it is located at the end of Great Prospekt (Bolshoy Prospekt) on Vasilyevsky Island, on the Gulf of Finland. It is the port of call of all Northern European cruises. The only

regular crossing now operating is between Stockholm and St Petersburg.

→ **BY TRAIN**
(See Regional Transportation p. 283).

BRIDGES

St Petersburg's 300 or so bridges form an intergal part of its architectural heritage. Between them they link the 42 islands that make up the city. Between April and November – when the rivers are not frozen – the swing bridges (20 in total) stay raised for part of the night in order to let commercial vessels through. You are advised to be aware of the bridge opening and closing times to avoid being stranded on the wrong island. The opening times of the bridges listed below should be verified by calling 063 between 8am and 10pm.

■ **SWING BRIDGE LIFTING TIMES**
Alexandra Nevskogo
1.30–5.05am
Birzhevoy
2.10–4.50am
Bolsheokhtinsky
2–5am
Bolshoy Krestovsky
2.05–3.55am and 4.40–5.20am
Bolshoy Petrovsky
1.25–2am and 5–5.45am
Dvortsovy
1.50–2.55am and 3.15–4.50am
Elagin I
by special order
Elagin II
by special order
Elagin III
by special order
Grenadersky
2.45–3.45am and 4.20–4.50am
Kamennoostrovsky
2.15–3am and 4.05–4.55am
Kantemirovsky
2.45–3.45 am and

4.20–4.50am
Lazarevsky
1.55–2.35am and
4.45–5.20am
Leitenanta Schmidta
1.40-4.55am
Liteiny
1.50–4.40am
Sampsonievsky
2.10–2.45am and
3.20–4.25am
Trotsky
1.50–4.50am
Tuchkov
2.10–3.05am and
3.35–4.45am
Ushakovsky
2.15–2.55am and
3.55–4.30am
Volodarsky
2–3.45am and
4.15–5.45am

CARS

→ **DRIVING**
■ **DRIVING LICENSE**
You are advised
to carry an
international
driving license.

■ **HIGHWAY CODE**
Roundabouts:
cars entering the
roundabout have
right of way over
those already
engaged.

■ **SPEED LIMITS**
In built-up areas:
37 miles/hr (60km/hr)
On the road:
56 miles/hr (90km/hr)

■ **ALCOHOL LEVELS
IN THE BLOOD**
Zero tolerance.

■ **GASOLINE**
After Jan 1, 2003,
the price of gasoline
in Russia rose from
20% to 30%.

■ **TRAFFIC JAMS**
Traffic and
congestion are
severe, especially
in the city center in
the rush hours,
between 8am–10am
and 5pm–8pm.

■ **PARKING**
Parking in the city
center is unmarked
and free of charge.
There are some
attended parking lots,
charged by the hour,
near the major hotels
and tourist sites.

■ **RESCUE SERVICE**
Tel. 320 90 00

→ **CAR RENTAL**
Not necessary if
you're planning to
stay in the city.

■ **CONDITIONS**
You must be over
21 and have held a
driving license for
at least a year.

■ **PAYMENT**
By credit card
(Amex, Visa, DC,
Mc/Ec, JCB, Hertz
Charge Card).

■ **CAR RENTAL
AGENCIES**
Prices average
US$115–150 per
day. Make sure you
have full insurance.
Astoria-service
Borovaya Ulitsa
11/13
Tel. 812 112 15 83
Avis
Konnogvardesysky
Bul. 4
Tel. 812 312 63 12
Rex
Kievskaya Ulitsa 3,
Office 206
Tel. 812 320 6662
www.rexlux.spb.ru/
Executive car
2 linia 35
Tel. 812 213 11 21

Hertz
– Pulkovo airport
terminals 1 and 2,
11am–11pm
– Malaya Morskaya
Ulitsa 23
Tel. 812 324 32 42
www.hertz.spb.ru

CHILDREN

If your children are
accompanying you,
take them to:
■ **ST PETERBURGSKY
TSIRK** (Circus)
Reki Fontanky nab. 3
Tel. 812 314 84 78
www.circus.spb.ru
Ticket office
11am–7pm

■ **CENTRAL LEISURE
PARK (ELAGIN ISLAND):**
giant wheel,
rowing boats...

■ **VICTORY PARK
"PRIMORSKY"**
(Krestovsky Island):
tennis courts,
rollerskating rink,
dolphins, ponies.

■ **ZOO** and other
attractions in
Alexandrovsky Park.

■ **ZOOLOGICAL
MUSEUM**
One of the largest
natural history
museums in
the world.

EMERGENCIES

■ **AMBULANCES**
Tel. 03
■ **FIRE BRIGADE**
Tel. 01
● **POLICE (MILITSIA)**
Tel. 02 or 164 97 87
for foreign visitors
■ **GAS LEAK**
Tel. 04
■ **SOS ON THE ROAD**
Tel. 812 320 90 00
■ **ALL-NIGHT
DRUGSTORE**
9pm–8pm
Tel. 812 311 20 77
■ **LOSS OR THEFT**
Go to the police
station nearest to the
place of loss or theft
in order to make a
declaration and
obtain an official
police report (Tel. 02)
which you will need

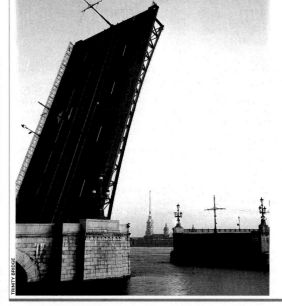

TRINITY BRIDGE

277

to submit to your consulate for lost documents, or to your insurance company.

Loss of luggage:
Luggage retrieval service
Pulkovo 2 Airport, open 24 hours
Tel. 812 324 37 87

FINDING YOUR WAY

Nothing could be simpler than finding your way around the center of St Petersburg, where the main tourist attractions (the Admiralty, Peter and Paul Fortress, St Isaac's Cathedral) and the canals provide you with clear landmarks. Out of the center, it is a little more difficult to find your bearings and you need to pay more attention.

→ TOPOGRAPHY
In the heart of St Petersburg (the oldest part of the city), the streets are laid out in a radial system, the main arteries fanning out from a central point while the canals curve around them. Later, more outlying areas were constructed mainly to an orthogonal design, dividing the whole area into a network of streets running at right angles to each other and forming "microdistricts" bound by the main arteries radiating out from the center.

→ SIGNPOSTS
Although the city has readopted many of the pre-revolutionary street names, the streets still tend to be known by both their Soviet and post-

NEVSKY PROSPEKT

Soviet names. Newly installed signs are now often sponsored by commercial companies; don't be surprised to find the trademark of a distinctly Western company displayed under the name of the street.

→ STREET NUMBERING
In theory, all streets are numbered starting from the Neva. In practice, in the majority of cases, the direction of street numbering varies from area to area. Guidelines are as follows:

■ in the mainland area of the city (south of the Neva): from north to south and from west to east;

■ on Vasilyevsky Island: from south to north and from east to west;

■ on Petersburg Island (also known as Petrograd Side): from south to north and from west to east.

FOOD AND DRINK

→ BISTROS
You will find several cheap bistro and fast-food chains.

→ BRASSERIES AND BREWERIES
There are a great number of brasseries in the city, and several brands of beer are produced in St Petersburg (Baltika, Nevskoye, Stepan Razin).

→ CAFÉS
The number of cafés in the city center is growing rapidly, and many now offer a fine selection of coffees, teas and cakes.

→ RESTAURANTS
There is a wide range of cuisine available in St Petersburg: the most common are Russian and Georgian, then Korean, Chinese and Latin-American.

→ RUSSIAN CUISINE
"Russian cuisine," writes travel journalist Jo Durden Smith, "is a mixture of elements of various origins: its starters (*zakusky*) come from a German and Scandinavian tradition imported by Peter the Great. Its noodles, ravioli (*pelmeny*) and tea derive from the Mongols; its buckwheat *kasha* from central Asia; its shish kebab (*shashlyk*) from the Caucasus; its *borshch* from central Europe – with the whole mix made more sophisticated and varied by imported 19th-century French chefs. Ice-cold vodka is traditionally drunk with *zakuski* (and often throughout the meal). Local beers are now excellent (try, for instance, Baltika no. 7). Georgian red wines are rather sweet to the Western palate, but you could try *kinsmarauli*, Stalin's favorite wine, as well as a dry white called *tsinandali*. Of Russian champagnes, the best is brut (the dryest); it's an agreeable alternative to its distant French cousin which, like all imported wines in Russia, is very expensive. French wines, for all this, are part of the old Russian tradition. Both Ivan the Terrible and Peter the Great had a fondness for Burgundy; and the Hotel Grand Europe, before the Revolution, is said to have had the finest champagne cellar in the world."

→ GLOSSARY
Bitky: meatballs.
Borshch: beetroot soup, potatoes, cabbage and meat.
Goluptsy: small meat-stuffed cabbage.
Kulibiak: salmon or meat pie.

Upp. case	Low. case	Phon.
А	а	a
Б	б	b
В	в	v
Г	г	g
Д	д	d
Е	е	ié
Ё	ё	io
Ж	ж	j
З	з	z
И	и	i
-	й	ï
К	к	k
Л	л	l
М	м	m
Н	н	n
О	о	o
П	п	p
Р	р	r
С	с	s
Т	т	t
У	у	ou
Ф	ф	f
Х	х	kh
Ц	ц	ts
Ч	ч	tch
Ш	ш	ch
Щ	щ	chtch
-	ъ	-
-	ы	y
-	ь	-
Э	э	è
Ю	ю	iou
Я	я	ia

Okhroshka:
  cold soup.
Pelmeny:
  a type of ravioli.
Pirozhky: small
  meat or cabbage
  pies.
Po-Pojarsky: poultry
  meat in flat pies).
Shashlyk:
  meat kebab.
Shchy:
  cabbage soup.
Ukha: fish soup.
Zakusky: varied
  hors d'œuvres.

HEALTH

→ **PREVENTION**
Avoid drinking tap water and bathing in lakes or pools (risk of leptospirosis, or Weil's disease). Be aware of the expiry dates on food packages (especially frozen food) and avoid "homemade" vodka and other spirits sold at kiosks and street stalls.

→ **MEDICAL CENTERS**
The local *poliklinika* will handle many most routine treatments, but doctors and nurses may not speak English. Many tourist hotels have their own doctors (inquire at the front desk).

■ **POLIKLINIKA #2**
Moskovsky
Prospekt 22
Tel. 812 292 62 72

■ **GASTELLO HOSPITAL**
Gastello Ulitsa 22
Tel. 812 291 79 60

■ **MEDICAL CENTERS FOR FOREIGN VISITORS**
American Medical Center
Serpukhovskaya
Ulitsa 10
Tel. 812 326 17 30
www.amcenters.com
Metro Teknolo-gitchesky Institut
Open 24 hours daily (office Mon.–Fri. 9am–6pm).
Private practice.
Euromed Clinique
Suvorovsky
Prospekt 60
Tel. 812 327 03 01
www.euromed.ru/en/
Private practice.

LANGUAGE

English is the foreign language most widely spoken by the population, especially by young people and staff in tourist locations. Russian is the official language, so if you want to be able to find your way around easily you will need to become familiar with the Cyrillic alphabet and its English phonetic transcription (see table, left).

MAIL

→ **POST OFFICES**
There are many post offices throughout the city. They can also be found in major hotels. Usually open 9am–8pm, closed one day a week.

■ **CENTRAL POST OFFICE**
(Glavpotchtamt)
Potchtamtskaya 9
(in the St Isaac's Cathedral district)
Tel. 312 83 02
and 312 80 39

■ **EXPRESS SERVICE**
DHL
Tel. 812 326 64 00
UPS
Tel. 812 327 85 40

■ **STAMPS**
US$0.66 for Europe.
US$1 for the US.
Sold at post offices.

MARKETS

→ **FOOD, FRUIT AND VEGETABLES**
Food markets are open daily. The products are generally fresher and cheaper than in stores.
■ **KUZNECHNY MARKET**
Kuznechny Per. 3,
Tel. 812 312 41 61
Mon.–Sat. 8am–8pm,
Sun. 8am–6pm
The largest market in the city center.

→ **ART AND ANTIQUES**
St Petersburg is known as the "antiques capital". There is a market on Konnyushennaya Square, near the Church of the Resurrection of Christ. There are also many sale-or-return stores, see Shopping p. 296.

→ **FLEA MARKETS**
The place to find anything from military belt buckles to antique china sets. They are on the outskirts of the city:
– Udelnaya Metro station, next to the railway tracks.
– Avtovo Metro station
– Marshala Kazakova Ulitsa 40 (Yunona Market, mostly for micro-electronics).

MONEY

→ **EXCHANGE**
Rubles cannot be converted on the open market. Exchange can only take place in Russia at bureaux de change, hotel receptions, in banks and in the larger stores.
Warning:
Do not take the risk of changing money on the black market, and beware of the numerous conmen operating in the city
.
■ **BANKS**
Usually open
Mon.–Fri. 9.30am–1pm and 2–4pm.
Alfa-Bank
Kanala Griboyedova
Nab 6/2
Association of the commercial banks of St Petersburg
Sadovaya Ulitsa 21
Tel. 315 65 09
Baltysky Bank
Sadovaya Ulitsa 34
and Nevsky Prospekt 85 (in the Moscow railway station building).
Menatep
Nevsky Prospekt 1
Promstroy bank
Nevsky Prospekt 140
Dumskaya Ulitsa 7
Sberbank
Nevsky Prospekt 153, 82 and 101, Liteyny Prospekt 7, Sadovaya Ulitsa 35

■ **FOREIGN-CAPITAL BANKS**
BNP-Dresdner Bank
Isaakyevskaya Pl. 11

279

Newspapers, nightlife, opening times, public holidays, religion

When in St Petersburg you do not need to dial the city code 812 before the seven-digit phone number.

■ **BUREAUX DE CHANGE**
Open daily 10am–8pm

→ **AUTO-TELLERS**
They are located in the city center, major hotels and banks. The maximum amount you can take out is set by your bank. Commission is 3%–4%.

→ **FORMS OF PAYMENT**
■ **CASH**
Although payment is often made in rubles, the US dollar, known as *kapusta* (cabbage), is the preferred local currency; it is a good idea to bring dollars with you in small denominations to use for tips – clean US$1, US$5, US$10 bills issued after 1990. As well as US dollars, euros are accepted for unofficial transactions such as the purchase of souvenirs.

■ **CREDIT CARDS**
Accepted in most restaurants, hotels, stores.
Warning:
Check all bills and receipts, and only use credit cards in reputable establishments. Beware of fraud.

■ **TRAVELER'S CHECKS**
They are not recommended as they are accepted only by banks and the commission is 5% to 7%, and sometimes more.

→ **COST OF LIVING**
Prices are volatile and inflation is rife. The tariffs applied to foreign visitors in tourist areas are those of Western Europe. Admission fees to sites and museums are higher than those charged to Russians in order

to finance the restoration of the national heritage, while allowing local people access to their own culture.
Cup of coffee: US$1.90
Pint of beer: From US$1.25
Bottle of wine: From US$12
Lunch: From US$4
Dinner in a restaurant: From US$19 per person
Museum admission fee: From US$6–12
Theater ticket: From US$30
Single room in a hotel: From US$60

NEWSPAPERS

→ **LOCAL NEWSPAPERS**
■ **IN ENGLISH**
The St Petersburg Times, a weekly publication for foreign residents, gives information on cultural events and is distributed free to hotels, restaurants and cafés.
www.times.spb.ru

■ **IN RUSSIAN**
Cultural magazines *Na Nevskom, Krasny journal, Sobaka.ru* (very trendy).
Dailies
Vecherny Peterburg, Smena, Sankt-Peterburgskiye Vedomosty.

→ **ENGLISH-LANGUAGE NEWSPAPERS**
Sold in hotels and at newsagents in the city center.

■ **IN ENGLISH AND RUSSIAN**
Pulse St Petersburg is a weekly publication that gives information on life in the city.

■ **IN ENGLISH**
Neva News and

Estate News (real estate in the Russian Federation and Eastern Europe) are both published monthly.

NIGHTLIFE

→ **ART AND MUSIC**
From permanent exhibitions to special events, there is always something to see or do in St Petersburg. Arts and music have always flourished here in the city that was known as the "Rock capital" during the Soviet era. Nightclubs, theaters, opera halls and cultural venues offer a wide range of concerts and shows all year round. (See Leisure p. 293, Celebrations, festivals and events p. 284).

→ **"WHITE NIGHTS"**
The widest range of events occurs in the summer, during the period of the "white nights", when nightlife becomes more intense and the city center is full of local people out on the streets until dawn (Vasilyevsky, Petrograd Side and Nevsky districts).

■ **INFORMATION**
From the Tourist Information Bureau, the Cultural Program Institute, or the local press.

■ **RESERVATIONS**
Ask at your hotel or at the venue itself.

OPENING TIMES

Vary greatly, but the standard opening times (with most places closing for lunch between 1–3pm) are:

■ **BANKS**
Mon.–Fri. 9.30am–1pm and 2–4pm

■ **BUREAUX DE CHANGE**
Daily 10am–8pm

■ **DEPARTMENT STORES**
8am–9pm (some stay open 24 hours)

■ **FOOD STORES**
8am–8pm or 9am–9pm

■ **OTHER STORES**
10am–7pm

■ **RESTAURANTS**
Times may vary, but restaurants usually serve until 10pm or 10.30pm. Russians tend to have lunch around 2pm and dinner between 9pm and 10pm.

■ **MUSEUMS**
See Places to Visit p. 300 for addresses and opening times.

PUBLIC HOLIDAYS

■ **JANUARY 1**
New Year's Day
■ **JANUARY 7**
Orthodox Christmas
■ **FEBRUARY 23**
Defenders of the Nation's Day
■ **MARCH 8**
International Woman's Day
■ **MAY 1 AND 2**
Labor Day
■ **MAY 9**
Victory Day (1945)
■ **JUNE 12**
Russian Independence Day
■ **NOVEMBER 7**
Reconciliation Day

RELIGION

■ **JEWISH**
Synagogue Lermontovsky Prospekt 104; Metro Baltiskaya

■ **MUSLIM**
Mosque, Kronversky Prospekt 7; Metro Gorkovskaya

■ **ORTHODOX**
– St Nicholas', Nikolskaya Pl. 1/3; Metro Ploshchad

Mira
– The Holy Trinity,
Nevsky Monastery
Metro Ploshchad
A. Nevsky

■ **PROTESTANT**
Lutheran Church,
Saltikov-Shedrine 8
Metro
Chernyshevskaya

■ **ROMAN CATHOLIC**
Our-Lady-of-Lourdes
Kovenski Prospekt 7
Metro Ploshchad
Vosstanya

SHOPPING

Make sure you are
given receipts and
that you keep them,
as you may be
required to produce
them by the Russian
customs when
leaving the country.

→ **WHAT TO BUY**
■ **GOLD AND SILVER**
objects, jewelry, and
clocks and watches.

■ **FURS** (*shapkas*),
scarves and shawls,
natural fabrics wool.
silk, etc. from
Central Asia.

■ **WOODEN OBJECTS**
Russian dolls
(*matryoshkas*),
lacquered boxes,
sculpted pictures...

■ **ST PETERSBURG
PORCELAIN**
from the Lomonosov
factory (originally the
famous imperial
works).

HELICOPTER TRIP ABOVE THE NEVA

BOAT CRUISE

VASILYEVSKY ISLAND

AVTOVO METRO STATION

■ **RECORDS**, cassettes
and CDs (classical or
folk music).

■ **RARE BOOKS**
in European
languages
(especially French)
in the numerous
second-hand
bookstores or stalls.

■ **ANTIQUES**,
paintings, etc.
Warning:
*Russian law
stipulates that you
can't export*

*antiquities that date
from before 1945,
especially icons.
Any antiques or
works of art taken out
of the country must
be authorized by the
Ministry of Culture
and have a certificate
of export. Otherwise,
customs officials
have the right to
seize goods and
demand that you
pay a fine.*

■ **VODKA AND CAVIAR**
A maximum of 7oz

(200g) of caviar per
person is allowed
through customs.
Warning:
*Buying vodka or
caviar from street
vendors may seem
like a smart move
because of the lower
price, but
you will have no
guarantee of
freshness or quality.*

→ **MAIN SHOPPING
STREETS**
■ **NEVSKY PROSPEKT**
and its commercial

galleries, Gostiny
Dvor and Passage.

■ **KAMENNO-
OSTROVSKY** and
BOLSHOY PROSPEKT
in the Petersburg
Island district.

TELEPHONE

→ **INTERNATIONAL
CALLS**
■ **TO THE UK**
Dial 8 (wait for a long
tone) then dial 10
(international access
code) then 44 for the
UK, the area code
(without the initial 0)
and number.

■ **TO THE US/CANADA**
Dial 8 (wait for a long
tone) then dial 10
(international access
code), 1 for the US,
the area code and
local number.

■ **INTERNATIONAL
OPERATOR**
Dial 077 (072 or 073
from your hotel).

→ **NATIONAL CALLS**
■ **CALLS WITHIN
ST PETERSBURG**
When phoning within
the city, you do not
need to dial the area
code 812.

■ **CALLS TO OTHER
RUSSIAN CITIES**
Dial 8 and wait for a
long tone then dial
the city code and
number.
Information for calls
outside the city:
070.
National city codes:
Moscow: 095
Novgorod: 8162
Ekaterinburg: 3432

→ **PUBLIC
TELEPHONES**
There are many
public phone booths
in the streets, in
museums and hotels.
You are advised to
buy an International
Phone card (sold at
Metro stations and
newsagents) as it will
be much cheaper
than using the normal
city network.

→ CALL CENTER

(*Tsentralniye Mejdugorodniye Telefonniye Punkt*)
Bolshaya Morskaya Ulitsa 28 (next to Palace Square, by Nevsky Prospekt)
Tel. 069
Open 24 hours
Business center (located inside the Call Center) for Internet and fax
Open 9am–9pm.

TIPPING

In restaurants and cafés, bills include a 10–15% service charge, but it is customary to leave a tip by rounding up the amount billed. In taxis, tipping is not usual, unless you wish to show special appreciation.

TOURS AND EXCURSIONS

Guided tours are usually in Russian. If you require a tour in English or have any specific request (expect to pay a lot

more), contact the Tourist Information Bureau or a tour operator (see Useful addresses p. 283).

→ BOAT TOURS

Trips run between April and November.

■ CRUISES DOWN THE NEVA

Departures from in front of the Hermitage; in front of the Admiralty (opposite the bronze cavalier); at the Peter and Paul Fortress by the gateway to the Neva; and also near the *Aurora*.

■ CANAL TRIPS BY WATER-TAXI

Departures from the quay on the Moyka Canal every night during the 'white nights'; from the Griboedov Canal (water-taxi trips through the Kolomna); and on the Fontanka Embankment, near the Zelieni, Kazansky and Anitchkov bridges.

■ TRIPS TO PETERHOF

Hydrofoil trips to Peterhof embark opposite the main entrance of the Hermitage.
Duration: 30 mins.
Tel. 812 325 51 20

■ EXCURSIONS TO KRONSTADT

Hydrofoil trips to Kronstadt embark opposite 34, Makarova Naberejnaya.
Duration: 35 mins.
Tel. 812 328 22 23

■ LASTOCHKA OMNIBUS-BOAT

Cruise in style in 19th-century interiors. Reserve ahead (Kronversky Bridge, near the Peter and Paul Fortress)
Tel. 812 327 25 07

→ COACH TOURS

Operators offer many itineraries and thematic tours. Information, reservations and departures from one of the following three stations in the city center: Palace Square, Kazan Square or near the Ruska Portik (next to Gostiny Dvor).

→ TRAMWAY TOURS

You can visit St Petersburg in one of the streetcars that have served the city faithfully for over a century.

■ RESERVATIONS

St Petersburg Tramway Museum
Sredny Prospekt 77
Tel. 812 321 5405/06

→ HELICOPTER TOURS

■ BALTIC AIRLINES (BALTYSKYE AVIALNY)

Nevsky Prospekt 7/9
Office no. 12
Tel. 812 571 00 84
A 15-minute flight in a MI-8. Departures from the strip situated between the Peter and Paul Fortress and

Kronverk; April–Nov., Sat.–Sun. and public hols. Price: around US$40.

TRANSPORTATION AROUND THE CITY

→ BUS, TRAMS AND METRO

St Peterburg has over 290 bus, trolleybus and tramway routes, 4 Metro lines and 57 stations, each reflecting the spirit of the time when it was built (do not miss Ploshchad and Vostanya at Avtovo).

■ MAP OF THE METRO

(See Map G p.336)
Maps are displayed at the entrance of every Metro station (these are in Russian only). Bilingual city and transportation maps are available from some kiosks in the city center, hotels, bookstores and the Tourist Information Bureau.

■ TICKETS

You must buy Metro tickets at station ticket offices, and bus and tramway tickets when boarding. Fares: around US$0.15 at time of going to press but inflation goes up quickly. Various special passes are also available.

■ OPERATING TIMES

Buses and tramways run between 6am and midnight. The Metro operates between 5.45am and 0.15am, roughly every 1–5 minutes.

→ PRIVATE SHUTTLES

The numerous *marshrutnoye* taxis, indicated by an "express" sign, are just as convenient to get to the surrounding area: shuttles for Petrodvorets

(Peterhof) depart from Baltyskaya Metro station; shuttles for Pushkin (Tsarskoe Selo) depart from Moskovskaya Metro station.

→ TAXIS

"Official" taxis carry a meter with a black and white checkered band or a taxi sign on the roof.

■ FARES

US$1.39 per mile.

■ CALLING A TAXI

There is an additional charge for reserving a taxi.
Tel. 7 000 000, 068 or 080
City center:
Tel. 812 271 88 88

→ HITCHHIKING

Russian citizens looking for extra income will stop their car and offer rides to hitchhikers. It's naturally cheaper than official taxis, but always agree on the price before getting into the car.

REGIONAL TRANSPORTATION

→ BY RAIL

The Russian railway network is very efficient but journeys tend to be very long.

■ SCHEDULES

Are based on Moscow time (same as St Peterburg)

■ INFORMATION

There is one single information line for all railway stations (calls are only in Russian and there is a charge):
Tel. 055

■ RESERVATION AND TICKET OFFICE

Griboedov Canal 24
Mon.–Sat. 8am–8pm, Sun. 8am–4pm
Tel. 812 762 33 44 or 812 768 67 33

Baltic Station
Obvodny Canal 120
Metro Baltyskaya
Destinations: Peterhof, Oranienbaum (Lomonosov), Gatchina.

Finland Station
Lenin 6
Metro
Ploshchad Lenina
Destinations: Vyborg, Carélie.

Moscow Station
Nevsky Prospekt 85
Metro Ploshchad Vostanya or Mayakovskaya
Destinations: Moscow, northern, central and southern Russia.

Vitebsk Station
Zagorodny Prospekt 52, Metro Pushkinskaya
Destinations: the city suburbs (Tsarskoe Selo, Pavlovsk), southwest of Russia

Warsaw Station
Obvodny Canal 118
Metro Baltyskaya or Frunzenskaya

→ BY COACH

The coach network is very efficient and links the major Russian cities.

■ COACH STATION

(*Avtovokzal*)
Obvodny Canal 36
Tel. 812 766 57 77
Metro Ligovskaya, and a 20-minute walk

→ BOAT

■ BOAT TERMINAL

(*Retchnoy vokzal*)
Obukhovskoy Oborony Prospekt 195
Tel. 812 740 58 58 or 812 740 58 59 (tickets)
Metro Proletarskaya and a ten-minute walk.
The Meteor boats serve Petrodvorets. (See Tours and Excursions p. 282).

USEFUL ADDRESSES

→ CONSULATES

■ CANADIAN CONSULATE

Malodetskoselsky Prospekt 32
198013 St Petersburg
Tel. 812 325 84 48
Metro Tehnologichesky Institut
Email: spurb@dfait-maeci.gc.ca

■ BRITISH CONSULATE

Proletarskoy Diktatury Pl. 5
191124 St Petersburg
Tel. 812 320 32 00
Email bcg-spb@yandex.ru
www.britishembassy.gov.uk
Metro Elizarovskaya

■ AMERICAN CONSULATE

Furshtatskaya Ulitsa 15

191028 St Petersburg
Tel. 812 331 26 00
(331 28 88 for after hours emergencies)
http://stpetersburg.usconsulate.gov
Metro Chernyshevskaya

→ TOURIST OFFICES

■ TOURIST INFORMATION BUREAU

Pulkovo 2 Airport Arrival hall, or:
Sadovaya Ulitsa 14
Tel. 812 710 58 93
Fax 812 310 28 22
Open Mon.–Fri. 10am–6pm

■ CULTURAL PROGRAMS INSTITUTE

Rubinchteyna Ulitsa 8
Tel. 812 764 75 96
Open Mon.–Fri. 10am–6pm
www.spbculture.ru

→ TOUR OPERATORS

For accommodation, hotel reservations, tour arrangements, excursions, etc.:

■ DATE-ST PETERSBURG

Kanal Griboyedova 5
Tel. 812 312 40 59
Mon.-Fri. 11am–6pm

■ INTERCITY SERVICE

Nevsky Prospekt 30
Tel. 812 278 92 85
www.kmp.ru

→ INTERNET CAFÉ

QUO VADIS
Nevsky Prospekt, 24
Tel. 311 81 11
Open 24 hours day; connection fron US$2.
www.quovadis.ru

◆ CELEBRATIONS, FESTIVALS AND EVENTS

CELEBRATIONS AND FESTIVALS

DECEMBER–JANUARY	ARTS SQUARE	**SQUARE INTERNATIONAL FESTIVAL** *Concerts, exhibitions, competitions*
	CITY PALACES	**CHRISTMAS ENCOUNTERS** **IN THE PALMYRA OF THE NORTH** *Christmas and New Year's balls (Roman Catholic and Orthodox) in the city palaces*
FEBRUARY	PETER AND PAUL FORTRESS	**ICE SCULPTURE FESTIVAL** *On Fortress beach*
	THE CAPELLA	**VIVA LA MUSICA ANTIQUA!** *Early music festival*
	MARIINSKY THEATER	**INTERNATIONAL BALLET FESTIVAL** *Participants of the third International Ballet Festival (2003) included dancers from the American Ballet Theater, the Royal Ballet of Great Britain and Moscow Bolshoi, as well as Mariinsky's own ballet troupe*
MARCH	MUSEUMS, GALLERIES	**FROM AVANT-GARDE TO THE PRESENT** *International arts festival*
APRIL	CONCERT HALLS	**SERGEI KURIOKHIN INTERNATIONAL FESTIVAL** *Contemporary music festival*
MAY	PETERHOF	**FOUNTAIN OPENING FESTIVAL** *In Peterhof gardens*
	VARIOUS VENUES	**INTERNATIONAL MUSICAL SPRING** *Two weeks of contemporary academic music by leading Russian and international composers of the 20th century*
MAY 27	HISTORICAL SQUARES	**CITY CELEBRATIONS AND BRASS BAND FESTIVAL** **AND MONUMENTS** *Entertainment, concerts, etc.*
END MAY-EARLY JUNE	PETERHOF PALACE, PAVLOVSK, TSARSKOE SELO	**MUSICAL OLYMPUS** *One week. Gala parade of the winners of the world's most prestigious classical competition.*
MAY 31– JUNE 30	MARIINSKY THEATER	**STARS OF THE WHITE NIGHTS** *World-famous international festival of classic arts. Organized by the Mariinsky Theater, much attention is given to Russian opera*
JUNE	ST PETERSBURG MUSEUMS	**CONTEMPORARY ART IN TRADITIONAL MUSEUMS** *Exhibitions in several small museums*
JUNE 15–22	JAZZ PHILHARMONIA, MIKHAIL PALACE GARDENS	**SWING ON SUMMER NIGHTS** *International jazz festival*
	HOME OF THE MOVIES	**MESSAGE TO MANKIND** *International documentaries and short films*
JUNE 1–30	HERMITAGE THEATER AND CITY PALACES	**ST PETERSBURG'S PALACES** *International chamber music festival at Mikhail, Yusupov, Sheremetev, Menshikov and other palaces*
	HOME OF THE MOVIES	**FESTIVAL OF ALL FESTIVALS!** *International movie festival*
JULY	CLUBS, CAFÉS, ETC.	**OPEN YOUR WINDOWS!** *Rock festival*
SEPTEMBER	CONCERT HALLS	**EARLY MUSIC** *Classical music festival*
OCTOBER	CAPELLA, PAVLOSK, PETERHOF, MENSHIKOV, PHILHARMONIA HALL	**INTERNATIONAL EARLY MUSIC FESTIVAL** *Founded in 1998 as a joint initiative between the British Council and the ensemble Musica Petropolitana to celebrate the 300th anniversary of Peter I's "Great Embassy" to England. The Festival draws on the musical traditions of Western Europe, Russia and the East, and strives for the greatest possible degree of historical accuracy*
	THEATER BALTIC HOUSE	*International theater festival*

OTHER EVENTS

AUGUST	ON THE NEVA	**REGATTA (SAILBOATS)**
SEPTEMBER	GALLERIES, EXHIBITIONS HALLS	**FALL PHOTO-MARATHON** *Photography exhibitions*

Addresses

Key

♥ The editors' choice		☗ Quiet
C Central		☗ Terrace
Ⅲ Air conditioning		⚘ Views
≋ Swimming pool		☗ Park or garden
♫ Music		P Parking

◆ HOTELS

Hotels are listed alphabetically within each district. The ◆ symbol indicates the relevant map reference in the map section at the end of the guide. For a list of symbols, see page 285. Unless otherwise noted, all hotels accept credit cards.

AROUND NEVSKY PROSPEKT

Angleterre
Bolchaya Morskaya Ulitsa 39 ◆ **D** F2
Tel. 812 313 56 66
Metro Nevsky Prospekt
The Angleterre (refurbished in 2002), is linked to the adjacent Astoria Hotel by a gallery, and although it is more soberly furnished than its neighbor, its prices are more accessible. The bar on the first floor is a popular meeting point for St Petersburg locals. Opt for the rooms overlooking Saint Isaac's Square if there are any available. The gym is equipped with a small swimming pool and a sauna.
194 rooms
▣ **C** ✖

Astoria
Bolchaya Morskaya Ulitsa 39 ◆ **D** F2
Tel. 812 313 57 57
www.astoria.spb.ru
Metro Nevsky Prospekt
This establishment enjoys a superb location opposite Saint Isaac's Cathedral, a mere 10-minute walk from both the Nevsky Prospekt and the Mariinsky Theater. The hotel was built in 1912 and remained an oasis of elegance under the Soviet regime; more recently, it has been meticulously restored to form part of the Rocco Forte luxury hotel chain. A cozy atmosphere reigns in the bedrooms, with their old-fashioned bathrooms, and in the lounges, where Russian-style tea is served in the afternoons from a samovar.
215 rooms, plus suites
▣ **C** ☼

♡ Casa Leto
Bolchaya Morskaya Ulitsa 34 ◆ **D** F2
Tel. 314 66 22
Metro Nevsky Prospekt or Sadovaya
The immediate neighbor of the Astoria and Angleterre, set in an old collective apartment, is one of the few small family hotels to be found in Saint Petersburg. Its five, high-ceilinged rooms are named after the city's most illustrious architects, including Rastrelli, Rossi and Trezzini. They offer snug comfort, enhanced by their antique furniture.
5 rooms
▣ ◐ **C** ▥

Comfort-Hotel
Bolchaya Morskaya 25 ◆ **A** B5
Tel. 812 318 67 00
www.comfort-hotel.spb.ru
Metro Nevsky Prospect or Sadovaya
An ideal location, equidistant from the Nevsky Prospekt, Saint Isaac's Square and the Hermitage Museum, in one of the city's most elegant streets, a stone's throw from the family home of the writer Vladimir Nabokov. The rooms are comfortable but austerely decorated.
14 rooms
▣ **C** ◐

Corinthia Nevsky Palace Hotel
Nevsky Prospekt 57 ◆ **E** C4
Tel. 812 380 20 01
www.corinthiahotels.com
Metro Mayakovskaya
This used to be the Sheraton, and seems to have survived the transition to new management more or less intact. Behind the 19th-century neoclassical façade, the interior is modern, characterless yet comfortable. Outstanding breakfast buffet – you could spend all day here. The hotel's proximity to the railway station and the cheap winter packages it offers make it a favorite weekend base for Muscovites.
256 rooms
▣

Dostoevsky
Vladimirsky Pr. 19 ◆ **A** F6 / **E** C4
Tel. 812 331 32 00 or 812 331 32 01
www.dostoevsky-hotel.ru
Metro Vladimirskaya
A modern hotel, situated on the top three floors of a large cultural centre. Fitness studio and business center, Internet access in the rooms, sauna, restaurant and a relaxation zone with a stunning view of the Cathedral of Our Lady of Vladimir. The rooms are all well-equipped to cater for disabled persons.
207 rooms
▣ **C** ☼ **P** ♿

Hermitage
Millionaya Ulitsa 11 ◆ **A** C3
Tel. and fax.
812 571 54 97
Metro Nevsky Prospekt
Rooms available in an unusual old hotel once owned by Princess Gagarin. Sumptuous décor.

Grand Hotel Europe
Mikhailovskaya Ulitsa 1/7 ◆ **A** D5
Tel. 812 329 60 00
www.grand-hotel-europe.com
Metro Gostiny Dvor
The city's foremost luxury hotel stands on the Nevsky Prospekt, opposite the Gostiny Dvor shopping mall. Its façade, dating from 1824, is classified as a heritage site and its Art-Nouveau décor has been partially preserved, as evident in the stained-glass windows and wood trim in the Europe Restaurant. The lovingly refurbished rooms are divided into nine categories, according to their size, furnishings and view. This hotel is the flagship of Orient Express Hotels and is accustomed to receiving royalty and movie stars.
301 rooms
▣ **C** ☼

Korona
Malaya Koniuchennaya Ulitsa 7 ◆ **E** A3
Tel. 812 571 00 86
Metro Nevsky Prospekt
This little hotel right next to Kazan Cathedral opened in 2001 on the second story of an 18th-century building with a preservation order on it. It has only eight rooms, with no bar or restaurant, although breakfast is served in the rooms.
▣ **C**

Marshal
Chpalernaya Ulitsa 41 ◆ **E** D1
Tel. 812 579 99 55
www.marshal-hotel.spb.ru
Metro Chernychevskaya
This hotel, which is close to the Botanical Gardens and a 10-minute walk from the Smolny Convent, occupies a 19th-century building that was once the barracks for a cavalry regiment. Its comfortable rooms are all equipped with computers connected to the Internet.
18 rooms
▣

Hotels
- ▫ < US$125
- ▫ US$125–315
- ▣ > US$315

When in St Petersburg you do not need to dial the city code 812 before the seven-digit phone number.

Mercury
Tavricheskaya
Ulitsa 39 ◆ **E** E2
Tel. 812 325 64 44
Metro
Chernychevskaya
This building adorned with pediments was turned into a comfortable little hotel in the 1980s. It was originally designed to receive official visitors but it now also welcomes tourists – although there are only 16 rooms, so booking is essential. The subway station is 15 minutes away, but the Tauride Gardens are close by.
16 rooms
▫

Moskva Hotel
Pl. Aleksandra
Nevskovo 2 ◆ **E** E5
Tel. 812 274 30 01
or 812 274 00 52
Metro Ploshchad
Aleksandra or
Nevskovo
This hotel at the end of the Nevsky Prospekt, in front of the Alexander Nevsky Monastery, has the advantage of a subway station on its doorstep. Its gigantic, Soviet-style façade conceals comfortable rooms, although these are often reserved for groups. Its restaurants and bars have a reputation for providing good value for money.
777 rooms
▫

Neptun Best Western
Obvodnogo Kanala
Nab. 93a ◆ **E** B6
Tel. 812 324 46 10
www.bestwestern.com
Metro Pushkinskaya
Part of the new Neptun business center. Although near the city center this hotel is not very conveniently located: the nearest metro station is 10–15 minutes' walk away.

However, with a tennis court, gym, bowling alley, billiard room, squash court, full-size swimming pool and golf simulator, it has much to please those who like their hotel to offer more than just a bed.
69 rooms
▫ ▨▧

Neva
Ulitsa Tchaikovskogo
17 ◆ **E** C2
Tel. 812 278 05 04
Metro
Chernychevskaya
This modest hotel is tucked behind a façade decorated with telamons, just 10 minutes from the Summer Garden on foot. The rooms are simple but their price is appealing.
133 rooms
▫ ▣

Novotel St Petersburg Centre
Nevsky
Prospekt 102 ◆ **E** C4
Tel. 335 11 88
Metro Mayakovskaya
The most recent of the big hotels in the town center opened its doors in 2005. It has 233 rooms arranged over nine floors. The sober design style gets better on higher floors, where there is a good view. All modern comforts are offered (sauna, fitness studio) and the hotel is equipped with state-of-the-art communications technology.
▣ ▣ ▥ ▣

Oktiabrskaya
Ligovsky
Prospekt 10 ◆ **E** D3
Tel. 277 63 30
Metro Ploshchad
Vosstanya
The Oktiabrskaya Hotel stands on the Nevsky Prospekt, midway between the Admiralty and the Alexander Nevsky Monastery. True, it is very central, but its

proximity to Moscow Station means noisy crowds and traffic, and this will be, for many, a disadvantage. The historic 19th-century building, in pure Soviet style, is somewhat charmless but the rooms are being renovated.
Over 500 rooms
▫ ▣

Piaty Ugol
Zagorodny Pr. 13
◆ **E** B5
Tel. 812 380 81 81
Metro Vladimirskaya,
Dostoevskaya
This small family-run establishment is located in the Dostoevsky district. Internet access in the rooms, some of which have views of Our Lady of Vladimir.
27 rooms
▫ ▣ ▥ ▣

🕮 Pushka Inn
Reky Priajky Nab. 14
◆ **A** C3
Tel. 312 09 13
Metro Nevsky
Prospekt
This small hotel is installed in a narrow building on the banks of the Moika, next to the Pushkin Museum. It offers simple but comfortable rooms; those with a view of the river are the most attractive (and also the most expensive). Breakfast is served in the first-floor Pushka Inn restaurant, which is taken over by local customers later in the day.
27 rooms
▫ ▣ ▣ ▥ ▧

Radisson SAS Royal
Nevsky
Prospekt 49 ◆ **E** C4
Tel. 812 322 50 00
www.radissonsas.com
Metro Mayakovskaya
This hotel near Moscow Station (beyond the Fontanka) is set in an elegant 19th-century building that was originally commissioned by a

wealthy businessman (the hotel's restaurant bears his name). It boasts a highly popular bar that is extended in the summer by a terrace that spills on to the Prospekt. The bedrooms, which are spacious and very comfortable, attract both tourists and business people.
164 rooms
▫

Renaissance St Petersburg Baltic Hotel
Potchtamskaya Ul. 4
◆ **A** A5
Tel. 812 380 40 00
Metro Nevsky
Prospekt, Sadovaya
This member of the Marriott chain opened in 2004, a stone's throw from the futuristic post office building. The hotel's 19th-century façade gives way to an interior design of the utmost modernity. The rooms are furnished with refinement, and those on the upper floor offer a dizzying view of Saint Isaac's Cathedral.
102 rooms
▣ ▣ ▥ ▣

KOLOMNA DOSTRICT

Hotel Sovetskaya
Lermontovsky Pr. 43
◆ **D** E5
Tel. 740 26 40
Metro Baltiskaya
In keeping with the Soviet penchant for doing things on a massive scale, this 18-story hotel was built in the 1970s with no less than one thousand rooms! Those on the Fontanka wing have been refurbished and are comfortable and attractive. The view of the city and its monuments from the top floor is breathtaking.
Over 1000 rooms
▫ ▧

◆HOTELS

Hotels
- ⚬ < US$125
- ⚬ US$125–315
- ⚬ > US$315

Matisov Domik
Reky Priajky
Nab. 3/1 ◆ **D** D3
Tel. 812 495 04 62
Metro Sennaya
Ploshchad
This hotel on Matisov
Island, far from the
city center, is much
appreciated for its
tranquility and family
atmosphere. The
tastefully furnished
rooms are set in a
small house built
around a courtyard
bedecked with
flowers. A small
museum inside the
hotel displays
Russian antiques.
46 rooms
⚬ **C**

MALAYA OKHTA
Deson-Ladoga
◆ OUTSIDE MAP AREA
Shaumyana
Prospekt 26
Tel. 812 528 53 93
www.deson.lek.ru
Metro
Novocherkasskaya
Don't judge this hotel
by its plain concrete
façade. The interior is
a totally different and
thoroughly modern
story. The rooms are
light, large and
comfortable, with
pastel décor, and the
bathrooms are well
equipped. The hotel
is slightly east of the
city center, but close
to the metro station
and a five-minute bus
ride away from the
Alexander Nevsky
Monastery.
96 rooms
⚬

MOSKOVSKY
Hotel German Club
◆ OUTSIDE MAP AREA
Ulitsa Gastello 20
Tel. 812 448 51 94
www.germanclub.
narod.ru
Metro Moskovskaya
The hotel's website
summarizes the place
as "Russian
hospitality meets
German order". The
German Club is rather
out of the city center
but in a lively and
interesting district.

It occupies the third
and fourth floors of a
tall building typical of
the monumental
Muscovite
architectural style of
the Stalin era. The
rooms are plain,
spotlessly clean and
light, with a lot of pine
woodwork and high
ceilings. All in all, it's a
cozy place to stay and
worth the extra
journey.
16 rooms
⚬

PRIBALTIYSKAYA HOTEL

Pulkovskaya
◆ OUTSIDE MAP AREA
Pobedy Ploshchad 1
Tel. 812 140 39 00
Fax 812 140 39 48
www.pulkovskaya.ru
Metro Moskovskaya
Though it's located at
the end of Moskovsky
Prospekt, away from
the city center, it's still
quite handy for
getting in and out of
town. The
Pulkovskaya is on a
direct metro line to
the heart of the city;
Nevsky Prospekt
station is no more
than a 20-minute ride
away. The hotel is
also just 10–15
minutes away from
Pulkovo airport by
taxi. Built in the
1970s, this is again a
charmless
establishment, but
the rooms are
adequate, well
equipped and
inexpensive. The
hotel's lobby is
impressive and
facilities include two
restaurants, two
saunas, a tennis court
and a health club.
840 rooms
⚬

NEAR PETROGRAD
LDM
Ulitsa Profesora
Popova 47 ◆ **C** B3
Tel. 812 234 32 78
www.ldm.ru
Metro
Petrogradskaya
This (very ugly) hotel
stands next to the
LDM (Leningradsky
Dvorets Molodioy –
Leningrad Youth
Center). Built in 1975,
it contains leisure and
sports centers,
conference rooms
and concert halls
where music
festivals are held.
The picturesque view
over the Malaya
Nevka and the islands
compensates for the
fact that the nearest
metro station is a
good 15 minutes'
walk away.
201 rooms
⚬ ♫ ≋

VASILYEVSKY ISLAND
Hotel Shelfort
3 Linia 26 ◆ **D** E1
Tel. 812 328 05 55
Metro
Vasileostrovskaya
This small hotel
opened in 2001 on
Vasilyevsky Island,
behind the University
quay, in a residential
area with an
abundance of
consulates. There
are only six rooms
(spread over two
floors); two of them
have preserved their
tiled fireplaces.
Breakfast is served in
a cozy lounge.
6 rooms
⚬ ◻

Pribaltiyskaya
Korablestroiteley
Ulitsa 14 ◆ **B** A6
Tel. 812 356 30 01
www.pribaltiyskaya.ru
Metro Primorkskaya
This typical Soviet-era
concrete structure is
the biggest hotel in
the city, and it was
considered the best
when built in 1980.
The Pribaltiyskaya is
well maintained
inside, but it is distant
from the historic
center and rates are
steep. Half the rooms,
though, have striking
sea views since it
stands right on the
edge of the gulf, high
on a promontory.
The restaurants serve
Russian and Western
European food, and in
one, Neva, there is
live music every
evening. Hotel
facilities include
sauna, pool, gym,
massage, beauty
salon, bowling and
billiard hall, and a
nightclub.
1200 rooms
⚬ ≋ ≋ ♫

NEAR VYBORG
Saint Petersburg
Pirogovskaya
Nab. 5/2 ◆ **C** E5
Tel. 812 380 19 19
www.hotel-spb.ru
Metro Ploshchad
Lenina
One of the standard-
bearers of Soviet
architecture, on the
banks of the Neva
(just opposite the
Aurora cruiser), a
10-minute walk
from the subway
station. Despite
refurbishments, the
décor is still imbued
with the spirit of the
Brezhnev era. The
only rooms that offer
any real comfort are
those on the top
floors, with large bay
windows overlooking
the river, but they are
also the most
expensive. The hotel
relies on group
bookings.
410 rooms
⚬ ≋

Restaurants

- 🞄 < US$30
- 🞄 US$30–50
- 🞄 US$50–70
- 🞄 > US$70

Prices in restaurants are sometimes given as 'y.e.': eg 25 y. e. y. e. is a conventional monetary unit equivalent to US$1.

AROUND NEVSKY PROSPEKT

1913 God (Year 1913)
Voznesensky
Prospekt 13/2 ◆ **A** A6
Tel. 812 315 51 48
Metro Nevsky
Prospekt
Open noon–1am
With a classic interior, a relaxed, comfortable atmosphere and high-quality service, this place offers Western European cuisine and a range of very rich and varied Russian dishes.
🞄 C

Admiralteistvo (Admiralty)
Nevsky Palace Hotel
Nevsky
Prospekt 57 ◆ **E** C4
Tel. 812 380 20 01
Open Tue–Sat.
6am–10.30pm
Metro Mayakovskaya
Big, bustling hotel-restaurant where the maritime theme extends to the décor and menu. It is strongest on fish but the reliable menu covers Russian and Soviet classics including caviar, stolichny salad (meat, hard-boiled eggs, gherkins, peas, potato and onion, with mayonnaise), borsch and solyanka (a sharp soup of vegetables and meat or fish). The Georgian fillet of lamb with garlic and coriander sauce is particularly good. Background Russian folk and "urban romance" music.
🞄 C 🎵

Caviar Bar
Grand Hotel Europe
Mikhailovskaya Ulitsa
1/7 ◆ **C** F5
Tel. 812 329 60 00
Open 6am–11pm
Metro Gostiny Dvor
The Caviar Bar's posh, expensive menu is of course strong on caviar dishes but also includes other favorites of wealthy

Russians such as crab, sturgeon, pirozhky (pastry parcels stuffed with meat or cabbage) cooked in champagne. Regular customers here recommend the trout marinated in vodka. Tea is served in samovars, as Russian and gypsy music plays in the background.
🞄 C

RESTAURANT OF THE HOTEL EUROPA

Dvorianskoye Gnezdo (the Nobles' Nest)
Dekabristov
Pl. 21 ◆ **A** A5
Tel. 812 312 32 05
Metro Gostiny Dvor
Open noon– midnight
A restaurant situated in the tea house at the bottom of the Yusupov Palace garden. The atmosphere is both cozy and imperial at the same time; the excellent menu, original and imaginative, includes dishes taken from the cookbooks of the Yusupov princes. Classical music is performed in the small rotunda. There's a wide selection of high-quality wines.
🞄 C 🎵 🞄

Europa
Grand Hotel Europe
Mikhailovskaya
Ulitsa 1/7 ◆ **A** D5
Tel. 812 329 60 00
Metro Gostiny Dvor
Open Mon.–Sat.
7am–11pm; brunch
Sun noon–4pm
Russian and Western European cuisine, excellent choice of wines and cigars. Recommended for the lavish Sunday brunch, to be taken

lazily with plenty of semi-sweet Russian champagne. But even then, dress at the smart end of casual to feel at ease in this soaring grand, glass-ceilinged Art Deco dining room, where you can expect to see everyone who is anyone in St Petersburg (tie required in the evening).
🞄 C

Hermitage
Dvortsovaya pl. 8
◆ **E** A2
Tel. 314 47 72
Metro Nevsky
Prospekt
Open daily 12
noon–11pm
A striking location on the square by the Palace, within the

grounds of the old army headquarters (now an annex of the Hermitage Museum). This restaurant was opened for the celebrations marking the city's 300th anniversary, when its vast halls were used for a constant stream of official banquets. They now lie empty, although they have preserved their ornate décor. The menu combines Russian specialties and international dishes. Extensive wine list.
🞄

Kalinka-Malinka
Italianskaya ul. 5
◆ **E** B3
Tel. 314 26 81
Metro Nevsky
Prospekt
Open daily
noon–11pm
The décor, complete with log walls, seeks to recreate the atmosphere of a dacha, while the waiters and musicians all wear appropriate costumes. The menu features classic Russian dishes. This restaurant is very popular at night with the audiences pouring out of the theaters on the nearby Arts Square.
🞄 🎵

Kamelot
Bolshaya
Koniuchennaya Ul. 14
◆ **A** C4
Tel. 812 325 99 06
Metro Nevsky
Prospekt
Open noon– midnight
As the restaurant's name suggests, the décor here is inspired by Arthurian legend. Beneath the Gothic vaulting are tables spread with cloths illustrating the adventures of the Knights of the Round Table. Excellent European cuisine, with unusual and

generous dishes.
▣ C

Karavan
Voznesensky Pr. 46
◆ A A6
Tel. 812 310 56 78
Metro Sadovaya
Open noon–2am
Traditional Caucasian and Central Asian cuisine served in an oriental atmosphere. Dishes include Georgian shashlyk (skewered meat), Azerbaijani lulia-kebab (minced meat) and plov uzbek (pilau rice).
▣

Kolkhida
Nevsky
Prospekt 176 ◆ E E5
Tel. 812 274 25 14
Metro Ploshchad Alexandra or Nevskovo
Open from noon until the last customer leaves
The Kolkhida offers a traditional Georgian atmosphere, with staff dressed in national costumes. There's a wide selection of high-quality Georgian wines.
▣

Landscrona
Nevsky Palace Hotel
Nevsky Prospekt 57
◆ E C4
Tel. 812 380 20 01
Metro Mayakovskaya
Open 6.30pm–midnight
A particularly well-regarded gourmet restaurant serving a wide range of Mediterranean dishes with an Italian touch but also offering some more unusual dishes, such as oysters with caviar cooked in champagne. The game (shot by a professional hunter who is a member of the hotel's staff) is particularly recommended. The restaurant, on the eighth floor, offers fine views over the

rooftops of St Petersburg. Live vocal music.
⊞ ♨ ♫

La Strada
Bolshaya Koniuchennaya 27
◆ A C4
Tel. 812 312 47 00
Metro Nevsky Prospekt
Open noon–11pm
A glass-walled gallery

VALHALL RESTAURANT ON NEVSKY PROSPEKT

VALHALL RESTAURANT

in a picturesque courtyard set out in the style of an Italian street. The specialty here is pizza cooked in front of customers. This is also a good place for families: there is a special children's menu, and a children's room with toys and supervision by a nanny.
▣ 🗋

Masha i Medvyed
Malaya Sadovaya Ulitsa 1 ◆ A D6
Tel. 812 310 46 31
Metro Gostiny Dvor
Open 11am–11pm
Plain, simple basement restaurant with plain, simple cooking. Its chief boast is pike caviar with onion. Also serves pirozhky (pastry parcels stuffed with meat or cabbage) prepared

with beer, onion soup and kasha (grilled millet) with mushrooms.
▣ C

Matrosskaya Tichina (Seaman's Silence)
Ulitsa Marata 54/34
◆ E C4-5
Tel. 812 764 44 13
Metro Ligovsky Prospekt

Open noon– midnight
Exceptionally good fish dishes prepared by a highly regarded French chef. The atmosphere here evokes the sea: the sound of waves whispers in the background, waitresses are dressed as sailors, and there is a large aquarium from which you may select your fish.
▣

Nicolai
Bolshaya Morskaya Ulitsa 52 ◆ A B 5
Tel. 571 14 02
Metro Nevsky Prospekt
Open daily noon–11pm
This restaurant is set in a private hotel donated to the Architects' Union and rechristened the

House of the Architects, but it is nevertheless open to all. The building has lost none of its charm and its wood trim provides a delightful setting for sampling traditional Russian food such as beef stroganoff and shashlyks (kebabs).
▣

Onegin
Sadovaya Ulitsa 11
◆ A B3
Tel. 812 571 83 84
www.oneginspb.com
Open Sun.–Thur. 5pm–2am, Fri.–Sat. 5pm–5am
Metro Gostiny Dvor, Nevsky Prospekt
Fashionable restaurant-club serving Russian and European cuisine.
⊞

Russian Empire
Nevsky
Prospekt 17 ◆ A C5
Tel. 571 24 09
Metro Nevsky Prospekt
This restaurant is located in the elegant rooms of the Stroganoff Palace. The décor revels in the splendors of a bygone era (inlaid tables, fine porcelain crockery and silver cutlery) but these do not come cheap...
⊞

lunch

Senat-bar
Galernaya Ulitsa 1
◆ D E2
Tel. 812 314 92 53
Open noon–2am
Metro Nevsky Prospekt
A restaurant in the cellars of the Senate where the imperial archives were stored before the Russian Revolution. Spacious interiors with décor depicting archivists, busts and frescoes in the Empire style. Russian and Western European cuisine. Some of the dishes are cooked in front of

diners. *A very good place for lunch.*
🔲 🅲

Stroganovsky Dvor
Nevsky
Prospekt 17 ◆ **A** B4
Tel. 812 315 23 15
Metro Nevsky
Prospekt
Open noon– midnight
A café-restaurant in the glass-roofed courtyard of the Stroganovsky Palace. Noted for its buffet, a touch simple and stodgy but one of the bargains of the city when you happen to be very hungry. Buffet US$5 (open until 10pm).
🔲 🅲

Valhall
Nevsky Pr. 22/24
◆ **A** B4
Tel. 812 571 00 24
www.valhall.ru
Metro Nevsky
Prospekt
Open 10am–3am
In the heart of the city, opposite the Cathedral of Our Lady of Kazan, Valhall has become a renowned and popular restaurant. Russian, Western European and Scandinavian cuisine, in which northern dishes feature prominently: Norwegian salmon, Greenland prawns, steaks served "on a Viking shield". The décor features 9th-century armory, and the waitresses are dressed as Valkyries.
🔲 🅲 ♨

Za Stsenoy
(Behind the Scenes)
Teatralnaya
Ploshchad 18/10
◆ **D** F3
Tel. 812 327 05 21
Metro Sennaya
Ploshchad
or Sadovaya
Open noon–2am
This is the restaurant of the Mariinsky Theater, whose very first guest was Placido Domingo.

It has a bohemian atmosphere, and the dining room is pleasingly decorated with theatrical paraphernalia – curtains, mirrors and pointed shoes. Russian and Western European cuisine are served.
🔲

Zolotoi Ostap
Italianskaya Ulitsa 4
◆ **A** D4
Tel. 812 303 88 22
Metro Gostiny Dvor
Open noon– midnight
The entrance to the Zolotoi Ostap, located beside Arts Square, is guarded by a bronze statue of Ostap Bender, the hero of Soviet satirical literature. Within is a suite of dining rooms decorated in the Art Nouveau style. The menu features not only Russian and Western European dishes but Caucasian and Chinese specialties as well. Zolotoy ostap, the house specialty – veal steak stuffed with smoked salmon – is recommended.
🔲 🅲

Russkaya Rybalka
(Russian Fishing)
Iujnaya Doroga 11
Primorsky Victory
Park ◆ **B** B2
Tel. 812 323 98 13
www.russian-fishing.com
Metro Krestovsky
Ostrov
Open noon–9pm
Set amid greenery, this restaurant stands on stilts at the edge of a lake filled with trout and sturgeon. Fishing tackle can be hired on site and guests may catch their own fish, which are then prepared – smoked, grilled or baked in foil – according to individual taste. Guests have included Russian president

Vladimir Putin, who has entertained foreign leaders here. Prices are based on the weight of the fish caught: about US$7 per lb for trout and US$9 for sturgeon. There is no additional charge for cooking the fish.
🏢 🔳 🅾

Podvorie
◆ OUTSIDE MAP AREA
Flitrovskoye Chosse
16
Tel. 812 465 13 99
www.podvorye.ru
Open noon–11pm
Well-known country-style restaurant at the entrance to Pavlovsk Park. A favorite spot for company junkets and the banqueting of visiting VIPs – Vladimir Putin once celebrated a birthday here. Standard Russian dishes, good choice of Crimean wines. Live music. Cossack and gypsy shows. A Russian bear at the entrance offering visitors a shot of vodka sets the tone for a fun place.
🔲 🎵 🅾

Akvarel
Birjevoy Most ◆ **A** A2
Tel. 812 320 86 00
Metro Sportivnaya
Open noon–11pm
"Fusion" cooking with strong Thai and Japanese accents, to a high standard. Modern, light interior. Akvarel occupies a moored boat, with spectacular views of the city. Café above, restaurant below. Bar and dance floor, with DJs on Fridays and Saturdays, add to the lively atmosphere of this trendy venue.
🔲 ♨

Austeria
Peter and Paul
Fortress ◆ **C** C6
Tel. 812 238 42 62

Metro Gorkovskaya
Open noon–midnight
At the time of Peter the Great "austeria" meant "inn", and the restaurant's interior re-creates a 17th-century Dutch inn. The menu, with a strong emphasis on vodka, caviar and blinis, is typically Russian.
🔲

Flora
Kamennoostrovsky
Prospekt 5 ◆ **A** C1
Tel 812 232 34 00
Metro Gorkovskaya
Open noon–11pm
The depressing modern exterior conceals a delicate Art Nouveau interior where Ilya Lazerson, one of the city's great chefs, holds court. French and Russian dishes. The flower-filled "tropical" setting, complete with a little bridge and a live parrot, make this a fun place to escape on a freezing day. With live ballet shows on Fridays and Saturdays, Flora is one of St Petersburg's most entertaining restaurants. Note also the related café and shop nearby, at Malaya Posadskaya Ulitsa 18.
🔲 🎵

Gorny Oriol
Alexander
Park ◆ **C** B5
Tel. 812 232 32 82
Metro Gorkovskaya
Open noon– midnight
This family restaurant located opposite the zoo is a good place to come to sample a wide variety of Georgian dishes. Especially recommended are the famous shashlyk (skewered meat). House wine is served in pitchers. The terrace, open in summer, looks onto the zoo.
🔲 ♨ 🅰

◆ RESTAURANTS

Restaurants
- ■ < US$30
- ■ US$30–50
- ■ US$50–70
- ⊞ > US$70

Na Zdorovye

Bolshoy
Prospekt 13 ◆ **D** A5
Tel. 812 232 40 39
Metro Sportivanaya
Open noon–11pm
Exceptional kitchen.
"The utopia of
Russian cooking"
says one Russian
critic. The décor is a
mix of Soviet retro
and old Russian. The
menu likewise, but
with a few dishes
betraying a French
influence. Duck
breast and fried
goat's cheese jostle
with the salted
salmon and the
pork marinated in
kvass (a popular
Russian drink made
from fermented
bread). A cheerful
atmosphere,
with gypsy
entertainment.
■ 🎵

U Gorchakova

Bolchaya
Monetnaya Ulitsa 19
◆ **C** C4
Tel. 812 233 92 72
Metro Gorkovskaya
Open noon– midnight
The Gorchakova is
located in the fine
residence of Prince
Gorchakov, the
eminent 19th-century
Russian diplomat
and chancellor.
However, neither
the unusual and
eclectic décor nor
the menu match the
atmosphere of the
state rooms. It's
definitely worth a visit.
■

STRELNA

Restaurant Strelna
◆ OUTSIDE MAP AREA
(NEAR PETERHOF)
Sankt-
Petersburgskoye
Schosse 58A
Tel. 812 421 41 96
Open 11am–
midnight
From this restaurant
there is a magnificent
view of the Strelna
Palace. Taste Russian
and Causasian
cuisine, while
listening to the

musical
accompaniment. Be
sure to check out the
fish of the day.
■ 🍴

VASILYEVSKY ISLAND

New Island
Universitetskaya
Nab. (level with
1 Linia) ◆ **D** E1
Tel. 812 963 67 65
Metro
Vasileovskaya
A restaurant on a boat
moored near
Rumiantsevsky ramp
on University

VIEW OF VASILYEVSKY ISLAND

GRIBOYEDOV CANAL

Embankment. Enjoy
Russian and Western
European cuisine as
the boat makes its
way along the Neva,
passing a succession
of magnificent
riverside palaces.
The boat trips take
place only between
April and November,
when the river is
navigable; New Island
is ice-bound in winter.
Trips along the Neva
cost US$8, and
dinner about US$35.
■ 🍴

Restoran
Tamozhenny
Per. 2 ◆ **D** F1
Tel. 812 327 89 79
Metro
Vasileostrovskaya
Open noon– midnight
Opposite the entrance
to Peter the Great's
Kunstkammer on
Vasilyevsky Island.
Smart, restrained
interior by Andrei
Dmitriev, the most
original young
designer in the city –
he also designed the
Mariinsky Theater's
restaurant; spacious
area, with a menu
printed on recycled
banknotes, that will
suit all budgets. Good
service, excellent
atmosphere. The
kitchen attracts mixed
reports for its fancier
dishes, but the open
fire makes this a good
place to retreat for
blinis and dumplings
with tea on a cold
day.
■

Russkiy Kitsch
Universitetskaya
Nab. 25 ◆ **D** E1
Tel. 812 325 11 22
Open noon–2am
Metro
Vasileostrovskaya
The décor is
everything the name
suggests – a parody
of nouveau-riche bad
taste. Some of the
joke carries over into
the food: blinis with
asparagus, for
example. But the

French-influenced
cooking is serious,
and for this city is by
no means overpriced.
Six rooms, two
galleries behind glass,
dance hall.
■ 🎵

Staraya Tamozhnaya (Old Customs House)

Tamojenny Per. 1
◆ **D** F1
Tel. 812 327 89 80
Metro
Vasileostrovskaya
Open 1pm–1am
Exceptional kitchen.
Grand food, even
grander wine list, high
prices, French chef.
The mainly French
menu also salutes
some Russian
classics, including
blinis with black
caviar. Historical
touches to the décor
help to create the
sense of tradition in
this red-brick vaulted
chamber, a customs
point in the 18th
century. Two bars,
jazz in the evening.
An institution.
■

VYBORG

7–40
Bolshoy
Sampsonievsky Pr.
108 ◆ **C** D1-2
Tel. 812 246 34 44
Metro Lesnaya or
Chyornaya Rechka
Open Mon. 3pm–
11pm, Tue.–Sun.
noon–11pm
Exceptionally good
Jewish cuisine, with
a wide selection of
traditional dishes,
including tsimes and
forchmak. The food is
served on clay
crockery painted in
the style of Chagall.
Live violin music.
■ 🎵

CAFÉS

Bistro Le Français
Galernaya Ulitsa 20
◆ **D** E2
Tel. 812 315 24 65
Open 11am–1am
Traditional French cuisine. Bar with movie theater and videos of French movies for hire.

Che
Poltavskaya
Ulitsa 3 ◆ **E** D4
Tel. 812 277 76 00
Open daily 24 hrs
Metro Ploshchad
Aleksandra Nevskovo
or Ploshchad
Vosstanya
A trendy café with Latin-American and jazz music in the background. A huge choice of teas and cakes on offer.

Coffee-Break
Kanala Griboyedova
Nab. 22 ◆ **A** C5
Tel. 812 314 67 29
Open 9am–11pm
A café with a fine view of the Cathedral of Our Lady of Kazan. Wide selection of coffees, and black, green and red tea; delicious desserts. Exhibitions of contemporary painting.

Idiot
Nab. Reky
Moyky 82 ◆ **C** A6
Tel. 812 315 16 75
Open daily
11am–1am
Vegetarian cuisine. Cluster of noisy, cosily furnished basement rooms, a popular refuge for students and foreigners. Overflowing bookshelves and bizarre ornaments help to create the wonderfully eclectic atmosphere. The food is mainly but not solely vegetarian. Complimentary shot of vodka provided with each alcoholic drink, The full bar, which serves cocktails, makes this an excellent place for a late drink as well as for a leisurely lunch.

James Cook
Chvedsky per. 2
◆ **E** A3
Tel. 812 312 32 00
or 812 571 11 51
Two naval-themed rooms in this café, offering a good choice of teas and cakes. There's also a pub with a large selection of beers and savory dishes. Musical flavor: jazz, blues, country.

PUBS AND BARS

Mollie's Irish Bar
Ulitsa Rubinstein 36
◆ **A** F6
Tel. 812 319 97 68
Open noon–2am
An off-the-shelf Irish pub, and none the worse for that. Guinness, some 20 types of beer and a wide range of cocktails on offer. Some hot food, and hardwood stools. Friendly atmosphere. Popular with foreigners.

Podval Brodiatcheï Sobaki
Isskusstv pl. 5 (near Nevsky Pr.) ◆ **E** B3
Tel. 315 77 64
Open daily
11am–11pm
Metro Nevsky
Prospekt
The name of this café in a vaulted cellar literally means "stray dog". It opened in 1912 and numbered among its regular customers the poets Anna Akhmatova and Vladimir Mayakovsky; they still preside over it today, in the form of portraits hung along the walls. A pleasant stopover for a cup of tea after a visit to the Russian Museum.

Quo Vadis
Nevsky Prospekt 24
◆ **E** A3
Tel. 812 571 80 11
www.quovadis.ru
Metro Nevsky
Prospekt
Open daily 24 hrs
Internet café.

Shamrock
Ulitsa Dekabristov 27
◆ **A** A6
Tel. 812 318 46 25
Open noon–2am
Another Irish pub, located opposite the Mariinsky Theater, and again a fashionable place with a bohemian atmosphere. Beer from US$2.
◻ ▭ Ⓒ

Sunduk (Coffee)
Furchtatskaya
Ulitsa 42 ◆ **E** D2
Tel. 812 272 31 00
Open 10am–10pm
Three small rooms, one with a stage where jazz, blues and rock bands perform. Friendly, relaxed atmosphere. Beer from US$2.50; snacks from US$1 (cover charge US$1).
◻ 🎵

Tinkoff
Kazanskaya
Ulitsa 7 ◆ **A** C5
Tel. 812 314 84 85
www.tinkoff.ru
Open noon–2am
Microbrewery (the modern interior with a glass partition allows customers to watch the brewing in action) with fine beer and fair food, including a sushi bar. A St Petersburg institution. Big and often noisy (quieter at lunch), with live music and giant television screen. A trendy, vibrant place, popular with students.

LEISURE

CASINOS

Premier Casino Club
Nevsky Pr. 47 ◆ **A** F5
Tel. 812 315 78 93
Open 24 hours
Bars and Palkin restaurant: cozy atmosphere and good-quality Western European cuisine.

Taléon Casino Club
Reky Moiky
Nab. 59 ◆ **A** B5
Tel. 812 315 76 45
Open 24 hours
Located in the former residence of the Russian merchant Eliseev, with many rooms and a strong gambling atmosphere.

NEVSKY PROSPEKT
JAZZ PHILHARMONIA

Restaurants and concerts. Private functions some evenings.

Dom Kino (the Movie House)
Karavannaya Ul. 12
◆ **A** E5
Tel. 812 314 80 36
Open exclusively to members of the film-directors' union during the Soviet era, the Movie House is now a center for cinema enthusiasts. Events include screenings of European movies, retrospectives and film festivals.

OSTROVSKY SQUARE

SMOLNY CATHEDRAL

Sankt Peterburgsky Tsirk
Reky Fontanky Naberejnaya 3
◆ **A** E2
Tel. 812 314 84 78
www.circus.spb.ru
Ticket office open 11am–7pm
One of the oldest Russian circuses and one the most beautiful in Europe. Established in 1877, it was the first edifice of stone to be constructed specifically for circus performances.

Bielosselskikh-Bielozerskikh Dvorets
Nevsky Pr. 41
◆ **A** E5
Tel. 812 315 52 36
Chamber music performed in the Oak Room and Mirror Room of the Beloselsky-Belozersky Palace.

Filarmonia Dmitria Shostakovicha
◆ **A** D5
Home of the fine St Petersburg Philharmonic and of the smaller Glinka recital hall.

SHOSTAKOVICH (LARGE) PHILHARMONIC HALL (Bolshoy Zal):
Mikhailovskaya Ul. 2
Tel. 812 110 42 57
Ticket office open 11am–3pm, 4–7.30pm
GLINKA (SMALL) CHAMBER HALL (Maly Zal):
Nevsky Pr. 30
Tel. 812 311 83 33
Ticket office open 11am–3pm, 4–7pm
The Shostakovich Philharmonia's distinguished concert hall has an excellent orchestra. Major international musicians perform here. The Glinka Philharmonia also hosts several festivals, including an early music festival where all the pieces are performed on period instruments.

Kapella
Reky Moiky Nab. 20
◆ **A** C3
Tel. 812 314 11 53 or 812 314 10 58 (ticket office)
Ticket office open noon–7pm
An architectural jewel, St Petersburg's State Kapella is now a concert hall with a wide-ranging musical program.

Oktiabrsky
Ligovsky Prospekt 6 ◆ **E** D3
Tel. 812 275 12 73
Ticket office open 11am–8pm
The largest concert hall in St Petersburg, with a wide-ranging program of musical events.

Smolny Sobor (Smolny Cathedral)
Rastrelli Pl. 3/1 ◆ **E** F1
Tel. 812 271 76 32
Concerts of Russian church music.

Filarmonia Djazovoy Muzyki (Jazz Philharmonia)
Zagorodny Pr. 27
◆ **E** B5
Tel. 812 764 85 65
www.jazz-hall.spb.ru
Open: *Great Room* Tue.–Sun. 7–11pm; *Ellington Room* Tue., Fri., Sat. 8–11pm
Established in the 1980s by David Golochtchekin, the renowned jazz musician, this is the oldest jazz club in St Petersburg. Performers from all over the world are invited here, notably for the annual Swing on Summer Nights festival in June. Smart dress required.

JFC Jazz Club
Chpalernaya Ul. 33
◆ **E** C1
Tel. 812 272 98 50
www.jfc.spb.ru
Open daily 7–10pm
One of the best jazz clubs in the city, where international musicians perform all types of jazz. Knowledgeable audience. Drinks at reasonable prices.

Neo Jazz Club
Solianoy Per. 14
◆ **A** E3
Tel. 812 273 38 30
Open noon–midnight; concerts at 8pm
Soft jazz, duos and trios.Western European and Caucasus cuisine.

Fish Fabrique
Ligovsky Prospekt 53 ◆ **E** C5
Tel. 812 764 48 57
www.fishfabrique.spb.ru
Open 4pm–5.30am; concerts start around 10pm
All styles of music. One of the oldest-established underground clubs in St Petersburg, with a bohemian atmosphere. Table soccer and a terrace that's open in summer.

Griboyedov Club
Voronejskaya Ul. 2a
◆ **E** C6
Tel. 812 764 43 55
Open 6pm–6am (Fri., Sat., till 7am)
concerts at 10pm
A fashionable venue located in a disused air-raid shelter hung with Persian carpets. DJ.

Jimi Hendrix Jazz Club
Liteiny Prospekt 33
◆ **A** F4
Tel. 812 279 88 13
Open 24 hours daily

THEATERS ◆

A club by night and a café by day. Blues, rock'n'roll and Latino evenings.
A pleasant place for dinner with friends. Affordable prices. As space is limited, reservations must be made.

Luna (the Moon)
Voznessensky Pr. 46
◆ **A** A6
Tel. 812 310 16 16
Open 6pm–6am
Two levels, three rooms, restaurants, casino, bars and a dance floor. A varied range of evening performances, with high-class professional choreography. Smart dress required.

Manhattan
Reky Fontanky
Nab. 90 ◆ **E** B5
Tel. 812 713 19 45
www.manhattan.by.ru
Open 2pm–5am; concerts at 9pm (except Mon.)
Rock, blues and jazz. Internet café and billiards.

Money Honey and City Club
Sadovaya Ulitsa 13
◆ **A** E4
Tel. 812 310 05 49
www.moneyhoney.org
Open 11am–6am; concerts at 8pm
Rock music. A club on two floors, with two dance areas and two bars. It has a "saloon" feel, with fireplaces and photographs of rock stars on the walls. A mixed, sometimes lively clientele.

Ostrov
Letenanta Shmidta
Nab. 37 ◆ **D** D2
Tel. 812 328 46 49
Open Wed.–Sun.
10pm–6am
Located in a fine restored residence. Unusual décor and a rotating dance floor with special effects and DJ. A relatively wealthy clientele.

Plaza
Nab. Makarova 2
◆ **C** B6
Tel. 812 323 90 90
Open daily 24 hours
Located in a beautiful old building with a huge dance floor, restaurant and casino. Dancing and concerts in the evening. Fri.–Sat.: concerts. Sun.: DJ.

Port
Antonenko Per. 2
◆ **A** B6
Tel. 812 314 26 09
www.clubport.spb.ru
Open Wed.–Sat.
10pm–6am
Located next to

STAGE AT THE MARINSKY THEATER

AUDITORIUM OF THE MARINSKY THEATER

St Isaac's Square, opposite the Mariinsky Palace. The venue has a high-tech feel. There is a billiard room, several bars and dance floors, including an outsize one. A very mixed clientele and special student evenings.

Red Club
Poltavskaya Ulitsa 7
◆ **E** D5
Tel. 812 277 13 66
www.redclubonline.com
Open noon–6am; concerts at 8pm
A varied program, with an orientation

toward young rockers. Excellent acoustics. Two floors, with two bars, two stages and a billiard room. A quieter atmosphere than elsewhere.

ENTERTAINMENT CENTERS

Carnaval
Anichkov Palace
Nevsky Prospekt 39
◆ **A** E5
Tel. 812 310 99 88
Russian folk music and dance are performed by top professional companies.

THEATERS

Aleksandrinsky Theater
Ostrovskogo Pl. 2
◆ **A** E6
Tel. 812 710 41 03
Ticket office open
11am–3pm, 4–7pm;
Sat.–Sun. 4–6pm
A classical repertoire

Sankt Petersburg
Lenina Pl. 1 ◆ **C** E5
Tel. 812 542 15 25
or 812 542 09 44
Ticket office open
1–3pm, 4–7pm
Concerts, shows and all sorts of other entertainments are part of a wide-ranging program .

of plays performed in the magnificent setting of a theater designed by the great Carlo Rossi.

Baltisky Dom (Baltic house)
Alexander Park
◆ **C** C5
Tel. 812 232 62 44
Ticket office open
noon–3pm, 4–7pm
Having evolved from TRAM (Young Workers' Theater) and LenKom (Komsomol Leninist Theater), this theater is now the home of several small companies that are known for their experimental productions. It also hosts the annual Baltic House international festival, which takes place in October.

G. Tovstonogov's BDT (Grand Dramatic Theater)
Fontanky Nab. 65
◆ **E** B4
Tel. 812 310 92 42
Ticket office open
1–3pm, 4–7pm
This theater was revived by the eminent director G. Tovstonogov, who brought together the best actors of the Soviet era.The company's repertoire covers the major works of the Russian theater.

Konservatori Rimskogo-Korsakova
Teatralnaya Pl. 3
◆ **D** E3
Tel. 812 312 25 07
Ticket office open
11am–7pm
The Rimsky-Korsakov Conservatoire's opera and ballet theater is a show-case for its students and teachers. The theater also organizes various Russian and international festivals and competitions.

295

Maly (Mussorgsky Opera and Ballet Theater)

Iskusstv Pl. 1
(Arts Square) ◆ **A** D4
Tel. 812 595 42 84
or 812 595 43 05
(ticket office)
Ticket office open
11am–3pm, 4–6pm
(6–7pm for that day's
performance only)
*The former
Mikhailovsky Theater
is St Petersburg's
second most
important center of
opera and ballet. It
was once used only
by visiting foreign
companies,
particularly from Italy
and France, but now
puts on a range of
classic works
performed by
Russian singers and
dancers. The building
is worth a visit to see
the architecture and
décor alone.*

Maly Dramatichesky Teatr (Theater of Europe)

Ulitsa Rubinstein 18
◆ **A** F6
Tel.812 713 20 28
or 812 713 20 78
(ticket office)
Ticket office open
noon–7pm
*This theater's artistic
achievements and
innovative
productions have won
it a reputation
of European stature.
Its artistic leader, Lev
Dodin, was voted
Europe's most
outstanding director
three years ago. The
company goes on
frequent foreign
tours.*

Mariinsky Opera and Ballet Theater

Teatralnaya Pl. 1
(Theater Square)
◆ **D** E3
Tel. 812 714 43 44
or 812 714 12 11
Ticket office open
11am–2pm, 3–7pm.
Performances 7pm,
matinees 11.30am.
*The history of this
theater is closely
linked to Russian*

ARTS SQUARE

VIEW OF VASILIEVSKY ISLAND

*musical culture.
Formerly known as
the Kirov Theater, it
has reverted to its
original name and
continues to attract
the most highly
talented actors and
directors. With one of
the best orchestras in
the world, new
productions of the
great classical operas
and ballets are
particularly worth
seeing. As the main
companies have
gained such an
international
reputation they are
more likely to be
away touring in
spring and summer.
Winter is a better
time to find them in
St Petersburg. The
annual White Nights
festival (June)
regularly offers a
highly innovative
program. Note,
however, that ticket
prices are higher at
this time of year, the
high tourist season.*

St Petersburg Opera

Galernaya Ulitsa 33
◆ **D** E2
Tel. 812 312 39 82
or 812 315 67 69
Ticket office open
12–3pm, 4–7pm
*This young opera
company has already*

*won several awards.
Shows take place at
the Yusupov Palace
(Reky Moiky Nab.
94) or at the
Hermitage Theater
(Dvortsovaya Nab.
34). Its productions
have won praise for
their avant-garde,
nonconformist spirit.*

Teatr Muzikalnoy Komedy (Musical Comedy Theater)

Italianskaya Ul. 13
◆ **A** E5
Tel. 812 313 43 16
or 812 313 48 68
Ticket office open
11am–7pm
*This theater,
specializing in
operetta, puts on
magical productions
performed by a
company long
recognized as
distinctive masters of
the genre. The
theater has a
sumptuous interior.*

Zazerkalie (Children's musical theater)

Ulitsa Rubinstein 13
◆ **A** F6
Tel. 812 712 51 35
Ticket office open
noon–3pm, 4–7pm
*Although most of the
repertoire consists of
tales and fables, the
musical shows put on*

*here will appeal to
both children and
their parents.*

Soldat Udatchi (Soldier of Fortune)

Nekrassova
Ulitsa 37 ◆ **E** D3
Tel. 812 272 39 78
Open daily
11am–8pm
*Army equipment,
military decorations
and accessories.
Large selection of
knives.*

Antikvarnitsentr

Nalitchnaya
Ulitsa 21 ◆ **D** A2
Tel. 812 355 10 10
Open daily
11am–7pm
*One of the oldest-
established antique
shops in the city.
Large showroom with
a wide variety
of pieces.*

Lavka Stariovchtchika (Bric-a-brac)

9 Linia 26 ◆ **D** D1
Tel. 812 328 56 37
Open Mon.–Fri.11am–
6pm (3pm Sat.)
*All kinds of old
utilitarian objects,
including dinner
services and flatware,
samovars, coffee
mills and furniture.
Affordable prices.*

Panteleimonovsky

Pestelia
Ulitsa 13/15 ◆ **A** F3
Tel. 812 279 72 35
Open Mon.–Sat.
11am–7pm
*A wealth of beautiful
old decorative
objects and fine
porcelain.
Knowledgeable staff.*

Petersburg

Nevsky Prospekt 54
◆ **A** F5
Tel. 812 311 40 20
Open daily
10am–8pm
*A variety of objects
on sale at reasonable
prices.*

Rapsodia
Bolshaya
Koniuchennaya
Ulitsa 13 ◆ **A** C4
Tel. 812 314 48 01
Open daily 11am–
7pm
*Well-known for its
collection of icons
chosen by experts.
Many silver and
crystal pieces.*

Renaissance
Pestelia Ulitsa 8
◆ **A** F3
Tel. 812 273 54 04
Open daily
11am–8pm
*Decorative objects,
porcelain and bronze,
and a wide selection
of Empire furniture.*

Bukinist
Liteiny
Prospekt 59 ◆ **E** C3
Tel. 812 273 25 04
Open daily
10am–2pm, 3–7pm
*Wide range of
antiquarian and art
books. A browser's
paradise.*

Dom Knigi
(the Book House)
Nevsky Prospekt 62
◆ **A** B3
Tel. 812 318 65 46
Open daily 9am–
10pm (9pm Sun.)
*The largest bookstore
in the city, stocking
all kinds of books,
including illustrated
books, postcards,
and many books on
St Petersburg.*

Iskusstvo (Art)
Nevsky Prospekt 16
◆ **A** B4
Tel. 812 311 54 73
Open daily
10am–8pm
*Art books, including
illustrated books*

Belotchka
(Little Squirrel)
Sredny Prospekt 28
◆ **D** D1
Tel. 812 323 17 63
Open Mon.–Fri.
9am–8.30pm
(7pm Sat.)

*Lovely confectionery
shop. It takes its
name from the
famous nut candy.*

Sever
Nevsky Prospekt 44
◆ **A** E5
Tel. 812 311 25 89
Open Mon.–Fri.
10am–9pm,
Sat.–Sun. 10am–8pm
*An institution selling
all the best Russian
chocolate and candy.*

Zhar-Ptitsa
(Firebird)
Marata Ulitsa 70b
◆ **E** B5
Tel. 812 315 26 87
Open Mon.–Sat.
10am–6.30pm
*The retail outlet of
the great Russian
confectioners, the
Krupskaya. Huge
choice of delicious
eastern European
confectionery.*

Dom Tkanei
(the Fabric House)
Komsomola
Ulitsa 45 ◆ **E** D1
Tel. 812 542 43 43
Open daily
11am–7pm
*Wide selection
of European and
Central Asian fabrics,
as well as
good-quality,
inexpensive Russian*

NEVSKY PROSPEKT

*linen and lace and
bedlinen.*

Lena, Torgovy Dom
Nevsky Prospekt 50
◆ **A** F5
Tel. 812 312 32 34
Open daily
10am–9pm
*Wide range of
"exotic" furs from
various countries,
including
Scandinavia.*

Rot-Front
Bolshaya Morskaya
Ulitsa 34 ◆ **D** F2
Tel. 812 311 73 57
Open Mon.–Fri.
10am–7pm (6pm Sat.)
*The city's other
leading fur house.*

Salon de Tatiana
Kotegova
Bolshoy Prospekt 44
(on the coast at
Petrograd) ◆ **C** C4
Tel. 812 346 34 67
Open Mon.–Fri.
noon–8pm
*Classic clothes with
simple outlines, in
plain colors (white,
black and brown)
and natural fabrics
such as fine linen,
cashmere and taffeta.*

Tatiana Parfionova's
Fashion House
Nevsky

Prospekt 51 ◆ **A** F5
Tel. 812 713 36 69
Open Mon.–Sat.
11am–8pm,
Sat.–Sun. 11am–9pm
*One of the city's
most prestigious
fashion houses, with
a unique clothing
line. Fine fabrics and
a wide selection of
scarves and
embroidered chiffon
shawls.*

Art-Boutique
Mariinsky
Teatralnaya Pl. 18
◆ **D** F3
Tel. 812 326 41 96
Open Tue.–Sun.
11am–7pm
*Souvenirs of the
Mariinsky Theater,
unusual decorative
pieces and theatrical
objects, illustrated
books, postcards,
CDs and DVDs.*

Beluga Deluxe
Isskoustv Pl. 5
◆ **A** D4/**E** D4
Tel. 812 325 82 64
Open daily 9am–8pm
*Amber, malachite
and porcelain items
in a very upmarket
type of store.*

Krasni Oktiabr
Ulitsa Blokhina 8
◆ **C** B5
Tel. 812 238 84 99
Open daily
10am–6pm
*Palekh lacquered
boxes, Russian dolls,
shawls, Gjel crockery,
and amber and
malachite objects.*

Northway
Angliskaya nab. 36
◆ **D** E2
Tel. 812 312 20 62
Open daily
*Lacquer boxes, fur
hats, lace shawls and
amber jewels in a
luxurious setting.*

Stroganoff
Nevsky Prospekt 17
◆ **A** C5
Open daily
11am–8pm
*Contemporary art, art
glass and handicrafts.*

◆ SHOPPING

JEWELRY

Ananov Jewelry Showroom
Nevsky Prospekt 31
◆ A E5
Tel. 812 110 55 92
Open daily
10am–7pm
Large showroom with jewelry representing the major periods and styles of the Russian jeweler's art, including that of Fabergé.

Belage
Nevsky Prospekt 57
◆ A F6
Tel. 812 310 66 88
Open daily
11am–8pm
Upmarket jewelry.

Luvelirtorg
Flagship shop:
Novosmolenskaya
Nab. 1 ◆ B A5
Tel. 812 355 58 61
Open Mon.–Sat.
10am–2pm, 3–7pm,
Sun. 11am–6pm
A major chain of jewelry shops with branches in several dsitricts of the city.

Salon Bouré
Nevsky Prospekt 23
◆ A C5
Tel.812 311 75 34
Open daily
10am–8pm
High-quality jewelry, clocks and watches.

MUSIC

Klassika
Mikhailovskaya Ul. 2
◆ A D5
Tel. 812 710 44 28
Open daily
11am–9pm
*Located in the Philharmonia's ticket office, the shop specializes in classical music, including secondhand CDs, cassettes, vinyl records and old musical scores.
Mail order.*

Otkryty Mir (Open World)
Isaakievskaya Pl. 5
(near Nevsky
Prospekt) ◆ A A5
Tel. 812 311 59 76
Open Mon.–Sat.
11am–8pm,
Sun. noon–7pm
*Wide choice of classical music.
Mail order.*

Rock Island
Kirochnaya Ulitsa 8
◆ E C2
Tel. 812 273 07 22
Open Mon.–Sat.
11am–7pm, Sun. till
6pm
Rock music. The secondhand section has a large collection of vinyl records and original recordings of Soviet-era rock.

Severnaya Lira (the Northern Lyre)
Nevsky Prospekt 26
◆ A C5
Tel. 812 312 07 96
Open Mon.–Sat.
10am–8pm,
Sun. 11am–7pm
Musical instruments, scores, accessories and CDs.

PORCELAIN

Lomonosov Porcelain Shops
◆ E E4
– Nevsky Pr. 160
Tel. 812 277 48 38
Daily 10am–8pm
– Vladimirsky Pr. 7
Tel. 812 713 15 13
Daily 10am–8pm
– Obukhovskoy
Oborony Pr. 151
Tel. 812 560 85 44
Open daily
10am–7pm
Descended from the imperial porcelain factory established in 1744, Lomonosov still produces high-quality porcelain today.

SHOPPING ARCADES

Dom Leningradskoy Torgovly (DLT)
Bolshaya
Koniuchennaya
Ul. 21/23 ◆ E A3
Tel. 812 312 26 27
Open Mon.–Sat.
10am–9pm,
Sun. 11am–7pm
St Petersburg's third great historic arcade.

Gostiny Dvor
Nevsky Prospekt 35
◆ A D5
Tel. 812 710 54 08
Daily 9am–10pm
One of St Petersburg's oldest shopping arcades.

Passage
Nevsky Prospekt 48
◆ A F5
Tel. 812 311 70 84
Open Mon.–Sat.
10am–9pm,
Sun. 11am–7pm
Designed as a promenade, the arcade links Nevsky Prospekt and Italianskaya Ulitsa.

SPORT AND LEISURE

Medved (the Bear)
Sadovaya Ul. 55/57
◆ E A5
Tel. 812 310 83 77
Open Mon.–Sat.
10am–7pm (5pm
Sun)
Everything for hiking, shooting and fishing, which, particularly in the case of fishing through the ice in winter, are all popular leisure activities in Russia. High quality and inexpensive.

SUPERMARKETS

Kalinka Stockmann
Finliandsky Pr. 1
Vyborgskaya Stornoa
(Vyborg coast) ◆ C D5
Tel. 812 542 22 97
Open daily
9am–10pm

Magasin Elisseiev
Nevsky Prospekt 56
◆ A F5
Open daily 9am–9pm
A delightful shop whose Art Nouveau architecture has been preserved. Caviar and other Russian specialties.

Passage
Nevsky Prospekt 48
◆ A F5
Open daily
10am–11pm

Piatorochka
Nalitchnaya Ul. 32
◆ D A1
Vasilyevsky Island
Tel. 812 356 51 77
Open daily 9am–1am

Prima
26 Bolshaya
Morskaya Ulitsa
(near Nevsky
Prospekt) ◆ D F2
Tel. 812 314 82 75

Super-Babylon
Maly Pr. 54/56, PS
(Petrogradskaya
Storona, on the
Petrograd coast)
◆ C B4
Tel. 812 233 88 92
Open 24/7

VIDEOS

Na Lenfilme
Kamennoostrovsky
Prospekt 10 ◆ C C5
Tel. 812 232 28 40
Open daily
11am–8pm
For the widest choice of Russian and Soviet films (over 1,000 titles)

Directory

◆ PLACES TO VISIT

Places to visit are listed alphabetically. The symbol ▲ refers to a page number in the Itineraries, ◆ refers to the Map section and ★ means places that should not be missed.

ST PETERSBURG

ACADEMY OF ARTS Universitetskaya Nab. 17 Tel. 812 323 35 78/812 323 64 96	*Open Wed.–Sun. 11am–6pm.*	▲ *162* ◆ **D** E1-2
AKHMATOVA MUSEUM Fontanka Nab. 34 (entrance on Liteiny Pr. 53 or through the Sheremetev Palace) Tel. 812 272 22 11/812 272 57 58	*Open Tue.–Sun. 10.30am–5.30pm.* *Closed last Wed. of the month.*	▲ *237* ◆ **A** F4-5
ALEXANDER NEVSKY MONASTERY (Sculpture Museum) ★ Nevsky Pr. 179/2 Tel. 812 274 2635/812 277 1716	*Open April–Sep.: Fri.–Wed. 9.30am–7pm;* *Oct.–March: Fri.–Wed. 9.30am–5pm.*	▲ *253* ◆ **E** E5
APARTMENT OF ALEXANDER BLOK Dekabristov Ul. 57, Apartment 21, 23 Tel. 812 713 86 27/812 713 86 33	*Open Thur.–Mon. 11am–5pm* *and Tue. 11am–6pm.* *Closed last Tue. of the month.*	▲ *199* ◆ **D** E3

BELOSELSKY-BELOZERSKY PALACE
Nevsky Pr. 41
Tel. 812 315 52 36
– **MUSEUM OF THE DEVELOPMENT**
  OF RUSSIAN DEMOCRACY
  Tel. 812 571 17 06
	Open daily 1pm–5pm. Guided tours only and
	musical evenings (call to enquire).
	
	– Visits arranged for groups of more than
	10 people
		▲ *238*
		◆ **A** F5

BOTANICAL GARDENS **AND MUSEUM** Professora Popova Ul. 2 Tel. 812 234 17 64	*Open 11am–4pm. Closed Fri.*	▲ *153* ◆ **C** C3
BREAD MUSEUM Ligovsky Pr. 73 Tel. 812 764 11 10	*Open Tue.–Sat. 10am–5pm.* *Closed last Tue. of the month.*	▲ *244* ◆ **E** D4
CABIN OF PETER THE GREAT (Domik Petra) Petrovskaya Nab. 6 Tel. 812 232 45 76	*Open Wed.–Sun. 10am–4pm.*	▲ *151* ◆ **C** D5
CATHEDRAL OF **OUR LADY OF KAZAN** Kazanskaya Pl. 2	*Open daily noon–6pm.*	▲ *217* ◆ **A** C5
CHURCH OF **THE RESURRECTION** Kanala Griboyedova Nab. 2a Tel. 812 315 16 36	*Open 11am–6pm.* *Closed Wed.*	▲ *228* ◆ **A** D4
CRUISER *AURORA* Petrogradskaya Nab. 4 Tel. 812 230 84 40	*Open Tue.–Thur. and Sat.–Sun. 10.30am–4pm.* *Free.*	▲ *152* ◆ **C** D5
DOSTOEVSKY MUSEUM ★ Kuznechny Per. 5/2 Tel. 812 571 40 31	*Open Tue.–Sun. 11am–6pm.* *Closed last Wed. of the month.*	▲ *240* ◆ **E** C4
ELAGIN PALACE (Museum of Decorative Arts of the 18th and early 19th c.) Elagin Island Tel. 812 430 11 31	*Open Wed.–Sun. 10am–6pm.*	▲ *154* ◆ **B** E1
ENGINEERS' CASTLE Sadovaya Ul. 4 Tel. 812 313 41 73	*Open Mon. 10am–4pm and* *Wed.–Sun. 10am–5pm.*	▲ *229* ◆ **A** E3-4
ETHNOGRAPHIC MUSEUM Ingenernaya Ul. 4 Tel. 812 313 44 21	*Open Tue.–Sun. 10am–6pm.* *Closed last Fri. of the month.*	▲ *228* ◆ **A** D4
HERMITAGE MUSEUM ★ (also known as Winter Palace) Dvortsovaya Nab. 36 Tel. 812 571 34 20/812 710 96 25 *www.hermitagemuseum.org*	*Open Tue.–Sat. 10.30am–6pm (5pm Sun.)* *A part of the Morozov collection (Pierre* *Bonnard, Maurice Denis...) is now in the rooms* *of the army and the guard headquarters, on* *Palace Square, opposite the Hermitage.*	▲ *168* ◆ **A** B3

*When in St Petersburg you do not need to dial the city code 812
before the seven-digit phone number.*

KUNSTKAMMER Universitetskaya Nab. 3 Tel. 812 328 14 12/812 328 01 18	*Open Tue.–Sun. 11am–6pm.* *Closed last Tue. of the month.*	▲ *160* ◆ **A** A3
LOMONOSOV MUSEUM Universitetskaya Nab. 3 Tel. 812 328 10 11	*Open Tue.–Sun. 11am–5.30pm.* *Closed last Tue. of the month.*	▲ *160* ◆ **A** A3
MARBLE PALACE Millionaya Ul. 5 Tel. 812 312 91 96	*Open Mon. 10am–6pm, Wed.–Sun. 10am–5pm.*	▲ *184* ◆ **A** D2
MENDELEEV MUSEUM (The Twelve Colleges) Mendeleevskaya Linya 2 Tel. 812 328 97 44	*Open Mon.–Fri. 11am–4pm.*	▲ *159* ◆ **C** E1
MENSHIKOV PALACE ★ Universitetskaya Nab. 15 Tel. 812 323 11 12	*Open Tue.–Sun. 10.30am–4.30pm.* *Guided tours only (call for information).*	▲ *161* ◆ **D** E1
MUSEUM OF DECORATIVE AND APPLIED ARTS Solianoi Per. 15 Tel. 812 273 32 58	*Open Tue.–Sun. 11am–5pm.*	▲ *188* ◆ **A** E3
MUSEUM OF LITERATURE (Pushkin House) Naverejnaya Makarova 4 Tel. 812 328 05 02	*Open Mon.–Fri. 10.30am–4.30pm. Guided tours only, by appointment (Tel. 812 108 4761). A must for Russian literature aficionados.*	▲ *158* ◆ **B** F6
MUSEUM OF THEATER AND MUSIC (Fountains House) Fontanki Nab. 34 Tel. 812 272 44 41	*Open Wed.–Sun. noon–5pm.* *Closed last Wed. of the month.*	▲ *236* ◆ **A** F4-5
MUSEUM OF POLITICAL HISTORY Kubysheva Ul. 2–4 Tel. 812 233 71 13/812 233 70 52	*Open 10am–6pm.* *Closed Thur.*	▲ *150* ◆ **C** D5
MUSEUM OF THE ARCTIC AND ANTARCTIC Marata Ul. 24a Tel. 812 117 25 49/813 113 27 81	*Open Wed.–Sat. 10am–5pm, Sun. 10am–6pm.*	▲ *241* ◆ **E** C4
NABOKOV'S HOUSE AND MUSEUM Bolshaya Morskaya Ul. 47 Tel. 812 315 47 13	*Open Tues.–Sun. 11am–6pm.*	▲ *198* ◆ **D** F2
NAVAL MUSEUM Birgevaya Pl. 4 Tel. 812 328 25 02	*Open Wed.–Sun. 11am–6pm.* *Closed last Thur. of the month.*	▲ *157* ◆ **A** A3
PETER AND PAUL FORTRESS ★ Revolyutsy Pl. Tel. 812 238 03 29, 812 238 05 11 or 812 232 94 54	*Open 11am–5pm.* *Closed Wed. and last Tue. of the month.*	▲ *146* ◆ **A** B-C1
PHARMACY MUSEUM 16/18 Linaya 7 Tel. 812 323 22 69	*Open Mon.–Sat. 8am–8pm.*	▲ *164* ◆ **D** D1
PORCELAIN MUSEUM Obukhovskoy Oborony Pr. 151 Tel. 812 560 83 00	*Open Tue.–Sat. 10.30am–5pm, Sun. 10.30am–4pm.* *Department of the Hermitage Museum.*	
PUSHKIN MUSEUM AND HOUSE Reki Moiky Nab. 12 Tel. 812 571 35 31	*Open Wed.–Mon. 11am–5pm.* *Book in advance for guided tours.*	▲ *182* ◆ **A** C3
THE RIDING SCHOOL (The Manège) Isaakievskaya Pl. 1 Tel. 812 314 82 53	*Open for displays Fri.–Wed. 11am–7pm.*	▲ *194* ◆ **A** A5
RIMSKY-KORSAKOV MUSEUM Zagorodny Pr. 28 Tel. 812 315 39 75	*Open Wed.–Sun. 11am–6pm.* *Closed last Fri. of the month.*	▲ *239* ◆ **E** C4-5
RUSSIAN MUSEUM ★ Ingenernaya Ul. 2 Tel. 812 595 42 40/812 314 34 48	*Open Mon. 10am–5pm, Wed.–Sun. 10am–6pm.* *Closed Tue.*	▲ *225* ◆ **A** D4

When in St Petersburg you do not need to dial the city code 812
before the seven-digit phone number.

RUSSIAN VODKA MUSEUM Konnogvardeisky Bl. 5 Tel. 812 312 34 16/812 312 91 78	*Open daily 11am–10pm.*	◆ **D** F2
ST ISAAC'S CATHEDRAL Isaakievskaya Pl. 1 Tel. 812 315 97 32	*Museum open Thur.–Tue. 11am–6pm.* *Panoramic visit 11am–5pm.*	▲ *195* ◆ **A** A5
ST NICHOLAS' CATHEDRAL ★ Nikolskaya Pl. 1/3	*Open daily 7am–7.30pm.*	▲ *204* ◆ **D** F4
ST PETERSBURG HISTORY MUSEUM (Engineers' Building) Alexandrovsky Park 7 Tel. 812 232 02 96	*Open Wed.–Sun. 11am–5pm.* *Closed last Thur. of the month.*	▲ *149* ◆ **C** C5
SHALYAPIN HOUSE (Museum of Russian Opera) Graftio Ul. 2b Tel. 812 234 10 56	*Open Wed.–Sun. noon–6pm.* *Closed last Fri. of the month.*	▲ *153* ◆ **C** B2
SMOLNY CATHEDRAL **AND MONASTERY** Rastelli Pl. 3/1 Tel. 812 271 91 82	*Open Fri.–Wed. 11am–5pm.* *Guided tours by appointment (Tel. 812 271 9421).* *Concerts (Tel. 812 271 7632).*	▲ *246* ◆ **E** F1-2
SMOLNY INSTITUTE Proletarskoy Diktatury Pl. Tel. 812 276 14 61	*Open Mon.–Fri. 10am–4pm.* *Guided tours only, by appointment.*	▲ *250* ◆ **E** F2
STROGANOV PALACE 17 Nevsky Pr. Tel. 812 117 23 60	*Open Mon. 10am–5pm, Wed.–Sun. 10am–6pm.* *Waxworks exhibition, 'The Romanov Family',* *open Mon.–Fri. 11am–8pm (9pm Sat.–Sun.);* *guided tours (Tel. 812 571 39 44).* *Porcelain gallery (annexed to the Russian* *Museum): open Mon. 10am–5pm, Wed.–Sun.* *10am–6pm.*	▲ *215* ◆ **A** C5
SUMMER GARDEN ★ Kutuzova Nab. 2 Tel. 812 314 03 74/812 314 04 56	*Open May–Oct.: daily 10am–9pm;* *Nov.–March: daily 10am–6pm. Closed the* *last Mon. of the month and in April.*	▲ *186* ◆ **A** E3
SUMMER PALACE Kutuzova Nab. Tel. 812 314 04 56	*Open Wed.–Mon. 10am–5pm.* *Closed last Mon. of the month and* *Nov.–early May.*	▲ *187* ◆ **A** E2
SUVOROV MUSEUM Kirochnaya Ul. 43 Tel. 812 279 39 14	*Open Mon. 10am–4.15pm, Tue. and Fri. 10am–* *5.15pm, Sat.–Sun. 10am–6.15pm. Closed Wed,* *Thur and last Monday of the month.*	▲ *252* ◆ **E** E2
THEATER MUSEUM Ostrovsky Pl. 6 Tel. 812 311 21 95	*Open Thur.–Mon. 11am–6pm, Wed. 1–7pm.* *Closed last Fri. of the month.*	▲ *231* ◆ **A** E6
WATER MUSEUM Chpalernaya Ul. Tel. 326 53 45	*Open Wed.–Sun. 10am–6pm.* *Closed last Sun. of the month.*	▲ *251* ◆ **E** E1
WINTER PALACE see **HERMITAGE**		
WRITERS' WALKWAYS MAUSOLEUM (Literatorskiye Mostki) Rastannya Ul. 30 Tel. 812 766 23 83	*Open April–Oct.: Fri.–Wed. 11am–7pm;* *Nov.–March: Fri.–Wed. 11am–5pm.*	▲ *244* OFF MAP
YUSUPOV PALACE Reki Moiki Nab. 94 Tel. 812 314 98 83	*Open Tue.–Sun. noon–5pm.* *Open daily 12–5pm* *Guided tours obligatory* *Closed first Wed. of the month*	▲ *202* ◆ **D** E-F3
ZOOLOGICAL GARDENS Alexandrovsky Park 1 Tel. 812 232 48 28/812 232 82 60	*Open Tue.–Sun. 10am–7pm.*	▲ *151* ◆ **C** C5
ZOOLOGICAL MUSEUM Universitetskaya Nab. 1 Tel. 812 328 01 12	*Open Sat.–Thur. 11am–6pm.*	▲ *158* ◆ **D** F1

AROUND ST PETERSBURG OFF MAPS

GATCHINA

GATCHINA PALACE Tel. 271 1 34 92	*Museum open Tue.–Sun. 10am–5pm.* *Closed last Tue. of the month.*	▲ 272

ORANIENBAUM

CHINESE PALACE Tel. 812 422 37 53/422 80 16 Tel. 812 422 47 96 (head office)	*Open April–Oct.: Mon. 11am–4pm, Wed.–Sun.* *11am–5pm; Nov.–March: daily 11am–4pm.* *Closed last Mon. of the month.*	▲ 262
JAPANESE PAVILION (Great Palace) Tel. 812 423 16 35	*Open April–Oct.: Mon. 11am–4pm, Wed.–Sun.* *11am–5pm; Nov.–March: daily 11am–4pm.* *Closed last Mon. of the month.* *Permanent exhibition of porcelain.*	▲ 262
ORANIENBAUM ESTATE (Menshikov Palace) Tel. 812 423 16 27	*Open April–Oct.: Mon. 11am–4pm, Wed.–Sun.* *11am–5pm; Nov.–March: daily 11am–4pm.* *Closed last Mon. of the month.*	▲ 262
PETER III'S PALACE Tel. 812 422 37 56	*Open April–Oct.: Mon. 11am–4pm, Wed.–Sun.* *11am–5pm; Nov.–March: daily 11am–4pm.* *Closed last Mon. of the month.*	▲ 263
"SLIDING HILL" (Katalnoy Gorky Pavilion) Tel. 812 422 37 58	*Closed for renovation.*	▲ 263

PAVLOVSK

PALACE Tel. 812 470 21 56	*Open Sat.–Thur. 10am–6pm.* *Closed Fri.*	▲ 268

PETERHOF ★

BENOIS MUSEUM Dvortsovaya Plochtchad 8 Tel. 812 427 50 39 (Bus 351, 356, 359)	*Open Sat. and Sun. 10am–4.30pm.* *Closed for restoration.*	▲ 261 ▲ 261
CATHERINE WING Nijny Park Tel. 812 427 91 29	*Open May–Oct.: Fri.–Wed. 10.30am–5pm;* *Nov.–April: Sat.–Sun. 10.30am–4pm.*	▲ 261
COTTAGE Alexandria Park (Buses 351, 356, 359) Tel. 812 427 99 53	*Open June.–Sep.: Tue.–Sun. 10.30am–5pm.* *Closed last Tue. of the month.* *Open Oct.–May: Sat.–Sun. 10.30am–5pm.*	▲ 257
GREAT PALACE Razvodnaya Ul. 2 (buses 351, 356) Tel. 812 427 95 27	*Open Tue.–Sun. 10.30am–4pm.*	▲ 260
HERMITAGE PAVILION Nijny Park Tel. 812 427 53 25	*Open May–Oct.: Tue.–Sun. 10.30am–5pm;* *Nov.–March: Sat.–Sun. 10.30am–4pm.*	▲ 260
MARLY PALACE Nijny Park (West side) Tel. 812 427 77 29	*Open May–Oct.: Tue.–Sun. 10am–6pm;* *Nov.–April: Sat.–Sun. 10am–4pm.* *Closed the last Monday of the month.*	▲ 260
MONPLAISIR Nijny Park Tel. 812 427 91 29	*Open Sat.–Sun. 10.30am–5pm.* *Closed Oct.–end May. Imperial spa and Chinese* *gardens.*	

STRELNA

STRELNA PALACE Berezovaya Alleya 3 Tel. 812 438 53 60	*Open 10am–5pm. Closed Wed. and during official* *receptions. Guided visits only.*	▲ 256
PETER I RESIDENCE Tel. 812 421 41 31	*Open Tue.–Sun. 10.30–5pm (4pm in winter).* *Closed last Tue. of month.*	

TSARSKOE SELO

ALEXANDRA PALACE Tel. 812 466 66 69	*Open Mon., Wed.–Sun. 10am–5pm.* *Closed last Fri. of the month.*	▲ 267
CATHERINE PALACE Sadovaya Ul. 7 Tel. 812 466 66 69	*Open April–Oct.: Wed.–Mon. 10am–5pm (4pm* *Nov.–March). Closed last Mon. of the month.* *Guided tours (Tel. 812 465 5308 for information).*	▲ 264
PUSHKIN LYCEUM Tel. 812 476 64 11	*Open Wed.–Mon. 10.30am–4.30pm. Closed last* *Fri. of the month. Visits by appointment only.*	

◆ USEFUL WORDS AND PHRASES

URBAN VOCABULARY

Avenue: *prospekt*
Bridge: *most*
Bus: *avtobus*
Car: *mashina*
Canal: *kanal*
Cathedral: *sobor*
Courtyard: *dvor*
District: *rayon*
Garden: *sard*
House: *dom*
Left: *nalevo*
Palace: *dvorets*
Passage: *proyezd*
Pedestrian crossing: *perekhod*
Quay: *naberezhnaya*
Right: *napravo*
River: *reka*
Square: *ploshchad*
Station: *vokzal*
Stop (bus, etc.): *ostanovka*
Street: *ulitsa* (small street: *pereulok*)
Suburbs: *prigorod*
Taxi rank: *stoyanka taxi*
Terminal (bus, etc.): *stantsiya*
Ticket: *bilet*
Train: *poyezd*
Tramway: *tramvay*
Trolley-bus: *troleybus*
"Watch out!": *ostorojno!*
Where is ...?: *gde nakhoditsa*

TRADES/STORES

Baker's: *bulochnaya*
Bank: *bank*
Café: *kafe*
Closed: *zakryto*
Delicatessen: *gastronom*
Department store: *univermag*
Food store: *producty*
Gas station: *stantsiya tekhnicheskogo obslujivanya*
Gasoline: *benzin*
Hospital: *bolnitsa*
Jeweler: *yuvelirniye izdeliya*
Market: *rynok*
Open: *otkryto*
Patisserie: *konditerskaya*
Pharmacy: *apteka*
Post office: *pochta*
Restaurant: *restoran*
Souvenirs: *souveniry*

Stamp: *marka*
Telephone: *telefon*
Tobacco, cigarettes: *tabak, sigarety*

NIGHTLIFE

Chamber music: *kamernaya muzyka*
Club: *klub*
Concert: *kontsert*
Evening: *vecher*
Exhibition: *vystavka*
Go to the theater (to a concert): *poyty v teatr (na kontsert)*
Guide: *ekskursovod*
Movies: *kino*
Nightclub: *nochnoy klub*
Museum: *muzey*
Music: *muzyka*
Program: *programma*
Theater: *teatr*
Ticket: *bilet*
Visit: *poseshcheniye* (or *vizit*)

FOOD

"The bill, please": *schet, pojaylusta*
Beef: *goviadina*
Beer: *pivo*
Bread: *khleb*
Breakfast: *zavtrak*
Cheese: *syr*
Cold: *kholodnyï*
Cool: *svejiye*
Dinner: *ujin*
Drink: *oit*
Eat: *yest*
Fish: *ryba*
Fruit juice: *sok*
Ham: *vechina*
Hot: *goriashiye*
Lunch: *Obed*
Menu: *menu*
Mineral water: *mineralnaya voda*
Pork: *svinina*
Potatos: *kartofel*
Rice: *ris*
Salt: *sol*
Sugar: *sakhar*
Veal: *teliatina*
Waiter: *ofitsiant*
Wine: *vino* (white wine: *bieloye vino*, red wine: *krasnoye vino*)

CAFÉS

Café: *kafe*
Cake: *pirog, pirojnoye, tort*
Capuccino: *kapuchino*
Coffee: *kofe* (large black/small black coffee:

bolchoy/malenkiye kofe, strong coffee: *krepkiye kofe*)
Dessert: *dessert*
Expresso: *espresso*
Green tea: *zelioniye tchay*)
Lemon tea: *tchaye s limonom*
Sweet: *sladkiye*
Tea: *tchaye*
Turkish coffee: *kofe po vostochnomu*
White coffee: *kofe s molokom*
Without sugar: *bez sakhara*

MONEY

Autoteller: *bankomat*
Bureau de change: *obmen valuty*
Buy: *kupit'*
Car rental: *prokat mashin*
Cheap: *dioshevo*
Convertible currencies: *SKV (CKB)*
Credit card: *kreditnaya kartochka*
Expensive: *dorogo*
How much is ...?: *skolko stoyt?*
Make a reservation: *zakazat'*
Money: *dengui*
Rent (to): *sniat*

ACCOMMODATION

Cleaning lady: *gornichnaya*
Day: *dien*
Double bedroom (two beds): *nomer*
Hotel: *gostinitsa*
Rent an apartment (a room): *sniat kvartiru (komnatu)*
Night: *notch*
Single room (one bed): *odnomestniye nomer dvukh-mestniye*
What's the price for one night?: *skolko stoyt odna notch?*
Youth hostel: *obshchejitiye, hostel*

CONVERSATION

Do you speak English?: *vy govorite po anglisky?*
Good-bye: *do svidanya (poka, fam.)*

Good evening: *dobriye vetcher!*
Hello!: *dobryï dien* (Hi!: *privet!*, between friends only)
I don't understand: *ya ne ponimayu*
I'd like ...: *ya khotel by*
Madam/Sir: Madam/Sir (or start the sentence with the phrase "Please")
No: *niet*
Please: *pojaylusta*
Please excuse me: *izvinite*
Thank you: *spassibo*
Yes: *da*

DAYS

Monday: *ponedelnik*
Tuesday: *vtornik*
Wednesday: *sreda*
Thursday: *chetverg*
Friday: *piatnitsa*
Saturday: *subota*
Sunday: *voskresseniye*
Holiday: *vykhodnoy dien*
Week: *nedelia*
Weekend: *vykhodniye* (or *weekend*)

MONTHS

January: *yanvar*
February: *fevral*
March: *mart*
April: *aprel*
May: *may*
June: *iyun*
July: *iyul*
August: *avgust*
September: *sentiabr*
October: *oktiabr*
November: *noyabr*
December: *dekabr*

COUNTING

1: *odin*
2: *dva*
3: *trY*
4: *chetyry*
5: *piat*
6: *shest*
7: *sem*
8: *vosem*
9: *deviat*
10: *desiat*
20: *dvadtsat*
21: *dvadtsat odin*
30: *tridtsat*
50: *piatdesiat*
100: *sto*
1000: *tysiacha*

◆ BIBLIOGRAPHY

ESSENTIAL READING

◆ DOSTOEVSKY (F.): *Crime and Punishment*, trans. Pevear (R.) and Volokhonsky (L.), Everyman's Library, London and Alfred A. Knopf, New York, 1993
◆ KELLY (L.) ed.: *St Petersburg – a travellers' companion*, Constable, London, 1981
◆ KROPOTKIN (PRINCE PIOTR): *Memoirs of a revolutionist*, Dover Publications Inc., New York, 1971
◆ OMETEV (B.) and STUART (J.): *St Petersburg: portrait of an Imperial city*, Cassell, London, 1990
◆ PIPES (R.): *Russia before the revolution*, Weidenfeld & Nicolson, London and Alfred A. Knopf, New York, 1934
◆ PUSHKIN (A.): *The Captain's Daughter and other stories*, trans. Debreczeny (P.) and Volokhonsky (L.), Everyman's Library, London and Alfred A Knopf, New York, 1994.
◆ WILMOT (M.) AND (C.): *The Russian Journals of Martha and Catherine Wilmot*, ed. M. of Londonderry and Hyde (H.M.), Macmillan & Co., London, 1934

GENERAL INTEREST

◆ CLARKSON (J.D.): *A History of Russia from the Ninth Century*, Longmans, London, 1961
◆ FALLOWEL (D.): *One hot summer in St Petersburg*, J. Cape, London, 1994.
◆ GUNTER (J.): *Inside Russia Today*, Hamish Hamilton, London, 1958
◆ HINGLEY (R.F.): *A Concise History of Russia*, Thames & Hudson, London, 1972
◆ MARSDEN (C.A.): *Palmyra of the North. The first days of St Petersburg*, Faber & Faber, London, 1942
◆ MILLER (W.M.): *Russians as People*, Dutton, NY, 1961
◆ REED (J.): *Ten Days that Shook the World*, Modern Books, London, 1928
◆ SIMPSON (C.): *This is Russia*, Hodder and Stoughton, London 1965
◆ WILTSHIRE (S.): *Floating cities: Venice, Amsterdam, Leningrad – and Moscow*, M. Joseph, London, 1991

HISTORICAL ACCOUNTS

◆ COXE (W.): *Travels into Poland, Russia, Sweden and Denmark, interspersed with historical relations and political inquiries*, S. Price et al., Dublin, 1784
◆ CUSTINE (MARQUIS A.L.L. DE): *Letters from Russia*, trans. and ed. Buss (R.), Penguin Books,
Harmondsworth, 1991
◆ HERZEN (A.): *My Past and Thoughts*, trans. Garnett (C). and Higgens (H.), Chatto & Windus, London, 1968
◆ MASSON (C.F.P.): *Secret Memoirs of the Court of Petersburg*, P. Wogan, Dublin, 1801
◆ PALÉOLOGUE (M.): *An Ambassador's Memoirs 1914–1917*, trans. F.A. Holt, London 1924–5
◆ PARKINSON (J.): *A Tour of Russia, Siberia and the Crimea, 1792–1794*, London, 1971
◆ VAN DER POST (L.): *Journey into Russia*, Penguin Books, Harmondsworth, 1965

IMPERIAL RUSSIA

◆ BADDELEY (J.F.): *Russia in the Eighties*, Longman & Co., London, 1921
◆ BARROW (SIR J.): *The Life of Peter the Great*, William Tegg, L, 1874
◆ ANTHONY (K.): *Memoirs of Catherine the Great*, Alfred A. Knopf, New York and London, 1927
◆ GREY (I.): *Peter the Great, Emperor of all Russia*, J.B. Lippincott & Co., PA and NY, 1960
◆ HINGLEY (R.F.): *The Tsars*, Corgi, London, 1973
◆ MASSIE (R.K.): *Peter the Great, his Life and World*, Phoenix Press, London, 2001
◆ MAZOUR (A.): *The First Russian Revolution, 1825*, University of California Press, Berkeley, 1937
◆ MOSSE (W.E.): *Alexander II and the Modernisation of Russia*, Collier, NY, 1962
◆ OLDENBOURG (Z.): *Catherine de Russie*, trans. Carter (A.), Heinemann, London, 1965
◆ SCHUYLER (E.): *Passages from the life of Peter the Great*, Sampson, Low & Co., London, 1881
◆ TROYAT (H.): *Catherine the Great*, Phoenix Press, London, 2000; *Ivan the Terrible*, Phoenix Press, London, 2001

THE REVOLUTION

◆ CARR (E.H.): *The Bolshevik Revolution*, 3 vols., Macmillan, New York, 1951–3
◆ CONQUEST (R.): *The Great Terror: Stalin's Purges in the Thirties*, Macmillan, London, 1968
◆ DEUTSCHER (J.): *Stalin*, Penguin Books, Harmondsworth, 1966
The Unfinished Revolution. Russia 1917–1967, George Macauley Trevelyan Lectures, OUP, Oxford, 1967
◆ HINGLEY (R.F.): *Russian Revolution*, Bodley Head, London, 1970
◆ LUKACS (J.): *A History of the Cold War*, Doubleday,
New York, 1962
◆ MCKEAN (R.B.): *St Petersburg between the revolutions: workers and revolutionaries*, Yale University Press, New Haven (Conn.), 1989
◆ MANDEL (D.): *The Petrograd Workers and the Soviet Seizure of Power*, Macmillan, London, 1984
◆ PHILBY (K.): *My Silent War*, MacGibbon & Kee, London, 1968
◆ TROTSKY (L.): *My Life*, Grosset & Dunlap, NY, 1960
◆ SALISBURY (H.E.): *The 900 Days: The Siege of Leningrad*, Harper & Row, New York, 1969
◆ WADE (R.A): *Red Guards and workers' militias in the Russian Revolution*, Stanford UP, Stanford, 1984
◆ WOLFE (B.D.): *Three Who made a revolution, Lenin, Trotsky, Stalin*, Dial Press, New York, 1961

SOCIETY

◆ BACH (M.): *God and the Soviets*, Thomas Y. Crowell, New York, 1958
◆ BATER (J.H.): *St Petersburg: Industrialisation and Change*, Edward Arnold, London, 1976
◆ BOURDEAUX (M.): *Religious Ferment in Russia. Protestant Opposition to Soviet Religious Policy*, Macmillan, London, 1968
◆ NEUBERGER (J.): *Hooliganism: crime, culture and power in St Petersburg*, UCP, Berkeley, c. 1993

ART AND ARCHITECTURE

◆ BILLINGTON (J.H.): *The Icon and the Axe: an interpretive history of Russian culture*, Alfred A. Knopf, NY, 1967
◆ COOKE (C.): *Architectural Drawings of the Russian Avant-Garde*, Museum of Modern Art, New York, 1990
◆ DESCARGUES (P.): *The Hermitage*, trans. Delavenay (K), Thames & Hudson, London, 1961
◆ ELLIOTT (D.): *New Worlds: Russian Art and Society 1900–1937*, Thames & Hudson, London, 1989
◆ KAHN-MAGOMEDOV (S.O.): *Pioneers of Soviet Architecture, the Search for new Solutions in the 1920's and 1930's*, Thames & Hudson, London, 1987
◆ OPOLOVNIKOV (A.) and (Y.), BUXTON (D.) ed.: *The Wooden Architecture of Russia*, Thames & Hudson, London, 1989
◆ RICE (T.T.): *A Concise History of Russian Art*, Thames & Hudson,
London, 1963
◆ SALMINA-HASKELL (L.): *Panoramic Views of St Petersburg, 1716–1835*, Ashmolean Museum, Oxford, 1993
◆ STRIZHENOVA (T.): *Soviet Costume and Textiles 1917–1945*, Thames & Hudson, London, 1991
◆ TOLSTOY (V.), BIBIKOVA (I.) and COOKE (C.) eds.: *Street Art of the Revolution*, Thames & Hudson, London, 1990

LITERATURE

◆ BIELY (A.): *St Petersburg*, trans. Cournos (J.), Grove Press Inc., New York, 1959
◆ BRODSKY (J.): *Less than One: Selected Essays*, Farrar, Strauss & Giroux, NY, 1986
◆ CHEKHOV (A.): *The Lady with the Dog*, trans. Pevear (R.) and Volokhonsky (L.), Everyman's Library, London and Alfred A. Knopf, New York, 1993
◆ DOSTOEVSKY (F.): *the Best Short Stories of Dostoevsky*, trans. Magarshack (D.), the Modern Library, NY, 1955
◆ GOGOL (N.): *The Overcoat and Other Stories*, trans. Garnett (C.), Chatto & Windus, London, 1923 *Tales of Good and Evil*, trans. Duddingion (N.), Everyman's Library, London and Alfred A. Knopf, New York, 1992
◆ GONCHAROV (I.): *Oblomov*, trans. Duddington (N.), Everyman's Library, London, Alfred A. Knopf, NY, 1992
◆ IGNATIEFF (M.): *The Russian Album*, Chatto & Windus, London, 1987
◆ MILLER (J. and K) eds.: *St Petersburg: Chronicles Abroad*; Chronicle Books, San Francisco, 1995
◆ NABOKOV (V.) trans.: *Eugene Onegin: a novel in verse by Alexander Pushkin*, trans. Nabokov (V.), Routledge & Kegan Paul, London, 1964 *Speak Memory – an Autobiography Revisited*, Weidenfeld and Nicolson, London, 1960
◆ PUSHKIN (A.): *Selected Poems*, trans. Thomas (D.M.), Secker & Warburg, London, 1982 *The Letters of Alexander Pushkin*, trans. Shaw (J.T.), Wisconsin, 1967
◆ SITWELL (S.): *Valse des Fleurs, a Day in St Petersburg and a Ball at the Winter Palace*, Faber and Faber, London
◆ TOLSTOY (L.N.): *Anna Karenina*, trans. Maude (L.) and (A.) Everyman's Library, London and Alfred A. Knopf, New York, 1992 *War and Peace*, trans. Maude (L.) and (A.) Everyman's Library, London and Alfred A. Knopf, New York, 1992

LIST OF ILLUSTRATIONS ◆

Bridgeman Art Library, London; *Karamzin*, anon., early 18th century, Pushkin House © V. Nesterov; *Dinner at the home of a bookseller*, title page of *Novosele*, Pushkin House © id.; Poster during the civil war, Bibl. Nat, St Petersburg © V. Baranovsky; *Learn, my son*, A. Kosolapov, 1974, Contemporary Art Museum of Tsaritsyno, Moscow © I. Boiko/APN. **56** Crucifix, 19th century, gold, enamel, © HEM/V. Terebenin/L. Heyfetc. **56–7** Iconostasis of St Isaac's Cathedral, St Petersburg, all rights reserved. **57** *Russian archbishop*, in *Collection of the clothing of different peoples…*, London, 1772, Bibl. Mun., Versailles © J. Vigne; *Russian baptism*, J.-B. Leprince, Musée du Louvre © R.M.N.; Preobrazhensky Cathedral, St Petersburg © V. Baranovsky; *Procession of the Cross*, V. Šurikov, oil on canvas © id. **58** *Saint Face*, icon, detail of the mouth and the whole © RM/V. Dorokhov. **58–9** *Life of Saint Serge of Radonega*, Moscow school, early 16th century, icon, RM © V. Baranovsky. **59** *Saint Face*, icon, detail of the eyes, © RM/V. Dorokhov.; *Christ in Majesty*, 16th century, icon, RM © V. Baranovsky.; *Trinity*, S. Ushakov, 14th century·icon, RM © id.; *Presentation of Christ at the Temple*, A. Rublev, late 14th–early 15th century, icon, RM © id.; *Our Lady of Kazan*, 19th century, icon of A. Akhmatova, Akhmatova Museum © id. **60** Bouquet of precious stones, J. Pauzié, St Petersburg, c. 1740, HEM © A. Sverdlov/ A.P.N.; Samovar, Tula, steel, bronze, cast iron, late 18th–early 19th century, © HEM/ V. Terebenin/L. Heyfetc; part of a harness, detail gold, emeralds, fabric, leather, metal, St Petersburg, c. 1730, © HEM/id. **60–1** The meeting of Melchisedec and Abraham, platter, gilded silver, Russia, 1721–5,© HEM/id. **61** Candelstick, Tula, steel, bronze, silver, late 18th–early 19th century, HEM© id.; chess pieces, Tula, steel, bronze, silver, late 18th century. © HEM/id.; Tabatière, J. Pauzié, St Petersburg, gold, silver, diamond, sapphire, quartz, mid 18th century, © HEM/id. **62** C. Fabergé, H. Oeberg, c. 1905 © V. Terebenin/L. Heyfetc; cornflowers and oatgrass, Fabergé, gold, enamel, diamonds rock crystal, © HEM/V. Terebenin/L. Heyfetc; cigarette case, Fabergé, gold, enamel and moonstone, UCAD, Paris. **62–3** Barbara Kelch Confectionary dish , Fabergé, enamel, gold, pearl and precious stones, priv. coll. © Edimédia. **63** Renaissance-style dish, Fabergé, rock crystal, silver, diamond, enamel, and gold, © HEM/V. Terebenin/L. Heyfetc; Goblets in the shape of an elephant, Fabergé, silver, © HEM/id.; Egg with the imperial coat of arms, gold, diamond and hard stone, priv. coll. © Edimédia; Statuette of kamerkazak Kudinov, Fabergé, colored stone, saphire, gold and silver, Pavlovsk © V. Terebenin/L. Heyfetc. **64** Plate, dish and sugar bowl from Empress Elisabeth's table service from the imperial works, 1756 © HEM/V. Terebenin/L. Heyfetc; Plate from Gureev table service, 1807 © HEM/id. **65** Marks of the St Petersburg pottery from 1749 to 1919, all rights reserved; Figurines, Gardner, c. 1820 © HEM/V. Terebenin/L. Heyfetc; Suprematism Service, S. Chekhonin, N. Sovietin, 1923 © APN; *Long live the Third International*, dish, M. Adamovitch © Edimédia; cup and saucer, Kuznetzov, Modern Style, © HEM/V. Terebenin/ L. Heyfetc. **66** Table and chairs from the reign of Peter the Great, Russia, © HEM/V. Terebenin/ L. Heyfetc; Russian Empire salon, Carelian birchwood © HEM/id. **66–7** Pedestal table, mosaic in malachite and gilded bronze, late 18th century. © HEM/id. **67** Fire guard, H. Gambs, 1794, Pavlovsk Palace © Alain de Gourcuff editor; armchair, Talachkino school, late 19th century © HEM/V. Terebenin/L. Heyfetc; desk, chair and pedestal table, Russian Jacob, early 19th century, © HEM/id.; Pedestal table, Tula, c. 1801 © HEM/id. **68** *Meyerhold*, Golovin, TM;

© V. Baranovsky; *Mariinsky*, 19th century © V. Terebenin/L. Heyfetc; Poster for the Mikhail Theater, 1895, TM; © V. Baranovsky. **68–9** *Gaudeamus* performed in Paris by the Maly Company © Gély/Bernand; **69** BDT poster for Shakespeare's *Henri IV*, 1971, TM © V. Baranovsky; *Self portrait*, Akimov, TM © id.; G. Tovstonagov during rehearsals for *Machekha Samanichnily*, Gorky Theater, 1982 © Y. Belinsky/APN. **70** Design for a costume for a *bacchante*, L. Bakst, 1911 © MNAM, Paris; *Diaghilev*, J. Cocteau, 1917, drawing, priv. coll. © Spadem, 1995 **71** *Nijinsky in l'Après-Midi d'un Faune*, L. Bakst, program for the Ballets Russes, May–June 1912 © G. Dagli Orti; *Ch.-L. Didelot*, anon. miniature, mid 19th century, TM; *Maria Taglioni, and her brother Paul*, in "La Sylphide", c. 1830, id.; *Costume designs for Béotiennes*, L. Bakst, 1911 priv. coll. © J.-L. Charmet. **72** *Balalaika player*, N. Bogdanov-Bielsky, 20th century, priv. coll. © Edimédia; *Russian musicians*, 1834, engraving © Roger-Viollet; *At the Novodievichy monastery*, K. Yuon, design sketch for the set design for *Boris Godunov*, Bakhrushkin Museum, Moscow © APN. **73** A. Khachaturian, D. Shostakovitch and S. Prokofiev © APN; *Stravinsky*, P. Picasso © RMN/SPADEM, 1995. **74–5** The pancake-maker, Lubok, Russia, 18th century, Bibl. Publ., Moscow © Edimédia; Film of the *Blini* recipe © E. Guillemot/Gallimard. **76** Specialties of St Petersburg © Gallimard. Vodka bottle *Sankt-Petersburg*. **78** Map of Peterhof, Peter the Great, Nat. Hist. Archives, Moscow; *Map of St Petersburg, c. 1700*, 19th century, IREMISE © Gallimard. **78–9** Peter the Great visiting the shipyards of St Petersburg, V. Serov © APN. **79** *General plan by Leblond, 1717*, 19th century, IREMISE © Gallimard. Plan of the Peter and Paul Fortress 1703 © SPHM/V. Terebenin/L. Heyfetc. **97** St Petersburg at sunset, M. Vorobiov, early 19th century, oil on canvas, RM © L. Heyfetc. **98–9** View of the Palace from the Peter and Paul Fortress, F. Alexeyev, early 19th century, TG © Scala; View of the Kutuzov docks and the Palace, B. Patersen, early 19th century © HEM/ V. Terebenin/L. Heyfetc. **100–1** Parade on the Marsovo Pole (Field of Mars), G. Chernetsov, ensemble and detail 1839, RM © L. Heyfetc; Neva Embankment in Front of the Fine Arts: Night, G. Chernetsov, c. 1830, RM © id. **102–3** Artist's apartments, Winter Palace, L. Premazzi, 1852–3, priv. coll. © Hazzlit, Gooden and Fox, London; Cimmerian Bosphorus Antiquities room, C. Ukhtomsky, © HEM/V. Terebenin/L. Heyfetc. Italian School gallery, E. Hau, c. 1853 © HEM/id.; History of Painting Gallery E. Hau, 1859 © HEM/ id. **104–5** Holy Week Fair on Admiralty Square about 1830, A. Benois, 1945, priv. coll. © F. Kerkessoff/ SPADEM and ADAGP, 1995; A.N. Benois, L. Bakst, oil on canvas, RM © V. Baranovsky. **106** The Fontanka and the Summer Garden, A. Ostrumova-Lebedeva, 1929, priv. coll. © V. Terebenin/ SPADEM, 1995; A. Ostrumova-Lebedeva, K. Samov, RM © The Bridgeman Art Lib., London; Columns of Our Lady of Kazan, A. Ostrumova-Lebedeva, 1903, priv. coll. © L. Heyfetc/ SPADEM, 1995. **107** Suprematism, Malevich, 1915, Réun. Mus, coll. Archives Nakov. **108** The Cock, Autumn, Larionov, 1912, TG, coll. id. **109** Suprematist Composition, Rozanova, 1916–17, RM, coll. id.; Portrait of Ivan Klium, Malevich, 1913, coll. id.; Peasants Carrying Fruit, Gontcharova, 1911–12, RM, coll. id. © ADAGP, 1995 **110** Supremus n°55, Malevich, 1916, coll. id.; The Carpenter, Malevich, 1930–1, RM., coll. id. **111** Orient and Occident, Filonov, 1912–13, RM, coll. id.; Movement in Space, Matiushin, 1920–2, coll. id.; Office Rozanova, 1915, RM, coll. id. **112** Monument to the Third International, V. Tatlin, 1920, coll. id.; Relief, V. Tatlin, 1914,

◆ ACKNOWLEDGEMENTS

V. Savik. **268** Hall of War, Pavlovsk © coll. Carpi/Alain de Gourcuff editor; *Grand Duke Paul Petrovitch*, B. Batoni after Batoni, c. 1782, Pavlovsk © Alain de Gourcuff editor; *Grand Duchess Maria Fyodorovna*, B. Batoni after Batoni, c. 1782, Pavlovsk © id.; Maria Fyodorovna's boudoir, Pavlovsk © coll. Carpi/Alain de Gourcuff editor; Pavlovsk, aerial view © V. Baranovsky. **269** Pavlovsk Palace © V. Baranovsky; Vestibule Egyptien, Pavlovsk © coll. Carpi/Alain de Gourcuff editor **270** One of a pair of small vases, Sèvres, 1782, Pavlovsk © Alain de Gourcuff editor; Throne Room, Pavlovsk © coll. Carpi/Alain de Gourcuff editor; curtain border, Lyon, c. 1780, Pavlovsk © Alain de Gourcuff editor. **270–1** Bedroom, Pavlovsk Palace © coll. Carpi/Alain de Gourcuff editor; French clock, 18th century, Pavlovsk Palace © V. Terebenin. **271** *Pavlosk Park*, H. Robert, 18th century , Pavlovsk Palace © Alain de Gourcuff editor; View of the Slavianka, Pavlovsk Park © V. Savik. **272** *View of Gatchina Palace seen from the square*, after Charlemagne, © SPHM/V. Terebenin/ L. Heyfetc; *The White Room, Gatchina Palace*, E. Hau, 1880 © Alain de Gourcuff editor; *State bedroom of Maria Fyodorovna, Gatchina Palace*, L. Premazzi, 1873 © id.; *View of Gatchina Park*, J. J. Mettenleiter, 1793, © id. **277** Opening of Trinity Bridge © V, Baranovsky. **278** Nevsky Prospekt, RR. **281** Helictopter tours of St Petersburg. © M. Borisov. Vasilyevsky Island © M. Borisov.Vasilyevsky Island © V. Baranovsky. Avtovo Metro station © A. and V. Terebenin. **282** Nevsky Prospekt, RR. **288** Pribaltiskaya Hotel © Pribaltiskaya Hotel. **289** Europa Restaurant, © ACFP. **290** Valhall Hotel © Valhall Hotel **292** Vasilyevsky Island © V. Baranovsky. Griboiedov Canal from Bank Bridge © V. Kokcharov. **293** Nevsky Prospekt, RR. Jazz Philharmonia, RR. **294** Ostrovsky Square © V. Baranovsky. Smolny, RR. **295** Stage curtain from the Mariinsky Theater, V. Baranovsky. Mariinsky Theater, RR. **296** Arts Square, RR. Sphinx quay © W. Buss. **297** Nevsky Prospekt © M. Borisov.

In some cases, we have been unable to trace the owners and publishers of some of the photographs and illustrations. We will be happy to acknowledge them if they make themselves known to us.

◆ Associated University Presses: Excerpt from "Tristia" #88 page 77, from Poems of Mandelstam by Osip Mandelstam, translated by R.H. Morrison © 1990 by The Associated University Presses. Reprinted by permission

◆ Farrar, Straus & Giroux, Inc.: Excerpt from "Less Than One" from Less Than One by Joseph Brodsky, © 1986 by Joseph Brodsky; excerpt from Turgenev's Literary Reminiscences, translated by David Magarshack, © 1958 by Farrar, Straus & Cudahy, Inc., copyright renewed 1986 by Elsie D. Magarshack. Reprinted by permission of Farrar, Straus & Giroux, Inc.

◆ Grove/Atlantic, Inc.: Excerpt from St. Petersburg by Andrei Biely, translated by John Cournos, © 1959 by Grove Press, Inc. Reprinted by permission of Grove/Atlantic, Inc.

◆ John Johnson (Authors' Agent) Limited: Excerpt from "The Bronze Horseman" from Selected Poems by Alexander Pushkin, translated by D.M. Thomas, © 1982 by D.M. Thomas (London: Secker & Warburg Ltd). Reprinted by permission of John Johnson (Authors' Agent) Limited.

◆ New Directions Publishing Corp.: Excerpt fom Futility by William Gerhardie, © 1971 by The Estate of William Gerhardie. Reprinted by permission of New Directions Publishing Corp.

◆ Princeton University Press: Excerpt from "Travels in Russia" by William Coxe from Seven Britons in Imperial Russia 1698–1812, edited by Peter Putnam, © 1952 by Princeton U. Press, copyright renewed 1980 by Princeton U. Press. Reprinted by permission of Princeton U. Press.

◆ Random House, Inc.: Excerpt from "White Nights" from The Best Short Stories of Fyodor Dostoyevsky by Fyodor Dostoyevsky, translated by David Margarshack, translation © 1955 by Random House, Inc. Reprinted by permission of Random House, Inc.

◆ Viking Penguin: Letter to M.P. Chekhova, Petersburg, Jan. 14, 1891, from The Letters of Anton Chekhov by Anton Chekhov, translated by Avrahm Yarmolinsky, translation copyright © 1947, 1968 by The Viking Press, Inc., © 1973 by Avrahm Yarmolinsky. Reprinted by permission of Viking Penguin, a division of Penguin books USA Inc.

◆ Vintage Books: Excerpt from Speak Memory by Vladimir Nabokov, © 1989 by The Estate of Vladimir Nabokov. Reprinted by permission of Vintage Books, a division of Random House, Inc.

◆ A.P. Watt Ltd and Chatto & Windus: Excerpt from "The Nevsky Prospect" from The Overcoat and Other Stories by Nikolai Gogol, translated by Constance Garnett, © 1923 by Mrs Edward Garnett. Reprinted by permission of A.P. Watt Ltd and Chatto & Windus on behalf of The Executors of The Estate of Constance Garnett.

Grateful acknowledgment is made to the following for permission to reprint previously published material:

Page numbers in **bold** refer to the Practical section.

◆ INDEX

Map section

◆ STREET INDEX

◆ STREET INDEX

Mejevoy (Kanal)
D B5
Melnitchnaya (Ulitsa)
E F6
Mendeleievskaya (Linia)
D E1 F1
Mendeleievskaya
(Ulitsa) **C** E3 F2
Metrostroievtsev (Ulitsa)
D E6
Mikhailova (Ulitsa)
C F5, **E** D1
Millionnaya (Ulitsa)
E A2, **A** C3
Minsky (Pereulok)
D E3
Mira (Ulitsa) **C** C4 D4
Mirgorodskaya (Ulitsa)
E E5
Mitchurinskaya (Ulitsa)
B B4, **C** D5
Mitrofanievskoye
Chose **D** E6 F6
Mochkov (Pereulok)
E A2, **A** C3
Moiseienko (Ulitsa)
E E3
Mojaiskaya (Ulitsa)
E A6
Mokhovaya (Ulitsa)
E C2, **A** F2 F4
Montchegorskaya
(Ulitsa) **C** A5 B5
Morskaya (Naberejnaya)
B A6 B3
Morskoy (Prospekt)
B E2 C2
Morskoy Slavy
(Ploshchad) **D** A3
Moskatelny (Pereulok)
E A4, **A** C6
Moskovsky (Prospekt)
E A5 A6
Mutchnoy (Pereulok)
A C6
Mytninskaya
(Naberejnaya)
C B6
Mytninskaya (Ulitsa)
E E3 E4
Mytninsky (Pereulok)
C B5 B6, **A** A1

N

Nakhimova (Ulitsa)
B A6 B6, **D** A1
Nalitchnaya (Ulitsa)
B B6 C4, **D** A1
Nalitchny (Pereulok)
B B6 C6, **D** A1
Narvsky (Pr.) **D** D6
Neichlotsky (Pereulok)
C E3
Nekrasova (Ulitsa)
E C3 D3
Nemansky (Pereulok)
B D6 E6, **D** C1
Nevelskaya (Ulitsa)
D B6
Nevsky (Prospekt)
E A3 E4, **A** B4 E5
Nikolsky (Pereulok)
D F4
Novgorodskaya (Ulitsa)
E E3 F3
Novoladojskaya (Ulitsa)
B E3
Novolitovskaya (Ulitsa)
C E2 F1
Novosmolenskaya
(Naberejnaya) **B** A5 B5

O

Obukhovskoy Oborony
(Prospekt) **E** F5 F6
Obvodnogo Kanala
(Naberejnaya) **D** D5 F5,
E B6 F6
Odoievskogo (Ulitsa)
B B5 D5
Ofitsersky (Pereulok)
B F4, **C** A5
Olgina (Ulitsa) **B** E2 F2
Opotchinina (Ulitsa)
D A2 B3
Oranienbaumskaya
(Ulitsa) **C** A4 B4
Ordinarnaya (Ulitsa)
C B3 C4
Orenburgskaya (Ulitsa)
C E4 E5
Orlovskaya (Ulitsa)
E F1
Orujeinika Fiodorova
(Ulitsa) **C** D6 E6, **E** B2,
A E2 F2
Oskalenko (Ulitsa) **C** A1
Ostumova (Ul.) **D** B1 B2
Ostrovskogo
(Ploshchad) **A** E6
Otchakovskaya (Ulitsa)
E E2 F2
Otchakovskaya
(Naberejnaya) **C** B1 C1

P

Paradnaya (Ulitsa)
D D2 D3
Pargolovskaya (Ulitsa)
C E1
Pavlogradsky (Pereulok)
E C6
Penkovaya (Ulitsa)
C D5, **E** B1
Perekupnoy (Pereulok)
E E4
Perevoznaya (Ulitsa)
D D3 D4
Pesotchnaya
(Naberejnaya) **B** F2,
C A3 B2
Pestelia (Ulitsa) **E** B2
C2, **A** F3
Petchatnika Grigorieva
(Ulitsa) **E** C5 C6
Petrogradskaya (Ulitsa)
B E2 F3
Petrogradskaya
(Naberejnaya) **C** D4
Petrovskaya
(Ploshchad) **B** D3
Petrovskaya
(Naberejnaya) **C** D5,
E B1, **A** D1
Petrovskaya Kosa **B** C3
Petrovsy (Pereulok)
B E4
Petrovsky (Prospekt)
B D3 E4
Pevtchesky (Pereulok)
C D4 D5
Pinsky (Pereulok)
C D4
Pionerskaya (Ulitsa)
B E3 F4
Pionerskaya (Ulitsa)
C A4
Pirogova (Pereulok)
D F3, **A** A6
Pirogovskaya
(Naberejnaya) **C** D3 D4
Pisareva (Ulitsa) **D** E3

Plutalova (Ulitsa)
C B3 B4
Podiezdnoy (Pereulok)
E B5 B6
Podkovyrova (Ulitsa)
C B4
Podolskaya (Ulitsa)
A A6
Podrezova (Ulitsa)
C B4
Polevaya (Alleia)
B E1 F1, **C** A2
Polozova (Ulitsa)
C B4
Poltavskaya (Ulitsa)
E D4 D5
Polustrovsky (Prospekt)
C F1 F2
Potshamtskaya (Ulitsa)
D E2 F2, **A** A5
Potiomkinskaya (Ulitsa)
C F6, **E** D1 D2
Povarskoy (Pereulok)
C C4
Pratchetchny (Pereulok)
D F3, **A** A6
Pravdy (Ulitsa)
E B5 C5
Priadilny (Pereulok)
D E4
Pribaltiskaya
(Ploshchad) **B** A6
Primorsky (Prospekt)
B E1, **C** A1
Profesora Popova
(Ulitsa) **C** A3 D3
Projektornaya (Ulitsa)
B D2 E2
Proletarskoy Diktatury
(Ulitsa) **E** F2
Pskovskaya (Ulitsa)
D D4
Pudojskaya (Ulitsa)
B F3, **C** A4 B4

R

Radichtcheva (Ulitsa)
E D2 D3
Raziezjaya (Ulitsa)
E B5 C5
Reky Fontanky
(Naberejnaya) **D** D4 F4,
E A5 B3, **A** E2 E6
Reky Iekateringofky
(Naberejnaya) **D** B6
Reky Karpovky
(Naberejnaya)
C B3 D3
Reky Krestovky
(Naberejnaya) **B** E1 F2,
C A2
Reky Moiky
(Naberejnaya) **D** F3 F2,
E A2 A3, **A** A6 D3
Reky Priajky
(Naberejnaya) **D** D3 D4
Reky Smolenky
(Naberejnaya)
B D5 E5
Remeslennaya (Ulitsa)
B E4
Rentgena (Ulitsa)
C C4
Repina (Ulitsa) **B** F6,
D E1
Repina (ploshchad)
D D4
Revelsky (Pereulok)
D E5
Reznaya (Ulitsa)
B F3, **C** A4

Rijsky (Prospekt)
D C5 E5
Rimskogo-Korsakova
(Pereulok) **D** D4 E4
Robespiera
(Naberejnaya)
C E6 F6, **E** D1
Romenskaya (Ulitsa)
E D6
Ropchinskaya (Ulitsa)
B F4, **C** A4 B5
Rozenshteina (Ulitsa)
D E6
Rubinshteina (Ulitsa)
A F6
Rukhina (Ulitsa)
B D2
Ruzovskaya (Ulitsa)
E A6 B6
Ryleieva (Ulitsa) **E** C2

S

Sablinskaya (Ulitsa)
C B5
Sadovaya (Ulitsa)
D F3 F4, **E** A4 B3,
A D6 E5
Sakharny (Pereulok)
C E4
Sanatornaya (Alleia)
B F1 F2, **C** A2
Sapiorny (Pereulok)
E D3
Saratovskaya (Ulitsa)
C E4 E5
Savinoy (Ulitsa) **B** E3
Savushkina (Ulitsa)
C A1
Sennaya (Ploshchad)
A A4
Serdobolskaya (Ulitsa)
C C1
Serpukhovskaya (Ulitsa)
E A6
Sestroretskaya (Ulitsa)
C A1
Severnaya (Doroga)
B B1 C1
Siezdovskaya (Linia)
B F5 F6, **D** E1
Siezdovsky (Pereulok)
D D2
Siezjinskaya (Ulitsa)
C B5
Sinopskaya
(Naberejnaya) **E** F3 F4
Smoliatchkova (Ulitsa)
C D3 E3
Smolnaya (Naberejnaya)
E F1
Smolnogo (Ulitsa)
E F1
Smolny (Prospekt) **E** F2
Soiuza Petchatnikov
(Ulitsa) **D** E3 E4
Solianoy (Pereulok)
E B2, **A** E2 E3
Sotsiallistitcheskaya
(Ulitsa) **E** B5 C5
Spasskiy (Pereulok)
E A4, **A** B6 C6
Sportivnaya (Ulitsa)
B E2 E3
Sred. Koltovskaya
(Ulitsa) **B** E3 F3
Srednegavansky (Pr.)
D A2 B2
Sredney Nevky
(Naberejnaya) **B** E1 F1
Sredniaia Podiatch
(Ulitsa) **D** F3

A

ULITSA IABLOTCHKOVA

MYTNINSKY PER.

A   B   C

KRONVERKSKAYA NABEREJNAYA

KRONVERKSKY STRAIT

KA

PR. DOBROLUBOVA

PETER AND PAUL CATHEDRAL

1 PETROGRAD SIDE
(PETERSBURG ISLAND)

PETER AND PAUL FORTRESS

BIRJEVOY MOST

ROSTRAL COLUMNS

NEVA

2 Birzevaya Ploshchad

DVORTSOVAYA NABEREJNAYA

MOCHOV PER.

ULITSA

HERMITAGE THEATER

MILLIONNAYA

NABEREJNAW

NABEREJNA

BIRJEVOY PROIEZD

ACADEMY OF SCIENCES

DVORTSOVY MOST

LARGE HERMITAGE

SMALL HERMITAGE

3 UNIVERSITETSKAYA NAB.

WINTER PALACE

MOIKA

ALEXANDER COLUMN

NABEREJNAYA REKY MOIKY

NABEREJNAYA REKY MOIKY

BOL. KONJUCHENNAYA UULITSA

ST MARY CHURCH

NABEREJNAYA ADMIRALTEISKAYA

Dvortsovata Ploshchad

ADMIRALTY

ALEXANDER GARDEN

ST PETER'S CHURCH

4 MONUMENT TO PETER I

Ploshchad Dekabristov

ADMIRALTEISKY PROSPEKT

NEVSKY PROSPEKT

ST ISAAC'S CATHEDRAL

MALAYA MORSKAYA ULITSA

KIRPITCHNY PER.

GOROKHOVAYA

ULITSA

STROGANOV PALACE

ASTORIA & ANGLETERRE HOTELS

MORSKAYA

MOIKA

RAZUMOVSKY PALACE

CATHEDRAL OF OUR LADY OF KAZAN

POCHTAMTSKAYA ULITSA

Isaakievskaya Ploshchad

NABEREJNAYA REKI MOIKY

NABEREJNAYA REKI MOIKY

5 FONARNY

BOLCHAYA

MONUMENT TO NICHOLAS I

PEREULOK ANTONENKO

PEREULOK GRIVTSOVA

KAZANSKAYA ULITSA

NABEREJNAYA KANALA GRIBOEDO

BANKOVSKY PER.

MOSKATELNY PER.

NABEREJNAYA REKY MOYKY

PEREULOK PIROGOVA

VOZNESENSKY PR.

MARIINSKY PALACE

MUTCHNOY PER.

PRATCHETCHNY PEREULOK

PEREULOK DEKABRISTOV

UL

KAZANSKY ISLAND

GRIBOYEDOV CANAL

SPASSKY PER.

GOROKHOVAYA ULITSA

6

0   330   660 ft
0   100   200 m

A   B   GRAJDANSKAYA UL   C

D   **E**   **F**

Troitskaya
Ploshchad

PETROVSKAYA NAB.

OSTROVSKY PROSPEKT

NABEREJNAYA KUTUZOVA

CHPALERNAYA ULITSA

1

LITEÏNY PROSPEKT

PETER THE GREAT'S
SUMMER PALACE

GAGARINSKAYA ULITSA

ULITSA   TCHAIKOVSKOGO

Suvorovskaya
Plochtchad

NAB. LELIAJEÏ KANAVKY

STATUE OF
KRYLOV

MOKHOVAYA ULITSA

NAB. REKY FONTANKY

ULITSA
ORUJEYNIKA FIODOROVA

STATUE OF
SUVOROV

GANGUTSKAYA UL.

2

SOLIANOY PEREULOK

MARBLE
PALACE

SUMMER
GARDEN

ULITSA PESTELIA

APTEKARSKY PER.

MONUMENT
TO THE HEROES OF
THE REVOLUTION

REKY MOIKY
REKY MOIKY

MOIKA

Koniuchennaya
Ploshchad

NAB. REKY FONTANKY

MOKHOVAYA ULITSA

3

UL. CHEKOVA

GRIBOIEDOV CANAL

CHURCH OF THE
RESURRECTION

ENGINEERS'
CASTLE

MIKHAILOVSKY
GARDEN

ZAMKOVAYA ULITSA

KLENOVAYA ULITSA

CIRCUS

KLENOVAYA ULITSA

LITEÏNY PROSPEKT

MIKHAIL PALACE

INJENERNAYA ULITSA

Ploshchad
Belinskogo

UL. BELINSKOGO

NAB. KANALA GRIBOIEDOVA
NAB. KANALA GRIBOIEDOVA

Iskusstv
Ploshchad (Arts Square)

SADOVAYA ULITSA

SHEREMETIEV
PALACE

4

ITALIANSKAYA ULITSA

MIKHAILOVSKY
RIDING SCHOOL

FONTANKA

St CATHERINE'S
CHRCH

ARMENIAN
CHURCH

ULITSA

ITALIANSKAYA

Manejnaya
Ploshchad

NAB. REKY FONTANKY

NEVSKY
PROSPEKT Ⓜ

GOSTINY
DVOR Ⓜ

UL.

KARAVANNAYA ULITSA

✚

NEVSKY PROSPEKT

DUMSKAYA

STATUE OF
CATHERINE II

5

ULITSA

SADOVAYA ULITSA

VORONTSOV
PALACE

Ploshchad
OstrovskoVo

ALEXANDRINSKY
THEATER

ANICHKOV
PALACE

NAB. REKY FONTANKY

VLADIMIRSKY PR.

LOMONOSOVA

UL. ZODTCHEGO ROSSI

GRAFSKY PEREULOK

ULITSA RUBINSHTEINA

DMITROVSKY PER.

SADOVAYA ULITSA

Ploshchad
Lomonosova

CHTCHERBAKOV PER.

VLADIMIR
CHURCH

6

D   **E**   **F**

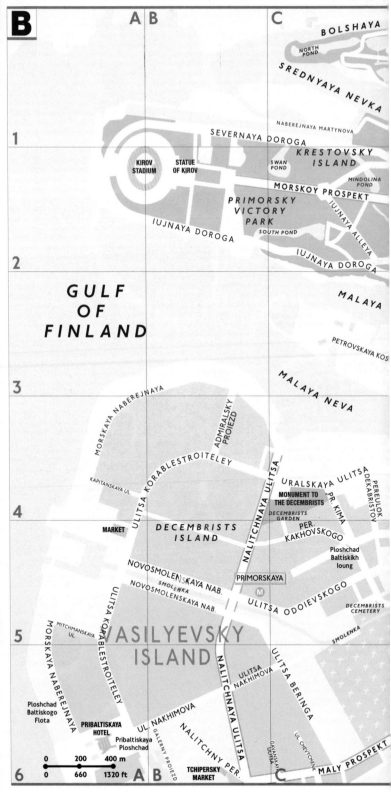

B

A B C

BOLSHAYA

NORTH POND

SREDNYAYA NEVKA

NABEREJNAYA MARTYNOVA

1

SEVERNAYA DOROGA

KIROV STADIUM

STATUE OF KIROV

SWAN POND

KRESTOVSKY ISLAND

MINDOLINA POND

MORSKOY PROSPEKT

PRIMORSKY VICTORY PARK

IUJNAYA DOROGA

SOUTH POND

IUJNAYA ALLEYA

2

IUJNAYA DOROGA

GULF OF FINLAND

MALAYA

PETROVSKAYA KOS

3

MALAYA NEVA

MORSKAYA NABEREJNAYA

ADMIRALSKY PROIEZD

ULITSA KORABLESTROITELEY

NALITCHNAYA ULITSA

URALSKAYA ULITSA

PEREULOK DEKABRISTOV

KAPITANSKAYA UL

MONUMENT TO THE DECEMBRISTS

DECEMBRISTS GARDEN

PR. KIMA

4

MARKET

DECEMBRISTS ISLAND

PER. KAKHOVSKOGO

Ploshchad Baltiskikh Ioung

NOVOSMOLENSKAYA NAB.

SMOLENKA

NOVOSMOLENSKAYA NAB.

PRIMORSKAYA

Ⓜ

ULITSA ODOIEVSKOGO

DECEMBRISTS CEMETERY

SMOLENKA

MORSKAYA NABEREJNAYA

MITCHMANSKAYA UL

ULITSA KORABLESTROITELEY

VASILYEVSKY ISLAND

NALITCHNAYA ULITSA

ULITSA NAKHIMOVA

ULITSA BERINGA

5

Ploshchad Baltiskogo Flota

PRIBALTISKAYA HOTEL

Pribaltiskaya Ploshchad

UL. NAKHIMOVA

GALERNY PROIEZD

NALITCHNY PER.

GVANDAKAYA ULITSA

UL. CHEYTCHEN

MALY PROSPEKT

0   200   400 m

0   660   1320 ft

A B

TCHIPERSKY MARKET

C

6

C

A B

C BELOOSTROVSKY

UL. OSKALENKO

CHICHMAROVSKY PEREULOK

UL. AKADEMIKA CHIHABBOGO

CHAIKOVSKAYA AKADEMIKA

SESTRORETSKAYA ULITSA

CHYORNAYA RECHKA Ⓜ

ULITSA AKADEMIKA KRYLOVA

NAB.

STAROBEL-SKAYA UL.

LISTCHANSKAYA ULITSA

ULITSA GRAFOVA

SERDOBOLSKAYA ULITSA

ULITSA

VAZASKY PEREULOK

TCHIORNO RETCHKY

TCHIORNAYA RETCHKA

UL. SAVUSHKINA

PRIMORSKY PROSPEKT

BOLSHAYA NEVKA

USHAKOVSKAYA NABEREJNAYA

NAB. BOLSHOY NEVKY

LETNIAYA ALLEYA

1 KITCHENS

TEATRALNAYA AL.

POLEVAYA AL.

BOLSHAYA AL.

2 BERIOZOVAYA ALLEYA

1 BERIOZOVAYA ALLEYA

SREDNIAYA AL.

SANATORNAYA ALLEYA

ZAPADNAYA NAB. MALO NEVKY

KAMMENY ISLAND

RESERVE

KAMENNOOSTROVSKY PALACE

KITCHENS

ORANGERY

OLDENBURG'S DACHA

GROMOV'S DACHA

LOPUKHINSKY GARDENS

ULITSA AKADEMIKA PAVLOVA

KAMENNOOSTROVSKY PROSPEKT

APOTHECARIES ISLAND

PROSPEKT MEDIKOV

2 BLUE DACHA

PROSPEKT DINAMO

NAB. REKY KRESTOVKY

MALAYA NEVKA NABEREJNAYA

VIAZEMSKY GARDEN

ULITSA GROTA

VIAZEMSKY PER.

ULITSA TCHAPYGUINA

APTEKARSKY PROSPEKT

PESOTCHNAYA

BAROTCHNAYA UL.

ULITSA DALIA

ULITSA PROFESORA POPOVA

NAB. REKY KARPOVKY

ULITSA PROFESORA

UL. LITERATOROV

NAB. REKY KARPOVKY

KAPROVKA

KAPROVKA

3 LEVACHOVSKY PR.

BOLSHAYA REZNAYA ULITSA

MALAYA ZELENINA ULITSA

GLUHAYA ZELENINA UL.

LODEINO-POLSKAYA ULITSA

PODOLSKAYA ULITSA

GAZOVAYA ULITSA

ULITSA VSEVOLODA VICHNEVSKOGO

BARMALEIEVA ULITSA

PLUTALOVA UL.

PODREZOVA ULITSA

ORDINAYA ULITSA

MALY PROSPEKT

ORDINARNAYA ULITSA

STATUE OF CHEVTCHENKO

STATUE OF POPOV

LENSOVETA CULTURAL CENTER

PETROGRADSKAYA

UL. LVA TOLSTOGO

PETROGRAD SIDE

KORPUSNAYA UL.

PIONERSKAYA UL.

ULITSA KRASNOGO KOURSANTA

BOL. ZELENINA

TCHKALOVSKY PROSPEKT

UL. LENINA

POLOZOVA ULITSA

PODKOVYROVA ULITSA

LAKHTINSKAYA ULITSA

GACHINSKAYA ULITSA

ORANIENBAUMSKAYA UL.

STRELNINSKAYA UL.

KOLPINSKAYA ULITSA

CHAMCHEVA

BOLSHOY PROSPEKT

BOLSHAYA PUCHKARSKAYA UL.

MALAYA PUCHKARSKAYA

UL. KROPOTKINA

KRONVERKSKAYA

UL. RENTGUENA

BOL. MONETNA

MALAYA MONE.

ULITSA DIVENSKAYA ULITSA

CHKALOVSKAYA Ⓜ

ROPCHINSKAYA UL.

4 JDANOVSKAYA UL.

JDANOVSKAYA ULITSA

MALAYA GREBETSKAYA ULITSA

MONTCHEGORSKAYA UL.

MALY PROSPEKT

PEREKOPSKAYA UL.

BERASNOSELSKAYA UL.

OFITSERSKY PER.

STATUE OF DOBROLUBOV

VVEDENSKAYA UL.

VOSKOVA ULITSA

SYTNINSKAYA UL.

SABLINSKAYA UL.

UL. MARKINA

SYTNY MARKET

ALEXANDER PARK

GORKOVSKAYA Ⓜ

STATUE OF STREREGUCHY

KAMENNOOSTROVSKY

5 PETROVSKY STADIUM

SPORTIVNAYA Ⓜ

BOLSHOY PROSPEKT

PROSPEKT DOBROLUBOVA

STATUE OF BLAGOIEV

UL. LIZY CHAIKINO

SEZJINSKAYA UL.

TATARSKY PER.

ZVERINSKAYA ULITSA

VLADIMIR CATHEDRAL

UL. BLOKHINA

UL. IABLOTCHKOVA

PLANETARIUM AUDITORIUM

KRONVERKSKY CANAL

MYTNINSKY PER.

KRONVERKSKAYA NABEREJNAYA

KRONVERKSKY STRAIT

PETER AND PAUL CATHEDRAL

PETER AND PAUL FORTRESS

TUBILEINY THEATER

TUCHKOV

PETERSBURG ISLAND

NAB. MAKAROVA

2 LINIA

TUCHKOV PER.

MALAYA NEVA

NAB. MAKAROVA

MYTNINSKAYA NAB.

HARE ISLAND

NEVA

ROSTRAL COLUMNS

Birjevaya Ploshchad

0	200	400 m
0	660	1320 m

A B C

6

FINLAND STATION
UL. MIKHAILOVA
ULITSA KOMSOMOLA
Ploshchad Lenina

NEVA

ARSENALNAYA NABEREJNAYA

NABEREJNAYA ROBESPIERA

D

E

F SMOLNAYA NABEREJNAYA

ULITSA KOMSOMOLA

UL. MIKHAILOVA

ORLOVSKAYA ULITSA

FORMAL GARDEN

UL. SMOLNOGO

ALEXSANDROVSKY INSTITUTE

1

PROSPEKT TCHERNYCHEVSKOGO
ULITSA
CHPALERNAYA ULITSA
ULITSA
POTIOMKINSKAYA UL.
CHERNY-CHEVSKAYA
UL.

STATUE OF DZERJINSKY
TAURIDE PALACE
TAURIDE GARDENS
STATUE OF YESENIN

TAVRITCHESKY PER.
KIKINY PALACE
STAVROPOLSKAYA ULITSA
TVERSKAYA ULITSA
OTCHAKOVSKAYA ULITSA

SMOLNY MONASTERY
UL. PROLETARSKOY DIKTATURY

PER. KVARENGY

SMOLNY CATHEDRAL

SMOLNY INSTITUTE

KIROCHNAYA ULITSA

KAVALERGARDSKAYA UL.

MARIINSKY PROEZD

SMOLNY PR.

ULITSA VOSSTANIA
ULITSA RADICHTCHEVA
SAPIORNY PER.
MALTSEVSKY MARKET
NEKRASOVA
OVENSKY PER.
OCTOBER CONCERT HALL
ULITSA VOSSTANIYA

VILENSKY PER.
PARADNAYA UL.
PRUDKY GARDENS

SUVOROV MEMORIAL

TAVRICHESKAYA ULITSA

SUVOROVSKY PROSPEKT

KIROTCHNAYA UL.

DEGTIARNY PEREULOK

ULITSA MOISEYENKO

NOVGORODSKAYA ULITSA

TULSKAYA ULITSA

TULSKAYA UL.

ULITSA KRASNOGO TEKSTILCHTCHIKA

2

FONTANNAYA

9
8
7
6
5
4
3
2

GRECHESKY PROSPEKT

SUVOROVSKY PROSPEKT

SOVETSKAYA ULITSA
SOVETSKAYA ULITSA
SOVETSKAYA ULITSA
SOVETSKAYA ULITSA
SOVETSKAYA UL.
SOVETSKAYA ULITSA

MYTNINSKAYA UL.

STARORUSSKAYA UL.

CHERNYCHEVSKY GARDENS

KIRILLOVSKAYA ULITSA

NOVGORODSKAYA ULITSA

SINOPSKAYA NABEREJNAYA

NEVA

MALOOKHTINSKY PROSPEKT
MALOOKHTINSKY PROSPEKT

3

PLOSHCHAD VOSSTANIYA
OKTIABRSKAYA HOTEL
MOSCOW STATION
OSPEKT
GONCHARNAYA UL.

SOVETSKAYA ULITSA

DEGTIARNAYA ULITSA

NEVSKY
KONNAYA

PEREKUPNOY PER.

ISPOLKOMSKAYA ULITSA
KHERSONSKAYA UL.

BAKUNINA
PROSPEKT

KHERSONSKY PROEZD

4

PIAT UGLOV

POLTAVSKAYA ULITSA
POLTAVKOVA
TCHAIKOVSKAYA UL.

TELEJNAYA ULITSA

PROSPEKT

ULITSA

KHERSONSKAYA UL.

ULITSA ALEKSANDRA NEVSKOVO

MOSKVA HOTEL

NEVSKOVO

ZANEVSKY PROSPEKT

NO-NAME ISLAND

TRANSPORTNY PEREULOK

KREMENTCHUGSKAYA ULITSA

MIRGORODSKAYA ULITSA

MONASTYRKA

KONSTANTINOGRADSKAYA ULITSA

METROPOLITAN GARDENS

PLOSHCHAD ALEKSANDRA

NEVSKY MONASTERY

NIKOLSKOYE CEMETERY

HOLY TRINITY CATHEDRAL

PR. OBUKHOVSKOY OBORONY

5

OMENSKAYA ULITSA
NEPETROVSKAYA ULITSA

ATAMANSKAYA ULITSA

ORTHODOX ACADEMY AND SEMINARY

NABEREJANA OBVODNOGO KANALA
OBVODNY CANAL

MELNITCHNAYA ULITSA

ULITSA

ZERKALNY PER.

GLAZURNAYA ULITSA

OBVODNOGO KANALA

GLINIANAYA

0   200   400 m

0   660   1320 ft

D

E

F

6

◆ PUBLIC TRANSPORTATION

F

GORKOVSKAYA Ⓜ

AURORE CRUISER

PETER AND PAUL FORTRESS

Troitsky most

MALAYA NEVA

Ⓜ VASSILEOSTROVSKAYA

Dvortsovy most

HERMITAGE

CHURCH OF THE TRANSFIGURATION

BOLCHAYA NEVA

AMIRALTY

Dvortsovaya Ploshchad

Iskusstv Ploshchad

NEVSKY PR. / GOSTINY DVOR Ⓜ

ST ISAAC'S CATHEDRAL

CATHEDRAL OF OUR LADY OF KAZAN

GRIBOEDOV CANAL

Sennaya Ploshchad

SADOVAYA / SENNAYA PLOSHCHAD

MARIINSKY THEATER

ST NICHOLAS CATHEDRAL

PUCHKINSKAYA Ⓜ

VITEBSK STATION

TEKHNOLOGICHESKY INSTITUT Ⓜ

0   250   500 m
1/23 000 · 1 cm : 230 m

A   B   C

TRAMWAY, BUS AND TROLLEYBUS NETWORKS ◆

G

PARNASKAYA

PROSPEKT PROSVESHCHENYA

OZERKY

UDELNAYA

KOMANDANTSKY PROSPEKT

PIONERSKAYA

STARAYA DEREVNYA

CHYORNAYA RETCHKA

DEVIATKINO

GRAJDANSKY PROSPEKT

AKADEMICHESKAYA

POLITEKHNICHESKAYA

PLOSHCHAD MUJESTVA

LESNAYA

VYBORGSKAYA

PLOSHCHAD LENINA

PETROGRADSKAYA

KRESTOVSKY OSTROV

CHKALOVSKAYA

SPORTIVNAYA

VASILEOSTROVSKAYA

PRIMORSKAYA

GORKOVSKAYA

NEVA

CHERNICHEVSKAYA

GOSTINY DVOR / NEVSKY PROSPEKT

PLOSHCHAD VOSTANYA / MAYAKOVSKAYA

SADOVAYA / SENNAYA PL.

PUSHKINSKAYA

DOSTOEVSKAYA / VLADIMIRSKAYA

LIGOVSKY PR.

NOVOCHERKASKAYA

LADOJSKAYA

TEKHNOLOGICHESKY INSTITUT

PL. ALEKSANDRA NEVSKOGO

PROSPEKT BOLCHEVIKOV

BALTISKAYA

FRUNZENSKAYA

ELIZAROVSKAYA

NEVA

ULITSA DYBENKO

NARVSKAYA

MOSKOVSKYE VOROTA

NARODNA

LOMONOSOVSKAYA

KIROVSKY ZAROD

ELEKTROSILA

AVTOVO

PARK POBEDY

PROLETARSK

LENINSKY PROSPEKT

MOSKOVSKAYA

OBUKHOVO

PROSPEKT VETERANOV

ZVIOZDNAYA

KURCHINO

RYBATSKOY

Legend

1 Kirovsko-Vyborgskaya Line	⬤ Connections possible
2 Moskovsko-Petrogradskaya Line	○ Stations
3 Nevsko-Vasileostrovskaya Line	
4 Pravoberejnaya Line	

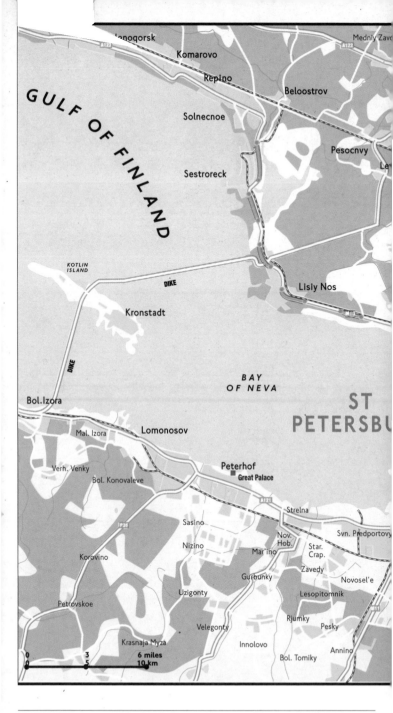

GULF OF FINLAND

Ianoqorsk
Komarovo
Repino
Beloostrov
Solnecnoe
Pesocnvy
Le
Sestroreck

KOTLIN ISLAND
DIKE
Lisiy Nos
Kronstadt
DIKE

BAY OF NEVA

ST PETERSBU

Bol.Izora
Mal. Izora
Lomonosov
Verh. Venky
Bol. Konovaleve
Peterhof
Great Palace
Strelna
Sasino
Nov. Hob.
Svn. Predportovy
Nizino
Mar'ino
Star. Crap.
Korovino
Zavedy
Novosel'e
Gurbunky
Lesopitomnik
Uzigonty
Petrovskoe
Rjumky
Pesky
Velegonty
Krasnaja Myza
Innolovo
Annino
Bol. Tomiky

0   3   6 miles
0   5   10 km

ST PETERSBURG IN FIGURES
The cultural and tourist capital of Russia and the country's second-largest city after Moscow. Built on the Neva delta, the city consists of 42 islands linked by some 300 bridges.
LATITUDE
Lying at 60°, it is the largest megalopolis at this latitude.
SURFACE AREA
540 square miles. Administrative subdivision (*oblast*): 772 square miles. 20 districts (*raion*):
Admiralteisky
Vasileostrovsky
Vyborgsky
Kalininsky
Kirovsky
Krasnogvardeisky
Krasnoselsky
Moskovsky
Nevsky
Petrogradsky
Primorsky
Frunzensky
Tsentralnyy
Puchkinsky
Pavlovsky
Lomonosovsky
Petrodvortsovy
Kronchtadsky